SHARIAH

WHAT EVERYONE NEEDS TO KNOW®

SHARIAH

WHAT EVERYONE NEEDS TO KNOW®

JOHN L. ESPOSITO
NATANA J. DELONG-BAS

OXFORD
UNIVERSITY PRESS

OXFORD
UNIVERSITY PRESS

Oxford University Press is a department of the University of Oxford. It furthers
the University's objective of excellence in research, scholarship, and education
by publishing worldwide. Oxford is a registered trade mark of Oxford University
Press in the UK and certain other countries.

"What Everyone Needs to Know" is a registered trademark
of Oxford University Press.

Published in the United States of America by Oxford University Press
198 Madison Avenue, New York, NY 10016, United States of America.

CIP data is on file at the Library of Congress
ISBN 978-0-19-932506-1 (pbk.); 978-0-19-932505-4 (hbk.)

1 3 5 7 9 8 6 4 2

Paperback printed by LSC Communications, United States of America
Hardback printed by Bridgeport National Bindery, Inc.,
United States of America

Some of the material in this book appeared previously, and in different form,
in the following:
Esposito, John L. 2002. *Unholy War*. New York: Oxford University Press.
Esposito, John L. 2011. *What Everyone Needs to Know about Islam*.
New York: Oxford University Press.
Esposito, John L. 2013. *The Future of Islam*. New York: Oxford University Press.
Esposito, John L. 2016. *Islam: The Straight Path*. New York:
Oxford University Press.

*John Esposito: For my brothers, Louis and Richard Esposito
and my sister, Susan Brown
Natana DeLong-Bas: For Dad and Ruth, who are always
there no matter what.*

CONTENTS

2 Shariah: The Big Picture   31

3 Shariah Courts   54

ACKNOWLEDGMENTS

This project has drawn on the talents of many contributors. We want to thank our student researchers Molly Wartenberg, Aamina Shaikh, Mona Mogahed, Nathan Lean, and especially Jason Welle and Tasi Perkins. We were especially fortunate to have colleagues in the US and overseas who agreed to read and review drafts for chapters of the book: Asifa Quraishi Landes, Jonathan Brown, Mohammed Fadel, Tamara Sonn, Khalid Masud, and Kathleen Moore. As with all his publications, John's wife and partner, Jean Esposito, read the entire manuscript multiple times, providing advice, input and editing. Natana is grateful to her husband, Christophe, and children, Aurora and Gabriel, who lived with and believed in this project from its conception through its development and conclusion. Without the supportive environment they created, the book never would have seen the light of day.

Oxford University Press provided an excellent team. Special thanks to Cynthia Read, Executive Editor, who believed in the importance of this project from the outset, reviewed the manuscript and provided critical and constructive feedback. Drew Anderla, editorial assistant, provided quick and efficient assistance when needed. Nicholas Hunt shepherded the manuscript through the copyediting stages and production and kept us on schedule.

SHARIAH

WHAT EVERYONE NEEDS TO KNOW®

INTRODUCTION

Shariah: What Everyone Needs to Know provides informed answers to many questions and charges that surround the debate over Shariah and Islamic Law. As its title indicates, we have written for a broad nonspecialist audience as well as for policymakers, political commentators, religious leaders, and students.

Because this book is written for a general audience, we have minimized Arabic terms, professional jargon, and footnotes and have sought to simplify our language and level of detail in discussing difficult concepts. At the same time, because of the controversy over Shariah, when describing charges and countercharges, we have included more specific detail than might have been expected in responding to particularly contentious issues. In addition, our format in this questions-and-answers book requires some repetition so that various answers will be self-contained. While this allows the reader to jump from topic to topic more randomly, we nevertheless encourage readers to start with Chapters 1 and 2, which provide basic perspectives on Shariah that make topics in subsequent chapters easier to read and understand.

The eleven chapters of this volume cover key areas of Islamic law and the hot-button issues that arise today. In all of these chapters, we discuss both historical and contemporary interpretations as well as variations across countries and law schools, and between Sunnis and Shia. Our goal is to highlight the complexity, diversity, and flexibility of Shariah and its interpretation over time and space in order to show Islamic law as a living, dynamic process, ideally guided by the quest to uphold the common good (*maslahah*), human dignity, social justice, and the centrality of the community. At the same time, we critically note where these ideals have not been upheld and where and how reformers are seeking change.

Throughout the book it is clear how much power and authority the word "Shariah" carries. Historically, the word Shariah has been used not only in traditional Islamic law (*fiqh*) that guides Muslim lives but also to refer to laws created by rulers that were not derived from scripture, but were practical regulations for such areas as fair marketing, certain taxes, public safety, and security, all developed to maintain public order. This kind of governance was called "*siyasa* [government policies or laws] *Shariah*" because of the common belief that Shariah's purpose was to ensure the welfare of the people. So too, as will be discussed, the common good measured in terms of preserving people's right to practice religion as well as faith, property, and dignity, is known as *maqasid al-Shariah* (principles or objectives of Shariah).

Chapter 1, "Shariah and Islamic Law: Myths and Realities," sets the Shariah controversies in a broader frame, delineating the multiple players and events that have led to public fears of Shariah and Islamic law as threatening our American legal system. It provides a more complex picture of critiques and condemnations of Shariah and Islamic law, as well as the spiritual meaning and purpose of Shariah as seen through Muslim eyes, past and present. Chapter 1 explores why so much fear is associated with Shariah and whether we need to protect American law from some impending threat. It compares the practice of Islamic law with other religious laws in America and presents data on Muslim attitudes toward Shariah, domestically and internationally, as well as data on Muslim attitudes toward living in the United States successfully.

Chapter 2, "Shariah: The Big Picture," deals with the multilayered meanings of the powerful word, Shariah, looking at the term's origins and meaning; how Shariah is viewed by Sunnis and Shia; and how Shariah plays a key role in legal renewal and reform. This chapter also explores why it is important to distinguish between Shariah (unchanging principles and values originating from revelation) and Islamic law (human interpretations that are subject to change). We also highlight the objectives Shariah is intended to fulfill (*maqasid al-Shariah*) in discussing the ways that diverse law schools can provide jurists as well as individual Muslims with legal rulings relevant to varied environments and changing circumstances.

Chapter 3, "Shariah Courts," focuses on the way Shariah courts work in comparison to other legal systems as well as on the roles of qadis (judges) and muftis (legal scholars and experts) in the development of Islamic law. Understanding the strengths and weaknesses of Shariah courts and how they have radically changed over time provides us with greater knowledge of current challenges and opportunities.

Chapter 4, "The Five Pillars of Islam and Community Life," elaborates on the prominent place held by the Five Pillars in Islamic legal literature, as they are always discussed in the opening chapters of legal works. The pillars represent the fundamental principles of both personal and collective faith, worship, and social responsibility that unite all Muslims. The strong moral and action-oriented force of the Five Pillars blends the theological with the legal and reinforces the sense of a worldwide community.

Chapter 5, "Women, Gender, and the Family," focuses on Muslim family law, which governs the rights and responsibilities of men and women in marriage, divorce, and inheritance. Throughout the ages, the family unit has been regarded as the foundation of Muslim society and many view family law as a reflection of an idealized Islamic past. Due to this view, family law has remained the most controversial and most resistant to reforms needed to reflect substantial changes in family structures and the roles of women and men in a modern, globalized world.

In Chapter 6, "Government, Law, and Order," we see that throughout history, while the examples of Muhammad as head of state and Shariah principles have been reference points, diverse models of government and law have existed. Although many changes through the ages have occurred, an idealized vision of a Muslim ruler and state governed by Islamic law remains a powerful influence even in contemporary times. Nevertheless, there are many competing visions of how Islam, Islamic law, and political power should function in a modern state and how different models impact civil law, democracy, pluralism, and the lives of Muslims who are now living in non-Muslim countries.

Chapter 7, "Freedom and Human Rights," discusses the major human rights challenges that Muslim countries and societies face today, including representative government; equal rights for women; freedom of religion, speech, and expression; and freedom of the press. Although majorities of Muslims strongly favor and desire these basic freedoms, debates abound today over limiting criticism of Islam and controlling freedom of speech and criticism of rulers. Ultra-conservative religious leaders as well as religious extremists misuse the traditional crimes of blasphemy and apostasy to condemn and silence those with whom they disagree. Militant extremists in some Muslim countries target and attack other Muslims and religious minorities. Muslim reformers struggle to move beyond medieval interpretations of Islamic law to use Shariah values and tools for reforms to address contemporary needs.

Chapter 8, "War, Peace, and the Common Good," discusses political Islam as a significant factor in the politics of mainstream and extremist rulers, political activists, and both mainstream (nonviolent) and terrorist movements who draw on interpretations of "jihad" or "struggle" and Shariah to justify both nonviolent civil resistance and violent aggression. This chapter reviews the use and abuse of jihad and its varied applications as well as the guidelines Islamic law provides to combatants throughout history, citing criteria in Islamic law for a just war, and safety for noncombatants. In addition, the chapter reviews legal arguments for the legitimacy or illegitimacy of martyrdom and suicide bombing as it explains why Islamic law condemns terrorist movements like Al Qaeda and ISIS as un-Islamic.

Chapter 9, "Criminal Law and Justice," describes how politics, power, and patriarchy have influenced the development of narrow legal codes and harsh penalties justified in the name of "Islamic" legitimacy. The chapter explains what "hudud" means and how it has been implemented past and present. It compares the original rationales and goals of Islamic criminal laws with contemporary hudud punishments for murder, theft, and illicit sex, and describes forgotten limits and requirements. It cites the many key Shariah principles on the common good, justice, and protection of life and property, and explains why just treatment for women in sexual crimes, honor killings, and domestic violence has been lost.

Chapter 10, "Islamic Finance in a Global World," notes Islam's links with trade and commerce originating from Muhammad's caravan trade experience. The Quran's emphasis on the common good, including social justice, honesty in the marketplace, and enjoyment of material possessions, as well as helping those in need, provided a foundation for Islamic law in trade and contracts, property rights, and interest or usury. Shariah principles inform Islamic banking and interest-free financial transactions, charitable giving, and modern microfinance projects. Islamic financial principles guide Muslims on property management, banking, loans, and contracts. Internationally, Shariah principles that emphasize long-term planning, financial moderation, and preserving resources for future generations strongly contrast with Western capitalist-driven development and economic inequality as well as with the Muslim world's vast income disparities, underdevelopment, and failure to support widespread social welfare.

Chapter 11, "Science, Bioethics, and Human Life," describes the Quran's view of humans as God's (Arabic, Allah's) representatives responsible for all of God's creation, including plant and animal life. Shariah principles promote the value of human life and Muslims' responsibility to preserve and protect the body, both matter and spirit. This chapter details the significant influence of these values on Islamic legal views, Islamic bioethics, and individual conscience when dealing with environmental issues and medical research and practice. It covers contemporary legal debates on cloning, stem cell research, and genetic engineering as well as bioethical issues of family planning, abortion, organ donation, and euthanasia.

We hope that this approach of providing both historical and contemporary examples and developments and coverage of a variety of themes will make a useful and constructive contribution to public conversations and reform efforts, and to the ongoing work of building bridges of understanding between the West and the Muslim world.

1

SHARIAH AND ISLAMIC LAW

MYTHS AND REALITIES

For many in the West today, "Shariah" is a word that evokes fear—fear of a medieval legal system that issues draconian punishments, fear of relegation of women and religious minorities to second-class citizenship, fear of Muslims living as separate communities who refuse to integrate with the rest of society, and fear that Muslims will seek to implement Shariah in the West. These fears are reinforced by sensational media headlines, interest groups, lobbies, and politicians who believe in and warn of a clash of civilizations between Islam and the West. Yet opinion polls and lived realities, both in Muslim-majority countries and in the West, paint a more complex picture of Islam and what Shariah means to Muslims and the varied roles Muslims want it to play in the public sphere.

Many Muslims maintain that observing Shariah is central to Islam and to their lives. They see Shariah as upholding the values of good governance, representative government, the public interest, social justice, human freedoms and rights, and individual accountability. These conflicting visions of Shariah as a threat versus a source of guidance and protection raise major questions about Shariah myths and Shariah realities that Chapter 1 discusses: Why is so much fear associated with Shariah? Is it very different from other religious laws found in Judaism, Christianity, and other faiths? Do Muslims in the United States and Europe want to replace Western laws with Shariah? Could Shariah ever be implemented in the West? Does Shariah pose a threat to Western values?

Where Does Fear of Shariah Come from?

Fear of Shariah, like fear of Islam, is associated with many international events and players, East and West, who have exploited the term for their own purposes. The emergence of global terrorist movements, especially Al Qaeda and ISIS, which claim justification for their militant jihads in the name of Shariah, reinforces the belief among many that Islam and all Muslims, not just extremist groups, are global threats. Second, self-styled "Islamic" governments like Afghanistan under the Taliban, Saudi Arabia, and Iran have implemented punishments like stoning women accused of adultery, amputating limbs of thieves, and executing those accused of apostasy or blasphemy. Third, ironically, the "clash of civilizations" promulgated by Al Qaeda and ISIS to strengthen their appeal to recruits is also reinforced by many Western politicians, far-right political commentators, and popular Christian televangelists who reinforce terrorists' hateful speech by predicting a looming clash of civilizations, epitomized by jihad and Shariah.

Mass media focus on "explosive, headline events" and sales ("If it bleeds, it leads") has resulted in an imbalance in news stories. Coverage of Islam and Muslims has overemphasized extremism and terrorist attacks with minimal mention of the broader context of Islam and the vast majority of mainstream Muslims globally. For example, news stories in 2015, after more than a decade of steady escalation, witnessed the all-time highest level of negative coverage. An analysis of media coverage in America and Europe by the global analytical media research institute Media Tenor found that over 80 percent of stories on Islam were negative. In the United States, the United Kingdom, and Germany, nine out of ten articles were negative. As a logical result, many have come to believe that there is a "clash of civilizations" between Islam and the West and fear a triple threat—political, civilizational, and demographic—that often reinforces a fear of Shariah. In Europe, worries about influxes of Muslim refugees and immigrants, Muslim birth rates outpacing those of "native" populations, and visible symbols of Islam's presence—veils, beards, "Islamic dress," halal meat, and mosques—give rise to concerns about the loss of native identity, culture, and civilization. Repeated terrorist attacks by those claiming inspiration from ISIS further fuel fear of a threat from within.

In the United States, fear of Islam and Muslims also focuses on identity issues, within the framework of foreignness and difference, exemplified most powerfully by deep concerns that Muslims, both terrorist and mainstream, seek to impose Shariah on the West. Fear of "radical Islamic terrorism" after the terrorist attacks of September 11, 2001, and "creeping Shariah" after the 2010 conflict over building an Islamic center near Ground Zero of the worst of those attacks in New York City have become widespread and pervade the American political landscape today. As documented by organizations such as the Center for American Progress and islamophobianetwork.com between 2001 and 2012, a small group of eight donors contributed more than $57 million to organizations promoting fear of Islam, Muslims, and, especially, Shariah as working to overthrow the US Constitution and legal system and install a radical Islamic caliphate that will punish and subordinate all non-Muslims. In 2016, the Council on American-Islamic Relations (CAIR) and the Center for Race and Gender at the University of California, Berkeley, examined support for radical organizations. Their report, "Confronting Fear," based on tax filings, showed that between 2008 and 2013, a US-based Islamophobia Network of some thirty-three groups had access to a total revenue of $205,838,077.

In both the United States and Europe, anti-Muslim activists and groups as well as far-right political parties and politicians have warned of a demographic explosion that would lead to Muslim dominance and an "Islamization" of countries. Concerns about the growing Muslim birth rate and the size of their communities have led to calls for restrictions on immigration.

This demographic myth is squarely overcome by the reality. The Pew Research Center estimates that Muslims constitute about 1 percent of the US population (3.3 million Muslims of all ages living in the United States in 2015) and that the share will double to 2 percent by 2050. Muslims currently constitute 6 percent of the European population, having grown about one percentage point per decade, from 4 percent in 1990 to 6 percent in 2010. This pattern is expected to continue through 2030, when Muslims are projected to make up 8 percent of Europe's population.

Like the demographic fear ("The Muslims are coming, the Muslims are coming"), the danger of Islamization and Shariah (dubbed "creeping Shariah") in the United States has also been based on a myth. In fact, no Muslim or Muslim organization has tried to implement Shariah to replace the Constitution or the American legal system. Yet, between 2010 and 2017, 120 anti-Shariah bills had been introduced in forty-two states. In 2017 alone, thirteen states introduced an anti-Shariah bill, with Texas and Arkansas enacting the legislation. Many of these efforts can be traced to a "lawfare" campaign against Islam begun by Israeli-American lawyer David Yerushalmi, who authored the model anti-Shariah legislation "American Laws for American Courts." Yerushalmi has been repeatedly criticized by the Anti-Defamation League, the American Civil Liberties Union, Jewish groups, and Roman Catholic bishops for his racially and religiously charged remarks not only against Muslims but also against immigrants, blacks, and women.

Yarushalmi's work is supported by institutions such as the Society of Americans for National Existence (SANE), which he founded, and like-minded individuals and their organizations, including Frank Gaffney's Center for Security Policy, Robert Spencer and Pamela Gellar's Stop Islamization of America, and Quran-burning pastor Terry Jones. Serious questions have been raised about the lack of evidence for their claims. Gaffney, for example, was one of the main drivers behind the rumors that President Obama was a Muslim and that the US government had been infiltrated by Muslims seeking to implement an alternative legal system. Spencer and Gellar were barred from entering the United Kingdom in 2013 because the British home secretary saw their presence as not conducive to the public good. However, in America, their anti-Muslim, anti-Shariah message, disseminated through neo-conservative public policy institutes and privately financed reports, has become part of mainstream American politics.

The US presidential elections in 2008, 2012, and 2016, as well as congressional elections, reinforced fears among American voters, particularly of Muslims supposedly wanting to implement Shariah in America. Republican candidates Donald Trump, Ben Carson, Rick Santorum, and Ted Cruz and former Speaker of the House Newt Gingrich criticized Islam and claimed that Muslims wanted to impose Shariah on Americans. Candidate Trump declared that "Islam hates us", Carson proclaimed that a Muslim should not be president unless he denounces his faith; to Santorum, Shariah is evil, and to Cruz it is an enormous problem; Gingrich labeled Shariah a mortal threat to the survival of freedom in the United States and the world as we know it and called for deporting Muslims who believe in Shariah. The anti-Islam and anti-Shariah climate rose to a crescendo in the Trump administration. Many of President Trump's key cabinet members, senior staff, and advisors, however different, subscribe to the belief that Islam is not even a religion but a dangerous political ideology that must be contained or eliminated. Influenced by this outlook, President Trump while still a candidate proposed creating a Muslim registry, greater profiling and monitoring of Muslims, and a ban on Muslim immigration. Muslims are puzzled and concerned about these fears. Major international poll reports (Gallup, PEW) verify that Shariah is central to the faith and spirituality of a majority of Muslims. However, as we discuss elsewhere in this volume, rather than "a clash" between Islam and the West, these polls report that majorities of Muslims admire the West for its representative governments, freedoms, economic prosperity, and security and that Muslims want these for their families and for themselves. At the same time, Muslims decry equating the faith of 1.6 billion Muslims with the belief of a fraction of the world's Muslims whose violence and terrorism taints them all, despite the fact that Muslims themselves constitute the majority of these terrorists' victims. The surge in anti-Muslim hate crimes, which rose in the United States 67 percent from 2014 to 2015, 78 percent from 2015 to 2016, and in the United Kingdom went up 500 percent following the Manchester attack, reinforces these fears.

Why Does Shariah Carry Deep Spiritual and Social Meaning for Muslims around the World?

Although many use the terms "Shariah" and "Islamic law" interchangeably, they are not the same thing. Shariah is not a formal legal system. It refers to God's law, sacred and unchangeable principles and values revealed in the Quran and the example (Sunnah) of Muhammad. Islamic law (*fiqh*) is the Muslim interpretation of those Shariah principles, the development of a vast body of laws or legal systems by jurists. While Shariah principles do not change, Islamic law is the product of human interpretations of Shariah in historical and social contexts and therefore can change in response to new challenges and circumstances.

A great deal of misinterpretation occurs when various actors hijack the term Shariah. Some associate Shariah's divine principles and religious authority to enhance their own agendas and garner support for harsh punishments and restrictions of human rights. Others, like Al Qaeda and ISIS, use their twisted interpretation of Shariah to enlist new recruits for terrorist actions protesting Western intervention as well as to justify their violent actions. Still others use the word to express the desire for laws that ensure justice and protection. Therefore, although the terms are often used interchangeably, Shariah and Islamic law are not the same thing. The distinction between divine law (Shariah) and its human interpretation, application, and development (Islamic law) is important to keep in mind throughout this book.

Today, Muslim reformists and scholars are giving great attention to identifying what portions of the law are Shariah and therefore sacrosanct and unchangeable and what are human interpretations (fiqh) that are subject to revision. In the face of rapid, worldwide change, debates increasingly swirl around the necessity of reforming and modernizing Islamic law while preserving Shariah values that reflect the common good (*maslahah*).

The meaning of Shariah, as well as the origin, development, and reform of Islamic laws through the centuries, will be covered in the answers and chapters that follow. These

answers address widespread misunderstandings about
Islamic law in the West as well as the need for Islamic legal
reforms required by the pressing political, social, and economic challenges in the Muslim world.

Is There a Need to Protect American Law from the Infiltration of Shariah?

The US Constitution already protects against infiltra-
tion by foreign law and ensures that domestic law takes
precedence over religious and foreign law. The First
Amendment to the Constitution protects freedom of
religion at the same time that it prohibits courts from
adopting any religious code as the law of the land. There
is also a precedent in American courts that foreign law
is used only when its application does not violate public policy. There is therefore no possibility of Shariah
becoming the law of the United States, just as there is
no possibility of Jewish or Roman Catholic canon law
becoming the law of the United States. In the past thirty-
five years, only seven cases have come to court in which
some "foreign law" (not necessarily Shariah) was honored. In another thirteen cases where Shariah principles
were introduced, they were all rejected either on trial or
on appeal.

The American Bar Association has opposed as unnecessary any legislation that enacts bans on foreign law or
Shariah, given that safeguards against foreign law infiltrating American federal and state law already exist and protect
against rules that are contrary to American foreign policy,
including discrimination on the basis of gender or religion.
The majority of cases involving foreign law or Shariah
that have been brought to American courts have focused
on contract agreement, interpreting contracts that cite foreign or religious law. Muslim Americans who want to use

Shariah are not asking the American legal system to adopt Islamic rules of conduct, penal or otherwise, but rather to look at the norms to which they have already agreed to be bound in a family or business agreement.

How Does Islamic Law Differ from Jewish Law or Christian (Roman Catholic) Canon Law in the United States?

Like Jewish law and Roman Catholic canon law, the development of Islamic law was the work of religious scholars (*ulama*), rather than judges, courts, or governments. These scholars used their judgment and techniques of interpretation of the Shariah, as well as their knowledge of legal principles, to develop rules and regulations governing the lives of Muslims. Many people of faith prefer faith-based mediation and arbitration as more consistent with their morals, religious beliefs, and community values. Some governments have proven willing to delegate certain legal functions to religious communities' courts or councils, but they retain the right to monitor and overturn decisions. In all cases, rulings must fit within the framework of national or regional law.

It is interesting to note that in Arabic the term Shariah is used to refer to any system of laws brought by a prophet and believed to reflect God's commands. Thus, Shariat Musa is used to refer to the way of Moses and Shariat al-Masih refers to the way of the Messiah (Jesus). This usage traces back to the tenth century when the Hebrew Bible was translated into Arabic by Jewish scholars who used the term Shariah for the Hebrew word "Torah." So too today, the Arabic name for God, Allah, is commonly used by both Muslims and Christians in predominantly Muslim countries, including in translations of the Bible by Christians in Malaysia, Indonesia, Turkey, Lebanon, Egypt, and Syria.

Today, Jewish, Catholic, and Muslim religious courts or advisory councils handle a variety of cases, including marriage, divorce, annulments, inheritance, and other internal community disputes. Catholics rely on canon law, Orthodox Jews on Halakhah, and Muslims on Islamic law. All decisions are subject to local, state, and federal law.

Although disputes sometimes make their way into US civil courts, the Supreme Court has ruled that judges may not interpret religious doctrine or rule on theological matters. Civil courts must either defer to the decisions of religious bodies or decide religious disputes based on secular law.

Despite positive examples of interaction between Jewish and canon law and the secular legal system, Muslim desires to follow Islamic law are often met with fear and opposition not only in the United States but also in Europe, Australia, and Canada. When, for example, in 2008 the Archbishop of Canterbury, Rowan Williams, raised the possibility of exploring what degree of formal accommodation might be given to minority communities and their legal and moral codes, his suggestion met with strong opposition. This was despite the fact that Shariah "councils" have been operating informally in the United Kingdom since the early 1980s, as have Muslim arbitration tribunals formed under the Arbitration Act in 1996. Both are unofficial bodies working on a purely voluntary basis; they have neither legal powers nor binding decision-making capacity. In the Netherlands, Roman Catholic, Protestant, and Jewish courts are recognized as conflict-resolution mechanisms, while Islamic courts of a similar type remain blocked. Similarly, although Australia has a Beth Din court for Orthodox Jews and Koori courts for indigenous persons, requests for Shariah courts have been strongly opposed. Finally, Canada has a long-established tradition of allowing faith-based arbitration for Christians and Jews that dates to the Canadian Arbitration Act of 1991 and even further back for private arbitration in Jewish Beth Din courts and Roman Catholic canon law courts. Yet, when the Islamic Institute of Civil Justice announced in 2004 its use of Shariah to arbitrate family and inheritance cases, it was met with opposition, and soon thereafter there was a halt of all voluntary faith-based arbitration in Ontario in 2005, including by Christians and Jews, in favor of one single law applying to all Canadians.

Why Do Majorities in Muslim Countries Want Shariah?

Many Muslims believe that Shariah is God's divine revelation. According to a Pew Research Center Poll (2013) conducted throughout Africa, Asia, and Europe between 2008 and 2012, the majority of Muslims in South Asia (73%), the Middle East/North Africa (MENA) (69%), and Central Asia (55%) believe that Shariah is the revealed word of God. Very strong minorities of Muslim populations elsewhere also believe this: 41 percent in Southern-Eastern Europe and 49 percent in Southeast Asia. By comparison, a much smaller minority believe that Shariah is a human construct based on the word of God: 31 percent in Southeast Asia, 28 percent in Central Asia, 26 percent in Southern-Eastern Europe, 22 percent in MENA, and 18 percent in South Asia, ranging from a high of 39 percent in Indonesia to a low of 8 percent in Pakistan. The issue is critical because divine revelation, the authority of God's word, carries stronger authority, influence, and sense of obligation than a human interpretation. Both majorities and strong minorities of Muslim populations do not make a clear distinction between Shariah as God's revelation and Islamic law, which is a human construct, the product of Islamic jurisprudence developed in responding to specific historical and social contexts. They instead equate Shariah with Islamic law and consider Shariah-Islamic law to be the revealed word of God. This is why Shariah plays such a central and authoritative role.

Major opinion polls have reported that majorities of Muslims want and expect Shariah, seeing it as important to their religious well-being and that of society. Gallup World Polls in 2006 and 2007 in thirty-five Muslim countries found that large majorities of Muslims, both women and men in many and diverse Muslim-majority countries, wanted Shariah as "a" source of law, but not "the sole source." Strong support for Shariah did not necessarily translate into a desire for theocracy. In fact, the majority called for democratic government that also incorporated Islamic values. The Gallup World Polls found that significant majorities in many countries said religious leaders should play no direct role in drafting a country's constitution, writing national legislation, drafting new laws, determining foreign policy and international relations, or deciding how women should dress in public or what is televised or published in newspapers. Those who supported a direct role for religious leaders limited this role to an advisory capacity rather than one exercising direct power.

The Pew Research Center Poll (2013) found that opinions about Shariah varied among Muslims globally. Majorities in Afghanistan (99%), South Asia (84%), Southeast Asia (77%), MENA (74%), and sub-Saharan Africa (64%) favored the establishment of Shariah as official law. Only very small minorities in Southern-Eastern Europe (18%), Central Asia (12%), and Azerbaijan (8%) agreed. No variations were found by gender, age, or education level, except in the MENA region, where Muslims aged thirty-five and older were found more likely to support implementation of Shariah than those aged eighteen to thirty-four.

What Are Muslims Asking for When They Call for Shariah?

Shariah means different things to different people. Just as there are those who are looking for full implementation of classical Islamic law and its punishments, so also there are others who want a more restricted approach—for example, giving Shariah jurisdiction in family matters but not criminal justice. Still others call for a more value-based and holistic approach to Shariah that looks at the common good (*maslahah*) and not punishment only. Some just want to be sure that no constitutional law violates Shariah principles and/or that the head of state is Muslim, while others see Shariah as a path to empowerment, rights, and the strengthening of families.

The Pew Research Center Poll found that the most critical factor in determining a population's relative support for Shariah seems to be the relationship between Islam and the constitutions or basic laws in any given country. Support runs higher in places where the constitution or basic laws favor Islam over other religions, such as in Afghanistan (99%), Iraq (91%), the Palestinian territories (89%), Malaysia (86%), Pakistan (84%), Morocco (83%), and Bangladesh (82%). In addition, support for Shariah in family matters was highest where religious courts were already in place. Ranging from a high of 94 percent in Egypt to a low of 66 percent in Indonesia, at least half of Muslims living in countries with religious courts said they believed that religious judges should decide family and property disputes By contrast, in countries where Islam is not legally favored, one-third or fewer supported Shariah as the official law of the land. Furthermore, in countries where secular courts oversee family matters, fewer than half said they believed religious judges should decide on family and property disputes, ranging from a high of 44 percent in Kyrgyzstan to a low of 6 percent in Bosnia-Herzegovina.

The Pew report also found differences of opinion as to which specific aspects of Shariah Muslims wanted to see implemented. Most were generally supportive of implementing Shariah in the domestic sphere, such as for settling family or property disputes, but they were far less supportive of severe punishments for crimes. Support for application of Shariah in the domestic sphere was highest in Southeast Asia (84%), South Asia (78%), MENA (78%), and Central Asia (62%). Those least in favor were in Southern-Eastern Europe (41%).

With respect to the question of what implementation of Shariah would mean for non-Muslims, the majority of those polled—64 percent in Southern-Eastern Europe, 60 percent in South Asia, 59 percent in Central Asia, 55 percent in Southeast Asia, and 51 percent in the MENA region—said that Shariah should only apply to Muslims and that non-Muslims should be free to practice their own religion. For example, in Pakistan although 84 percent of those polled favored implementation of Shariah as official law, fully 96 percent said that non-Muslims should be free to practice their religion—and that this was a good thing. Of the twenty-one countries surveyed, in only five—Egypt (74%), Kyrgyzstan (62%), Afghanistan (61%), Jordan (58%), and Indonesia (50%)—did a majority think that Shariah should be applicable to everyone.

What these statistics make clear is that while majorities wish to see Shariah implemented, there no clear consensus about what Shariah in the public sphere should look like. Moreover, opinions range considerably by country and by issue, making it difficult to assert any blanket statement about "Muslim opinions" or what is specifically meant when Muslims indicate support for Shariah.

How Does Shariah Play a Role in Muslim-Majority Countries Today?

As a central set of guidelines and principles intended to guide Muslim communal life, for many Muslims the concept of Shariah in public life represents a strong moral, emotional, and religious ideal as the blueprint for Muslim society. At a time when many Muslim-majority countries perceive themselves to be under threat from forces ranging from Western imperialism to domestic political challenges, an idealized vision of history in which strong, independent empires were ruled by Shariah provides a powerful alternative, a vision of authenticity and identity rooted in Islam that was once—and can again be—possible. Calls for the reimplementation of Shariah in the public sphere must be understood within that context. The challenge is that definitions of what Shariah is and what aspects Muslims want to have implemented in public life vary significantly.

Today, thirty-five countries incorporate Shariah into civil, common, or customary law so that the legal systems in most Muslim-majority countries can best be described as a hybrid of Islamic law and Western-inspired constitutions and legal codes. While there are countries such as Saudi Arabia and Iran that assert the primacy of Shariah and insist that all laws must be in compliance with it, the reality is that secular and Western influences, such as in civil and commercial law, are also apparent in these countries.

Is More than One Interpretation of Shariah Possible?

The Pew Research Center Poll found mixed responses to this question. In no region other than South Asia (62%) was there overall a clear minority or majority calling for a single interpretation, but there were strong majorities in specific countries in favor of a single interpretation, most notably

70 percent in Tajikistan and 67 percent in Afghanistan. By contrast, strong majorities in Morocco (60%) and Tunisia (72%) believe that multiple interpretations of the Shariah are possible. The smallest support for multiple interpretations was found in Kosovo (11%), Azerbaijan (15%), and Pakistan (17%). Overall, the greatest division in opinions was found in MENA, Central Asia, and Southern-Eastern Europe. In several countries—Turkey, Indonesia, and Iraq—the population was nearly evenly split. In other cases, very strong minorities said they simply didn't know whether there should be a single or multiple interpretations of Shariah—46 percent in Albania, 42 percent in Kosovo, and 35 percent in Uzbekistan. What this tells us is that although there may be majority support for including Shariah in the public sphere, opinions about whether it should be monolithic or varied in interpretation are quite mixed.

How Do Muslims Whose Countries Do Not Follow Shariah Feel about It?

Again, results vary by country and region with narrow majorities in Bosnia-Herzegovina and Kosovo (50% each) finding this to be a good thing, along with strong minorities elsewhere, such as 47 percent Azerbaijan, 42 percent Kazakhstan, and 41 percent Lebanon. On the other hand, majorities in South Asia (91% Pakistan, 84% Afghanistan, 83% Bangladesh), Southeast Asia (65% Malaysia and Indonesia), and much of MENA (83% Palestinian territories, 76% Morocco, 71% Iraq, 69% Jordan, 67% Egypt, 54% Tunisia) found this to be a bad thing.

Furthermore, opinions about the degree to which Shariah is already being followed in a given country's laws also vary. The only region where a majority of respondents indicated belief that the country's laws somewhat or very closely follow Shariah was Southeast Asia (58% in Malaysia and 54% in Indonesia). Other regions had mixed results. In South Asia, for example, 88 percent of those polled in Afghanistan believed the country somewhat or very closely followed Shariah, compared to only 48 percent in Bangladesh and 41 percent in Pakistan. In MENA most results hovered in the middle—56 percent in Iraq, 54 percent in Morocco, 41 percent in Jordan, 40 percent in Tunisia, and 39 percent in the Palestinian territories.

Ultimately, these statistics show that while the idea of Shariah in power is appealing to many, opinions vary significantly as to what, exactly, Shariah is, how it is to be interpreted, and which aspects are to be implemented.

How Do Muslims in the West Feel about Shariah?

The overwhelming majority of American Muslims understand Shariah as a matter of personal religious observance, not something they wish to see enforced by the government. They further say that they do not want to replace the US Constitution with Shariah and they do not seek to use Shariah to override secular laws. A 2016 poll by the Institute for Social Policy and Understanding found that only 10 percent of American Muslims said Islam should be a main source of law, while 27 percent said it should be a source, but not the only one. By way of comparison, 12 percent of Protestants said Christianity should be the main source of American law and 29 percent said it should be a source, but not the only one. More Muslims (55%) than Protestants (50%) said that religion should not be a source of American law at all.

American Muslims overall support the Constitution and value the freedom of religion all American citizens enjoy. Like members of other faith traditions, Muslims face the challenge of life and loyalty in a secular society where some laws and cultural practices differ from the teachings of their faith. Yet they also recognize that religious freedom—for both themselves and others—requires embracing secularism and an open society as the mechanisms that make such religious freedom possible. That means balancing their religious identity as Muslims with their cultural identity as Americans (something that ethnic Catholics, Hindus, and other immigrants have faced). It also means respecting the centrality of the rights of religious freedom and freedom of expression in this religiously diverse society. These rights cannot be voted away or curtailed—for anyone—without violating the First Amendment.

Muslims are most likely to pursue adherence to Shariah in family matters, but with the understanding that civil law must be followed as a primary obligation. For example, like many Christians who believe in the importance of a church wedding, but still must obtain a civil marriage license, many Muslims sign both an Islamic marriage contract (*nikah*) and obtain a civil marriage license in order to meet both their religious and civil obligations. Since the state recognizes only the civil marriage license as legally binding, several suits asking for recognition of marriages conducted in the United States with only Islamic ceremonies have failed because of the lack of a marriage license, along with missing markers normally considered evidence of a marriage, such as a change in last name and joint bank accounts, which are not common practices under Islamic law. Similarly, many Muslims realize the importance of obtaining both religious permission and a civil decree in the event of divorce because the state claims exclusive jurisdiction over the dissolution of marriage.

The First Amendment to the US Constitution prohibits the court from interpreting Islamic law or ruling on religious doctrine. It can only consider the legal requirements of the case, such as fairness and whether the contract breaches public policy or constitutional principles. In practice, considering Islamic law on any point would require interpretations agreed upon by Islamic scholars so that no expert knowledge of the subject on the part of the judge would be required. Since this rarely happens, attempts to argue on the basis of Islamic law typically fail in the American court system. In addition, the American legal system must follow certain public policy guidelines, such as considering the best interests of the child in child custody and guardianship cases or due process and equal treatment in cases of divorce. American judges are not bound to accept rulings on these issues from other countries unless these parameters are met.

In addition to commercial transactions, Islamic law is most often raised in American courts regarding divorce cases involving children, property, and/or long-term marriages. A common issue involves the dower or marriage gift assigned to a Muslim woman in the Islamic marriage contract. Under Islamic law, this gift is considered to be her personal property to which she is entitled as a term of the contract. If it is not specified in the contract, Islamic law stipulates that she must be assigned the equivalent amount for a person of her background, education, and other considerations.

Courts have differed as to whether the terms of the Islamic marriage contract qualify as a prenuptial agreement or contract law. Enforcing a dower or marriage gift under prenuptial agreements, which are not recognized in all US states, is not guaranteed. Considering the marriage gift as a term of a contract, especially if specific amounts are listed, has tended to have more success because it does not present a constitutional challenge or public policy issue. A vaguely described marriage gift has proven difficult to collect.

Some cases that come to American courts address comity issues. The principle of comity requires an American court to recognize a decision made in another country as a matter of reciprocity. Once that decision is recognized by an American court, it becomes law. In some cases, comity can be disadvantageous to a divorced woman. For example, a husband may claim that he divorced his wife in a country that does not support fair property division and support for a wife in divorce cases. However, although this represents a challenge to comity, if the divorce does not fulfill the requirements of due process under American law and was not recognized by an official body, the American court is not obligated to recognize it, which can work to the wife's advantage by requiring a divorce in an American court with terms more favorable to her.

Some imams (mosque leaders) are working to bridge private observance of Shariah with American civil law by drafting marriage contracts, in consultation with the prospective couple, that are then submitted to the court as consent orders. Having the court approve the agreement provides security for the future because the contract then becomes legally binding as a mutual agreement without raising concerns about the need to interpret Islamic law. Some imams and mosques even have standard marriage contracts with fill-in-the-blank provisions. This does not constitute the introduction of Shariah into the American court system, but it provides a mechanism that respects Islamic law while leaving power in the hands of the American courts.

Can Muslims in the West Be Loyal Citizens?

Much of the fear of a growing presence of Islam and Muslims in the West and eventual "take-over" of Western countries based on demographics is rooted in the question of whether it is possible to be both a good Muslim and a loyal citizen of a non-Muslim state. Many Muslims themselves sometimes wonder about their place in Western societies, particularly when they are increasingly subjected to scrutiny as potential security threats and even face travel bans. If some in the West ask whether Muslims can be loyal citizens of the West, some Muslims ask whether the West will truly accept their loyal citizenship or whether they will remain constantly under suspicion and surveillance as outsiders, even in their birth countries.

Historically, Muslims have always participated in the governance of the places where they have lived. Islamic law has long taught that Muslims may live anywhere, so long as they are free to practice their religion. Wherever they live, Muslims are expected to abide by the laws of that land unless doing so would violate their religious freedom. Today, Muslims serve in the US Congress and European parliaments, the military, government agencies, and police forces; they also have roles in state and local government and in the business, medical, legal, and educational communities. While a tiny minority of extremists seeks to disrupt society, the overwhelming majority of Muslims are law-abiding contributors to their host and home societies.

At the heart of issues related to Muslim loyalties is the degree to which Muslims can and should integrate into non-Muslim societies. Finding that road to integration, rather than choosing isolation or militancy, is facilitated by contemporary reformers' thoughts about questions of faith, identity, assimilation, religious pluralism, and tolerance.

The most influential reformist voices are Europeans who have faced the same questions, such as Tariq Ramadan of Switzerland, Mustafa Ceric of Bosnia-Herzegovina, and Timothy Winter (Abdal Hakim Murad) of Great Britain.

These reformers reject a polarized view of the world that posits "Muslims" against the "West" and advocate a synthesis of common values for establishing a European or American Muslim identity instead. Though recognizing distinctive religious and cultural differences, they nevertheless affirm the essential compatibility of Islam and the West.

Tariq Ramadan emphasizes that those living in the West are Muslim by religion, but they are also French, British, German, American, and so on by culture. Thus, rather than seeing themselves as religious minorities or perpetual victims, Muslims can focus on making a contribution to the society in which they are living according to the ethics of citizenship and remaining true to democratic principles. Ramadan takes a positive view of secularism as the mechanism by which all citizens can live together in religious freedom for all. He sees no inherent conflict between being European and being a Muslim. He embraces democracy, the rule of law, and open political dialogue. Yet he also observes that integration does not necessarily mean wholesale assimilation. While Muslims must accept the constitution, laws, and framework of their new countries, they must also be clear when they disagree with a law while also respecting it. Thus, if the hijab is prohibited by law, that law must be obeyed and an alternative to hijab found while nevertheless protesting the injustice of the law. At the same time, he insists that many so-called Muslim problems in Europe, such as crime, slums, and unemployment have nothing to do with religion and everything to do with social, economic, and educational inequalities faced by immigrant communities. He believes that social rather than religious solutions to these problems are needed.

Mustafa Ceric emphasizes that patriotism is a required religious duty and urges Muslims to embrace their European identity and be patriots of their countries in the name of Islam. At the same time, he calls upon European governments to facilitate Muslim integration into European society by accommodating and institutionalizing their religious needs. He notes the negative role of fear—both of European societies with respect to Muslims and of Muslims with respect to the experiences of poverty, isolation, and being outsiders to local culture. He cites freedom from poverty as particularly critical to Muslim European success. Ceric also calls for training European imams in Europe rather than importing imams from elsewhere. He believes that establishing a unified European-wide Islamic authority, similar to Bosnia's model, with an elected head or president of the ulama (religious scholars) would help to institutionalize Islam in a European setting, making it clear that Muslims are loyal citizens and contributors to European culture and civilization.

Like Ramadan and Ceric, Timothy Winter emphasizes that European and American Muslims have a vested interest in asserting their identities—not simply as Muslims but, more importantly, as European and American Muslims. He describes the need for acculturation, self-criticism, and reform, setting aside criticisms and resentments. Instead, he believes that Muslims need to locate and populate both spiritual and cultural space that is at once Muslim and European/American. He further charges Muslims to develop theological and social tools that identify and thwart extremism and that root citizenship in the rejection of militant, distorted ideologies.

A view of Muslims' place as citizens of America can be found in the Pew Research Center's 2017 poll of US Muslims. A number of findings regarding their lives reflect optimism and positive feelings about their citizenship in America. For example, 90 percent of the Muslims surveyed said that they are proud to be American and proud to be Muslim. In addition, 55 percent of Muslim Americans think

Americans are friendly toward US Muslims, compared to only 14 percent who believe that they are unfriendly. Fully 80 percent report satisfaction with the way things are going in their lives and a large majority believe in the American dream, with 70 percent saying that most Muslims who want to make it in America can succeed if they are willing to work hard.

All of these statements were made despite the acknowledgment overall by Muslims in this survey that they perceive a lot of discrimination against their religious group, and Muslim women, who have a higher level of concern than Muslim men, report in larger percentages that they have experienced discrimination personally. About three-quarters of Muslim Americans say that President Trump is unfriendly toward them and two-thirds say they are dissatisfied with the way things are going today. In stark contrast, in 2011 when Barack Obama was president, most Muslims were positive about the president and thought the country was headed in the right direction.

Muslims' view of their citizenship is linked to their identity as Muslims. The 2017 Pew survey reports that seven in ten Muslims say working for justice and equality in society is essential to what it means to be Muslim and a similar percentage report that there is no conflict between Islam and democracy. In an attempt to gauge views about violence in society, both Muslim Americans and the US public overwhelmingly reported rejection of violence against civilians to further a political, social, or religious cause, but three-quarters of US Muslims (76%) say it is never justified, compared to 59 percent of the general US public.

2

SHARIAH

THE BIG PICTURE

Shariah is a word that evokes condemnation from politicians, pundits, and others, yet it carries deep spiritual and social meaning for Muslims around the world.
Understanding the origin and development of Shariah
is critical to addressing widespread misunderstandings
about Islamic law in the West as well as Islamic legal
reforms being made in response to pressing political,
social, and economic challenges in the Muslim world.

Central to the development of Islamic law were schools
of law, established in the early centuries of Islam within
diverse historical, social, and cultural contexts. While there
is an underlying unity in Islamic law, there are also significant differences of opinion. Over time, Shariah blended
with Islamic as well as other forms of law, such as *siyasa
Shariah*, created by rulers for purposes of governance. As a
result, many came to label all of these laws as Shariah and
to think that to follow the law of the land was to follow
Shariah.

Today, Muslim reformers and scholars are giving great
attention to identifying what portions of Islamic law are
divine (*Shariah*), what its objectives or purposes (*maqasid
al-Shariah*) are, and what portions are human understanding (*fiqh*) and interpretations of Shariah. Whereas Shariah

is immutable and infallible, Islamic law (fiqh) is fallible and changeable. Fiqh is supposed to be guided by Shariah objectives (maqasid al-Shariah).

In the face of rapid, worldwide change, debates swirl around the necessity of reforming and modernizing Islamic law while preserving Shariah values that reflect the common good. This chapter addresses the key sources and legal mechanisms used to inspire and develop legal renewal and reform in the face of scientific and medical advances, economic and political forces, and calls for new women's and human rights that will impact jurists' decisions and the lives of Muslims around the world.

What Are the Origins and Meanings of Shariah?

Shariah literally means a "path" or "a way to life-sustaining water." It is mentioned only once in the Quran, in reference to Muhammad: "Then we placed you on a Shariah from the command, so follow it and do not follow those who do not know" (Q 45:18).

Shariah provides a set of principles or guidelines Muslims are to follow in order to live a faithful and observant life in this world and to receive eternal reward in the next world. It includes duties and responsibilities to both God (worship) and human beings (social transactions), giving it both private and public dimensions.

Shariah principles are found in two revealed sources—the Quran (God's revelation) and Sunna (reports on what Muhammad said and did). Muslims believe that rational thinking is a gift from God, but by itself it is incomplete. Muslims believe the Quran is the final, perfect, and complete revelation given by God to Muhammad between 610 and 632 CE, and then written down by his followers in the generation after his death. It represents the most important source of Shariah. The Quran requires both individuals and communities to implement God's will on earth by living a moral life, expanding and defending the faith and Muslim community, and establishing a just society. It enjoys the highest level of religious authority for Muslims.

The Sunna (Muhammad's example) is understood as the authoritative precedent of the Prophet, in effect how he lived out and explained the message of the Quran in daily life. It is transmitted through reports (*hadith*) by followers, both male and female, about what Muhammad said and did and the rulings he issued, as well as through the communal practices he established and even the methods of legal reasoning he passed on to his senior followers. The Sunna is considered a revealed source of law alongside the Quran, although its details and exact shape are not fixed like those of the Quran.

Shariah functioned as an ethical code that affected the social, educational, cultural, economic, and political practices in the Muslim community. Drawing on the Shariah, jurists were able to answer specific questions about just and unjust human behavior in the community, including "promoting good and preventing evil," in order to seek personal happiness and reward and to build strong communities. Rather than a map, Shariah is a moral compass or guide.

Today, the term "Shariah" is often used broadly to refer to the rules and regulations of Islamic law that govern the lives of Muslims. Islamic law includes devotional worship (prayer, fasting, pilgrimage), civil duties (contracts, marriage, divorce, inheritance), and penal and international law, and provides a common code of behavior and connection for all Muslim societies.

Although Muslims refer to Shariah as providing a comprehensive approach to life, it is not a formalized code of law or set of rules that are fixed in a specific volume or period of time. One cannot go to the library and check out the Shariah. Shariah is the source for the development of Islamic law which became a broad-based system of norms and the values that, along with local customs, guided the way of life in the Muslim community.

Are Shariah and Islamic Law the Same Thing?

Many people, Muslims and non-Muslims alike, use the terms Shariah and Islamic law, that is created by human beings, interchangeably. However, they are not the same thing. Shariah refers to the divinely inspired codes, guidelines, or principles (maqasid) Muslims are to follow in living out their faith, combining law, religion, and ethics. Islamic law, on the other hand, refers to the practical application of Shariah, in both real and hypothetical cases. To put it another way, Islamic law is the product of human reasoning in light of divinely revealed guidelines. The term fiqh, meaning "understanding" or "comprehension," is used to describe this science of jurisprudence, which requires deep understanding and knowledge for one to interpret and apply Shariah principles (maqasid) from the Quran and Sunna to create human-made laws. Fiqh is thus the body of Islamic law reflecting this understanding or comprehension of the Shariah principles.

Another type of law that existed in classical times, made by Muslim rulers, was called siyasa Shariah. These laws were not based on scripture, but on the rulers' personal judgments about how to maintain order and deal with practical needs in civil society, such as fair marketing, traffic control, or public security. Fiqh and siyasa operated in separate realms and Muslim rulers had no control over interpreting the Quran or Sunna. However, because these regulations were necessary to promote the community's welfare (*maslahah*) they came to be known as siyasa Shariah, Islamically legitimate because the ultimate purpose of the Shariah was to promote good governance and to foster the public good.

The development of Islamic law was critical because of Islam's primary emphasis on correct behavior or action (orthopraxy) rather than correct belief or doctrine (orthodoxy) for which Christianity came to be known. Historically, these humanly fallible legal interpretations came to be viewed as sacred and as unchangeable as the Shariah principles on which they were based. Jurists themselves sometimes used the term Shariah to refer to the human-made laws in order to highlight the divinely inspired principles that were at their core. This equation of Shariah with Islamic law has created confusion among both Muslims and non-Muslims alike.

Many scholars and reformers today are calling for greater attention to differentiating between Shariah principles or objectives (maqasid) and man-made law, or fiqh (Islamic law). While Shariah is sacred and unchangeable, as seen in beliefs and ritual worship, Islamic law is the product of human understanding and interpretations that occurred in specific historical contexts. These laws can and have changed over time and space. Part of the development, and at times diversity, of Islamic law was its ability to consider new situations and circumstances in human interactions and exchanges, and to focus on outcomes that promote justice and public welfare (maslahah), all while maintaining the consistency of maqasid al-Shariah as a set of principles. At certain points in history, claims that Islamic law was fixed and unchangeable threatened Islam's dynamism and ability to adapt to new circumstances that had been characteristic of the relationship between Shariah and developing Islamic law.

What Are the Sources Used to Develop Islamic Law?

The primary sources or guideposts for the development of Islamic law are the Quran and the Sunna, the example of Muhammad. These narrative reports (hadith) of what Muhammad said and did were used to exemplify, explain, and add to the Quran's principles and values.

Muslims believe that the Quran is God's revelation given to Muhammad between 610 and 632 CE and codified by his followers in the generation after his death. The Quran does contain about eighty verses that address strictly legal matters, but the Quran is not a law book as are biblical books such as Leviticus or Deuteronomy. Most of the Quran consists of broad guidelines and moral directives that are supposed to guide individual and communal human interactions. They sometimes modify and at other times replace or supplement earlier tribal laws.

Quran verses, such as "In God's Messenger you have a fine model for anyone whose hope is in God and the Last Day" (Q 33:21), highlight the importance of the Sunna. The Sunna was written down after Muhammad's death when many stories were narrated and collected about what Muhammad had said or done. Because Muslims believe that these narrative reports or prophetic traditions illustrate from the Quran what perfect living is, authentication of the hadith is viewed as critical to a correct understanding of their Islamic faith. Muslim scholars developed a science of hadith criticism to evaluate the authenticity of many hadith in circulation. The two most famous and authoritative collections of hadith revered by Sunni Muslims are the Sahih (Authentic) collections of al-Bukhari (d. 870) and Muslim (d. 875).

Shia Muslims also believe in the importance of the Sunna, but they look to different hadith collections, preferring those that can be traced to members of Muhammad's family, particularly Ali, Muhammad's cousin and son-in-law. Shia Muslims also look to the teachings of Ali and their Imams (Ali's male successors) as divinely revealed sources and infallible legal interpretation.

When there was no direct or relevant text in the Quran or Sunna, Muslim scholars or jurists used their intellect and reasoning to interpret and develop Islamic law. While Sunnis used analogical reasoning (*qiyas*) and consensus (*ijma*) of scholarly opinion for this purpose, Shia relied simply on the use of reason (*aql*).

Analogical reasoning (qiyas) draws on previous laws or answers that provide parallels to new situations or principles. A similar situation or principle provides guidance since what is true for one must also be true for the other. For example, the Quran's prohibition of drinking date wine led to a broad prohibition against alcohol altogether based on the altered mental state that all of these substances produce in those who drink them. Contemporary jurists have expanded this ban to include other substances, such as heroin and cocaine, which produce similar altered mental states. Therefore, this analogy is based on the similar outcomes produced by consuming these products.

The consensus of scholars (ijma) relies on a hadith reporting Muhammad's saying that "My community will never agree on an error." During Muhammad's lifetime, any legal question could be posed to him directly. After his death, the situation became more complicated. For some issues, such as worship requirements, the entire Muslim community's consensus was sought because all Muslims were expected to fulfill these duties. On other matters, particularly the growing need for legal rulings on new issues and problems, the community turned to those considered to be most informed in religious and legal matters. Thus, the consensus of scholars (ulama) was considered a safeguard for the unity and functionality of the community.

In addition to these legal mechanisms, other guiding principles are also used to interpret Islamic law. The Quran's strong emphasis on justice reflects the primary values and objectives (maqasid) that the jurist must uphold when using reasoning (*ijtihad*). The most important of these are juristic preference (*istihsan*), permitting the jurist to select the most appropriate interpretation for a given situation, and equity (*istislah*), allowing for exceptions to strict or literal legal reasoning in light of public welfare (maslahah), or the common good. These three principles often work in conjunction with each other. For example, if the outcome is to be more just and equitable (istislah), the legal mechanism of juristic preference (istihsan) permits a jurist to select the most appropriate interpretation for a given situation (even though it is a minority or weaker position) and therefore to override a stricter or more literal interpretation of the law. At the heart of the outcome would be the common good or public benefit (maslahah) of the decision. Ultimately, the purpose of these principles was both to assure that the law is not applied rigidly and that jurists have some flexibility in reaching decisions that justly address a specific set of circumstances. These principles also help to explain the multiplicity and diversity of interpretations in Islamic law.

Do Sunnis and Shia Share the Same Shariah?

Whether Sunnis and Shia have different Shariah depends on how one interprets the word. Sunnis and Shia both hold the Quran and Sunna (Muhammad's example) as primary sources of Islamic law. United in their common confession of one God, the Quran, and the Prophet Muhammad, they share the same Shariah in the sense of divinely inspired guidelines or principles. However, they have clear differences in their interpretations of Islamic law, rooted in their disagreement about legitimate leadership in the Muslim community after Muhammad's death.

Sunnis, who are approximately 85 percent of all Muslims, believed that leadership should pass to the most qualified person based on majority opinion. Abu Bakr, who was Muhammad's most trusted Companion and advisor, as well as his father-in-law, was widely respected by the community for his wisdom and piety. He was selected by majority consensus to serve as caliph, or successor as political and military head of the community. Although Abu Bakr's opinions about religious and legal matters were respected because of his close relationship to Muhammad, he was not considered to be infallible or to be a prophet.

Shia, 15 percent of all Muslims, believed that leadership should be hereditary. Muhammad did not have any sons who survived infancy. However, his daughter, Fatima, was married to Ali, Muhammad's cousin and closest living male relative. Shia believed that Muhammad had appointed Ali as his successor and thus Ali should have been appointed Imam (leader) after Muhammad's death, serving as both political and religious leader. They also believed that Ali's successors should also come from the family of the Prophet. Shia Imams, although not prophets, were regarded as inspired, infallible, and authoritative interpreters of God's will as expressed in Islamic law.

This disagreement about rightful leadership led not only to a political divide between Sunnis and Shia but also to differences between the Sunni and Shia interpretations of Islamic law. Sunnis saw the success and power of Sunni caliphs in Islamic history as validation of their claim to rule and a sign of God's favor for following God's guidance. Sunnis equated political success with the faithful upholding of Islamic law, thus making Islamic law central to Sunni claims to political legitimacy. Shia, as a perpetual minority, viewed history as a theater for their struggle as a righteous, oppressed, and disinherited community forced to constantly strive to restore God's rule on earth. They believed this is to be done through the implementation of Islamic law under their divinely appointed Imam.

Although Sunnis and Shia both look to the Quran and Sunna for guidance, they refer to different sources for Sunna. Sunnis look to the hadith collections of al-Bukhari (d. 870) and Muslim (d. 875), which record narratives from a variety of Muhammad's Companions and close friends, including those who became caliphs. Shia rely alternatively on the hadith collections traceable to Muhammad's family, particularly Ali, and his supporters. Although Sunnis accept hadith from Ali, Shia do not accept hadith from Abu Bakr and the other Sunni caliphs, whom they view as illegitimate usurpers of Ali's rightful position as leader.

Through the centuries, Sunnis and Shia each developed their own independent schools of law and used different methods to derive legal rulings from Shariah guidelines and principles. Sunnis use analogical reasoning (qiyas) and consensus (ijma), while Shia rely on reason (aql). Sunnis look to a variety of interpreters of the law, recognizing some as more authoritative than others, but Sunnis do not consider any interpreter of Islamic law, other than Muhammad, to be infallible. Shia, on the other hand, look to their Imams as infallible interpreters and rely on qualified religious scholars who serve as the Imam's authoritative, although not infallible, agents in his absence.

These differences in visions of leadership and law have often led to tension and even conflict between Sunnis and Shia. One major modern effort to overcome these tensions and assert the common beliefs of Sunnis and Shia is the Amman Message, issued in 2004. The Amman Message brought together the most highly recognized Sunni and Shia scholars to address several questions related to Islamic law. The most important outcome of this effort was mutual recognition of Sunnis and Shia as Muslims and mutual recognition of the validity of their main law schools and their commonly shared Shariah.

How Did Scholars and Jurists Create Islamic Law from Shariah Principles?

Maqasid al-Shariah, meaning divinely inspired guidelines or principles, comes from the Quran and Sunna (example) of Muhammad, both of which date to the seventh century. Islamic law, as the practical application of Shariah principles to real-life situations, began in the seventh century but has been in an ongoing process of creation that continues right through to our present age.

Because the Quran is not a law book and because new situations constantly arose, the Islamic legal system in the early period of Islamic history relied on legal specialists (muftis) for opinions (fatwas) on specific questions. These rulings represented a mufti's own authoritative reasoning and conclusions about the question, making fatwas distinct from Shariah. A fatwa is best understood as the mufti's answer to a question from members of the community or a judge (*qadi*) with a difficult case. In contrast to Western practice, the fatwas of distinguished scholars, rather than the decisions of judges, were collected and published. Thus, authoritative legal literature was formed not by precedents from law courts (as in the West) but primarily from answers given by distinguished muftis. Qadis, like muftis, were residents in their community well-versed in its customs and ways of life. The legal literature used by qadis as references addressed changing social conditions. The fatwas that were most relevant for current use became established and those that were less germane were gradually excluded.

Over time, certain jurists, who were often muftis or authors with deep legal knowledge, came to be considered pivotal scholars, and specific law schools were named after them. Their patterns of reasoning became examples for other jurists to use in approaching the sources. For Sunnis, the most important figures are Abu Hanifa (d. 767), Malik ibn Anas (d. 795), al-Shafii (d. 820), and Ibn Hanbal (d. 855). For Shia, the most important figures are Jafar al-Sadiq (d. 765) and Zayd ibn Ali (d. 740). Two other important figures in the development of Islamic law were Abdullah ibn Ibad (d. 708) and al-Zahiri (d. 883). All eight of the law schools named after these figures were recognized in the 2004 Amman Message as legitimate interpretations of Islamic law.

The legal schools represented an authoritative source that replaced the authority of any Muslim ruler or a single jurist. Masterful knowledge of the law established legal authority and this authority became the sole province of legal scholars rather than political rulers. A mastery of legal knowledge, known in later centuries as ijtihad or independent reasoning, has always been a key quality of Islamic law. A popular saying developed, that God would send a renewer of religion every century, implying that the interpretation of Islam and Islamic law were intended to remain dynamic.

Do Shariah Principles Allow Social Renewal and Reform?

While Shariah as a set of guidelines or principles remains unchanging, how these guidelines are interpreted has changed over time and space in accordance with society's needs and developments. Central to discussions about modernization and reform are the concepts of renewal (*tajdid*) and reform (*islah*) that call for fresh approaches to thinking about how Shariah principles can be applied most appropriately in a modern context to fulfill the common good (maslahah). Both are rooted in the Quran and Sunna (Muhammad's example).

The Quran uses the word "reform" to describe the preaching of prophets who called sinful communities to return to God's path. The Quran's command to Muslims to promote good and prevent evil (Q 3:104, 110) has served as the rationale for reform throughout Islamic history. Ongoing renewal is intended to help Muslims reform their societies in a way that keeps them faithful to Islam, while allowing for changing circumstances. There are several hadith in which Muhammad reassures his followers that God will send a renewer (*mujaddid*) in every century, making the ongoing process of renewal part of God's divine plan for humanity.

Historically, renewal and reform have been called for at times when there is a perceived disconnect between God's will and vision for society and the reality of the state of the world. Calls for renewal typically focus on returning to the ideal patterns revealed in the Quran and Sunna, while reinterpreting these sources (ijtihad) to address contemporary concerns. Efforts are focused on getting back to the authentic teachings, regulations, and social vision of the foundational sources and the norms of the early community—which represents a purer past. This is done by seeking to remove historical accretions, unwanted innovations, and, sometimes, established institutions that have been corrupting influences. Shariah, fiqh (jurisprudence, human interpretation of Shariah), and Islamic law, particularly the early legal manuals, are often conflated, however, which makes attempts at reform difficult, due to fears of ignoring or changing divinely inspired truth.

Islamic reformers often have to remind Muslims of this difference between Shariah and fiqh, distinguishing between divine, eternal truths, principles, and objectives (maqasid al-Shariah) on the one hand, and historically conditioned, human-made explanations and applications of these truths that are time and location-specific (laws), on the other. Ultimately, the purpose of reform is to bring society into greater conformity with Shariah principles in a way that is sensitive to the realities of real people living in complex, diverse, and constantly changing societies.

At times, the return to a purer past is pursued in a very literal way, by efforts to recreate the modes of behavior and belief from the idealized seventh-century community of Muhammad and his early followers (Salafi, forefathers). Salafis look to the first three generations of Muslims as the normative examples to be followed. Some do this at a personal, individual level, such as in how they dress or wear a beard, while others try to return the broader society to these patterns, sometimes through social activism and sometimes by seeking political power. Resistance to more progressive change stems from concerns about a loss or watering down of faith, identity, and values that could lead to weakening religious practice. Nevertheless, even the most conservative Salafis adopt some of the trappings of modern life, such as use of cell phones, computers, and modern transportation.

At other times, reformers focus attention on the spirit or value behind particular customs and norms in order to find appropriate ways to adapt them to contemporary circumstances. They see change as representing the dynamic nature of Shariah values (maqasid), not as opposing them. A Muslim's duties and obligations to God (worship) do not change. What is open to change in Islamic law are guidelines that involve social transactions and obligations, which function within dynamic and changing social and historical circumstances. Indeed, reinterpretation that addresses contemporary issues and needs in a way that fulfills the common good (maslahah) is regarded as an obligation.

Over the past two hundred years, questions of revival and reform have revolved around whether and how to accommodate new realities, such as modernization; secularism; technological, scientific, and medical advances; economic development; political ideologies; and women's and human rights. Early encounters with many of these ideas and phenomena were the direct result of the European colonial presence and its political and legal systems, and thus some Muslims were and remain hesitant to engage or embrace them, fearing Western influence and dominance that might lead them to lose their own identity, authenticity, and faith. However, others point to the long history of compatibility between Islam and science, technology, medicine, and reason when scientific exploration and discovery were understood to be true expressions and signs of faith. To recapture this dynamic relationship, they highlight the great Islamic reformers from the nineteenth and early twentieth centuries, such as Egypt's Muhammad Abduh and South Asia's Sayyid Ahmad Khan and Muhammad Iqbal, who exemplify successful marriages between Islam and modernity.

Today, most Muslim states, including Egypt, Sudan, Nigeria, Morocco, Iraq, Pakistan, Afghanistan, Malaysia, and Indonesia, have Western-inspired constitutions and legal codes that are blended with Islamic laws. These systems are the product of reinterpretation, adoption, or adaptation of Western models blended with Islamic belief and traditions to respond to the new challenges of modern life and society. At the same time, some legal reforms, particularly those addressing family law and women's rights, remain contested issues in many Muslim countries and communities. Some significant reforms in marriage and divorce laws have been implemented to protect and expand women's rights in many countries. However, some scholars argue that they have not gone far enough in securing women's rights as specified in the Quran, while others condemn them as having gone too far.

The total of eight different law schools emerging from the Sunni and Shia traditions (described in the above question), which today are all internationally acknowledged as legitimate interpretations of Islamic law, demonstrate a broad diversity of legal opinion. The various schools provide a spectrum of authority and legitimacy available to individual Muslims wanting to follow Shariah as well as reformers who are seeking legislation that both follows Shariah and promotes the common good in contemporary times.

To address concerns about how much reform is possible, twenty-first century scholars and reformers such as Tariq Ramadan, Mohammed Hashim Kamali, Jasser Auda, and Asifa Qureshi-Landes have called for invoking the ideal of maqasid al-Shariah (principles of objectives) as the guide for reform, placing the common good (maslahah) of the community at the heart of legal reforms. Some also maintain that lawmaking for the public good (siyasa Shariah) has historically functioned as an essential part of a Shariah legal system that fosters social renewal and reform because it promotes God's vision of a just society and thus defines what makes a government Islamic in modern times.

Why Do We Have Different Schools of Islamic Law?

The existence and development of different schools of thought in Islam emerged because early jurists lived in different geographic, social, historical, and cultural contexts. These law schools share a common basis in the Quran and Sunna (example of Muhammad), but vary in other sources and legal mechanisms.

During Muhammad's lifetime, his followers were able to ask him their questions directly. After his death, opinions were sought throughout the early Muslim community, with majority opinion, or consensus (ijma), being favored over individual opinions. However, because orthopraxy (correct conduct) is central in Islam, it soon became clear that religious scholars were needed both to guide the community and to provide consensus and a sense of continuity in legal interpretation. Consensus served to limit the power of individual interpreters. It also contributed to the creation of a relatively fixed body of laws.

Law schools developed as certain jurists became renowned for their interpretations and gathered many students and large followings. Jurists were known as *mujtahids*, or those engaged in reasoning (ijtihad) about the law. In many places, these scholars came to constitute a distinct class within Islamic societies. Over time, certain interpretations came to be more widely accepted than others and some disappeared. By the end of the eleventh century, the major law schools had emerged and become authoritative. These law schools share many points in common but also have distinctive differences that reflect their diverse geographic locations, local customs and practices, relationship to the state, and particular methods of reasoning of their founders.

Although different law schools exist, they do not necessarily oppose each other. Legal pluralism has always been the norm in Islam, so jurists typically consider a multiplicity of opinions, even when there are disagreements on an issue, in order to reach a conclusion. It is often possible to find scholars representing different law schools living and working in the same area.

What Are the Major Schools of Islamic Law and Where Are They Located?

Significant differences and rivalries among the various schools of Islamic law reflect both dynamism and diversity of interpretation across the world. The most important

Sunni law schools are the Hanafi, Maliki, Shafii, and Hanbali. The most important Shia law schools are the Jafari and Zaydi. Two additional important law schools are the Ibadi and Zahiri.

The Hanafi school, named for Abu Hanifa (d. 767), the largest Sunni law school, is followed by more than one-third of Muslims globally. The Hanafi school became dominant under the Abbasid Empire (750–1258) and was the official law school of the Ottoman Empire (1299–1923). It remains influential in the former Ottoman provinces, particularly in matters of family law, although most of these countries presently have predominantly secular legal systems. Today, it is the dominant law school in the Balkans, the Caucasus, the Central Asian republics, Afghanistan, Pakistan, India, Bangladesh, and China.

The Maliki school, named for Anas ibn Malik (d. 795), is the second largest Sunni law school, followed by about 25 percent of Muslims globally. Historically, it was the official law school of the Umayyad (756–1031) and Almoravid (eleventh century) dynasties in Spain and North Africa. Today, the Maliki school is the dominant school in West Africa, Morocco, Algeria, Tunisia, Libya, Sudan, Upper Egypt, Bahrain, the United Arab Emirates (UAE), and Kuwait and has a substantial minority presence in other parts of the Arab world.

The Shafii school was named for al-Shafii (d. 820), and is followed by about 15 percent of Muslims globally. Historically, the Shafii school was the official law school of the Ayyubid dynasty in Egypt (1174–1250) and was prominent under the Mamluk regime that followed (1250–1517). Today, the Shafii school is dominant in Egypt, the Palestinian territories, and Jordan, with significant followings in Syria, Lebanon, Iraq, Pakistan, India, and Indonesia, as well as among Sunnis in Iran and Yemen.

The Hanbali school, named for Ibn Hanbal (d. 855), is the smallest of the Sunni law schools, with about 5 percent of Muslims globally as adherents. The Hanbali School is known for its conservatism in ritual matters and its connection to the Wahhabi tradition. Today, the Hanbali school is the official law school in Saudi Arabia and Qatar and has a growing number of adherents in Palestine, Syria, Iraq, and elsewhere.

The largest Shia law school is the Jafari School, named for Jafar al-Sadiq (d. 748), the sixth Shia Imam. It represents about 10 percent of the global Muslim population. It is the only Shia law school accredited by al-Azhar University in Cairo, one of the most important Sunni educational institutions in the world. Today, the Jafari school is followed by both Twelver and Ismaili Shia, as well as Alawis, and is the majority school in Iran, Azerbaijan, Bahrain, and Iraq, with minority populations in Lebanon, Kuwait, Albania, Pakistan, Afghanistan, and Saudi Arabia.

The Zaydi school, named for Zayd ibn Ali (d. 740), is a minority Shia school that was the official law school for Zaydi states in Iran (864–1126) and northern Yemen (893–1962). Today, Zaydis are found mainly in Yemen, with a small population in Saudi Arabia.

The Ibadi school, named for Abdullah ibn Ibad (d. 708), was formed before Sunni and Shia identities became distinct. Historically, the Ibadis were found in several dynasties in Oman, where today they are the majority of the population, and Algeria. Smaller populations can also be found in East Africa (particularly Zanzibar) and parts of Libya and Tunisia.

The Zahiri school, named for al-Zahiri (d. 883), is considered to have become largely "extinct" by the fourteenth century, although its influence is still recognized by the four surviving Sunni law schools. Historically, it was prominent in Iraq, Syria, Egypt, Spain, and Portugal.

There are minority communities of Zahiris in Morocco and Pakistan today. Some, although not all, members of the Ahl al-Hadith movement in India also claim to follow the Zahiri school.

In 2004, faced with the challenge of militant extremists like Osama bin Laden and Al Qaeda who use Islam and issue or obtain fatwas (religious opinions or edicts) to legitimate their organizations and acts of terror and excommunicate Muslims who reject or do not support them, declaring them apostates, 200 Islamic scholars from over fifty countries signed the Amman Message in which they called for tolerance and respect among Sunnis and Shia in the Muslim world. They identified and recognized the underlying unity within the diversity of the eight law schools as well as major schools of theology and of Sufism (Islamic mysticism). Thus all their followers were to be accepted as Muslims and therefore could not be excommunicated from Islam (*takfir*) and declared apostates by militants and their fatwas who did not possess the qualifications or follow the methodology required to be a legitimate mufti capable of issuing a fatwa.

Are Jurists Required to Abide by the Rulings of Their Law School Alone?

Historically, belonging to a law school meant that jurists were generally expected to follow the legal manuals developed by their early law schools, especially those written by the founders. Jurists were also expected to use the legal mechanisms recognized or preferred by their school when issuing new rulings. These rulings, along with the legal precedents and traditions they established, formed the body of classical and medieval law.

By around the tenth or eleventh century, the majority of Sunni jurists believed that the most important legal questions had already been answered. This, they believed, diminished the importance of independent reasoning (ijtihad) in favor of following or imitating past scholarship (*taqlid*). They announced a so-called closing of the gates of ijtihad on this basis. There remained, however, those Sunni jurists, particularly members of the Hanbali School, who supported the continuous exercise of independent reasoning. Moreover, in practice, Sunni jurists and muftis continued to interpret Islamic legal texts, but called it "commentary" or "elaborations" of prior law rather than ijtihad. Shia jurists, because of their emphasis on the use of reason and intellect, have consistently maintained independent reasoning throughout history.

By the sixteenth and seventeenth centuries, many Sunni jurists began to challenge the practice of imitating past scholarship over concerns that this had led to stagnation in the law that did not meet the need for new developments or understandings. Throughout the Muslim world, eighteenth-century reform movements arose and called for returning to the Quran and Sunna (Muhammad's example) for legal reinterpretation. In the nineteenth and early twentieth centuries, some reformers called for a new approach to independent reasoning that would set aside strict adherence to the established Islamic law schools in favor of looking to a variety of legal schools for opinions that would support reform. This eclectic approach to choosing a juristic opinion has been applied over the past century, particularly in reforming personal status laws in Muslim-majority countries.

In the contemporary era, although there are still some conservative jurists who believe that imitation of the past and exclusive adherence to one's own law school must be respected, other reformist jurists emphasize reengaging independent reasoning to address contemporary issues and needs. They stress the importance of distinguishing between Shariah, as divinely revealed sources, and its human interpretations, as Islamic law (fiqh). While they recognize some issues such as religious duties and obligations related to worship as unchanging, they view others as open to change based on historical, social, and cultural contexts. Reflecting a widespread recognition, especially among Sunni schools, that other schools are both authentic and orthodox, some reformist jurists have worked to combine approaches and rulings from different law schools and jurists. This idea has roots in traditional Islamic legal history as well, as stated in the legal canon: There is no prohibition against changing legal rulings to fit changes in time and place.

Are Muslims Required to Abide by the Rulings of Only One Law School?

As in other faiths, the distinction between Muslim religious leaders and legal specialists on the one hand and laity on the other is important. Like laity in other religious traditions, many Muslims do not consider themselves experts in law or theology, although they believe in the importance of living a life in accordance with God's will.

Muslims conceive of Shariah and Islamic law as broad guidelines and ideas rather than defined codes. Jurists play an important role as resources or interpreters of Islamic law to whom Muslims turn when they have questions. While some might choose a religious scholar based on his affiliation with a particular legal school, others might make their choice based on the reputation and popularity of the scholar or the opinion of a specific law school. A Sunni might turn to the Grand Mufti of Al-Azhar University in Egypt as an authority, or to a prominent scholar and popular preacher, such as Yusuf al-Qaradawi, whose followers number in the millions globally. A Shia would likely turn to an Ayatollah or Grand Ayatollah, such as Ali al-Sistani, for guidance. A woman seeking divorce who is aware of the specificities of the schools of law might choose a Maliki jurist because the Maliki school offers the broadest grounds for divorce initiated by the wife.

Today, when Muslim scholars commonly consider opinions from multiple schools of law, self-identification with a particular school is often not a priority. Muslims identify themselves as Sunni or Shia rather than as followers of specific law schools. Most Muslims also tend to understand "Islamic law" in light of their own cultural, ethnic, or national background, rather than a particular school.

Many Muslims encounter Islamic law formally in family law matters (marriage, divorce, or inheritance) or in criminal or business law in countries where Islamic law is part of the official legal system. Outside of these official interactions, laypersons often decide for themselves how strictly to follow their understanding of Islamic law. An example would be how far observance of the ban on alcohol consumption extends. For some, simply avoiding alcoholic beverages might be considered good enough. Others might take a more comprehensive approach, scrutinizing the labels of items they purchase for indications of alcoholic content in a supermarket (such as noting the ingredient of white wine in mustard) or on the menu of a restaurant (looking for items prepared with wine or food items containing pork). Individual conscience often guides the believer in adhering to Islamic law.

3

SHARIAH COURTS

Rooted in the local community, Shariah courts played a pivotal role in Muslim societies through the ages. In this chapter, we look at the responsibilities of qadis (judges) and muftis (legal scholars and experts) not only in the courtroom but also in the broader Muslim community and in the continued development of Islamic law.

To understand Shariah courts we must consider questions such as how fatwas differ from court decisions; how strict rules of evidence and testimony protect defendants, especially women; and how Islamic law treats lying or concealing the truth. Discussions of the strengths and weaknesses of Shariah courts, how they differ from other legal systems and secular courts, and how they have changed due to the impact of European colonialism and the rise of capitalism provide valuable perspectives on current problems and opportunities. Finally, we see how reformers draw on approaches and rulings from diverse schools of law to craft arguments for legal reform.

How Does Islamic Law Cover Public and Personal Areas of Life?

Muslims often describe Islam as a comprehensive way of life. The areas covered by Islamic law address a wide variety of behaviors and interactions. They range from personal issues (hygiene and purification, dietary prescriptions, worship regulations, ritual guidelines, and dress) to more public requirements (criminal behavior, financial regulations—including business, commerce, banking and charity—military regulations, international law, and family law, including marriage, divorce, and inheritance). If Islamic law is included in the legal code of a country, it is most likely to appear in the area of family law, although it may also be included in criminal or commercial law, or in a constitution, typically alongside a bill of rights.

In personal matters, the degree to which an individual follows Islamic law is often, but not always, a matter of personal choice. For example, some Muslims might choose to avoid foods such as pork, ham, or bacon, while others might carefully examine labels to determine if products contain any pork. Some Muslims will only eat meat with a *halal* label, meaning that it was prepared according to Islamic legal requirements, similar to kosher requirements in Judaism.

In some cases, national laws might encourage, rather than require, particular behaviors. In Saudi Arabia, while no one is forced to attend the five daily prayers, a government regulation that requires stores and businesses to close during prayer times is intended to encourage people to do so. Other instances of regulating activities, such as the former ban on women driving in Saudi Arabia, are often perceived as matters of Islamic law when in fact they are really cultural practices.

National laws sometimes mandate what would typically be considered a personal choice in the West. For example, some countries require women to cover their hair but allow for a variety of methods and variations in fabrics and colors reflecting the woman's culture and heritage. In some Muslim-majority countries, women are free to choose whether to cover their hair and dress modestly, based on their own personal preferences. Other countries require a specific type of veiling for women in public, such as the chador (full-length black drape covering the head and pinned under the chin) in Iran in government offices and institutions or the burqa (full body covering with a mesh opening for vision) in Afghanistan. Some countries, such as Turkey until 2013, banned headscarves for women in public-sector jobs and schools. Egypt drafted a bill in March 2016 that would ban the niqab (full face covering) and burqa in public places and government institutions. Finally, some countries, although they are nominally secular, nevertheless have religious ministries to regulate different traditions, including Turkey's Diyanet, which oversees Turkish Muslims living in France in conjunction with France's Council for Muslim Religion.

Ultimately, the degree of freedom of choice on many issues varies significantly by country; there is no single version or position in "Islamic law."

What Five Categories Describe a Range of Human Behavior in Islamic Law?

Human beings are capable agents and are expected to make choices based on individual conscience. Islamic law provides guidelines for Muslim behavior rather than clearly articulated and enforceable rules. Muslim jurists developed a categorization of human behavior and actions that reflects a belief that not every action has eternal consequences or is to be viewed in a black and white manner. Islamic law places human actions into one of five categories: obligatory (*fard*), recommended (*mustahabb*), permitted (*halal*), discouraged (*makruh*), and forbidden (*haram*).

Obligatory actions such as following the Five Pillars of Islam (declaration of faith, prayers, almsgiving, fasting, and pilgrimage) are required of all Muslims. Those performing these actions will be rewarded in the after-life, while disobedience will result in punishment in the afterlife. Flagrant, public failures to abide by obligatory actions, such as public and deliberate breaking of the fast of Ramadan, may result in public censure in Muslim-majority countries.

Recommended actions such as extra prayers, fasting, or charitable giving beyond what is required are encouraged but not mandatory. Engaging in recommended actions will earn reward in the afterlife but failure to do so will not earn punishment.

Permitted actions carry no moral implications. They can be engaged in or not without reward or punishment.

While discouraged actions are not prohibited, they are nevertheless considered undesirable. Avoiding discouraged acts may earn a reward in the afterlife. Some jurists believe that divorce belongs in the category of discouraged acts, as Muhammad said that there was nothing God hated more among what was permissible than divorce.

Forbidden acts such as theft, murder, or apostasy, which are understood to have a negative impact on the security and well-being of the community, are punishable.

Historically, different law schools advocated different approaches to these categories. In the Hanafi school, any-thing that was not expressly permitted was forbidden in ritual matters (such as prayer or fasting), which narrows the range of what is considered permissible behavior. Coming from the opposite direction, the Hanbali school held that anything not expressly forbidden was permitted, thereby opening the door to a more expansive vision of permissible behavior. This approach proved particularly important in the development of commercial law.

In exceptional circumstances, namely, when a human life is at stake, something that is normally forbidden might become permissible if it would save that human life. One example would be the general prohibition against consuming pork products, which is often extended in practice to pig products in general. That prohibition can be overridden by medical necessity, such as in the case of a needed heart valve transplant when no human or mechanical heart valve is available. Heart valves from pigs have long been used successfully in such cases. Because the intent behind the act is to save a human life, some jurists, including the Saudi Fiqh Academy, have ruled that such a transplant is permitted under Islamic law, even though use of pork products would normally be forbidden.

Who Is Considered an Expert in Islamic Law?

The founders of the major schools of Islamic law were among the first to demonstrate comprehensive and systematic knowledge of many fields, including Arabic language and grammar, the Quran and Quranic exegesis, the Sunna (Muhammad's example), Shariah, logic, and jurisprudence (human reasoning/interpretation) as well as their application to legal matters in a way that resonated with and served as models for increasingly broad audiences.

Historically, legal expertise was gained through study of both the subject matter related to the Arabic language and religious sciences and the specific rulings and methods of one or more schools of Islamic law. One way to acquire this expertise was to be a student in a study circle with a recognized scholar, most famously in Mecca and Medina in what is today Saudi Arabia, but also available in other urban centers, such as Damascus, Syria, or Karbala, Iraq. Another method was to enroll in an institution and its programs, such as al-Ahzar University in Cairo, Egypt (founded in 972 CE), or al Karaouine (also spelled Al-Qarawiyyin), founded in 859 CE by a woman, Fatima al-Fihri, in Fez, Morocco—the oldest degree-granting university, known as a *madrasah*, in the world for Sunnis. Shia could study in *hawzas* (seminaries), such as those found in Qom, Iran, or Najaf, Iraq.

Although some experts preferred—and were often trained and qualified—to remain within their own school of Islamic law, others saw value in learning the teachings of different schools in order to have a variety of perspectives on a given issue and insight into the legal tools used to arrive at particular conclusions in specific contexts. The jurist was expected to formulate an informed ruling rooted in, although not necessarily limited to, this varied legal literature. The process of engaging the tradition while also formulating a fresh response for a new time and context is known as ijtihad (independent reasoning). Scholars differ about the degree to which genuine ijtihad was practiced after the tenth century CE, although they agree that it continued in various forms, despite attempts by some jurists to bolster their own authority, as well as the authority of the founders of the schools of law, by claiming that "the gates of ijtihad" had closed. By the eighteenth century, as the Islamic world increasingly encountered modernity, many jurists began to call for reviving the practice of ijtihad in order to revitalize the Islamic legal tradition. This activity continues in many places as new situations and discoveries, such as in medicine, technology, and commercial activities, call for new legal approaches and solutions.

Although there remain traditionally trained experts with strong popularity, such as Al-Azhar Grand Mufti Shawki Ibrahim Abdel-Karim Allem and Shaykh Yusuf al-Qaradawi (Qatar) for Sunnis or Grand Ayatollah Ali al-Sistani (initially trained in Iran and now operating out of Iraq) for Shia, perceptions of expertise and authority are changing in many places. Today, a handful of traditionally, formally trained women are recognized as legal experts, the most popular of whom for Sunnis are Dr. Suad Saleh and Dr. Abla El Kahlawy. Both are law professors and are recognized as legal experts by al-Azhar University in Egypt. Both also have their own popular satellite television programs. For Shia, pivotal formally trained female legal experts include Nosrat Amin and Zohreh Sefati, whose scholarship and expertise were recognized by their male peers as being of the highest rank.

Contemporary reformists argue that too much focus on the past inhibits fresh approaches to the law that are meaningful to the lives of everyday people today. The result has been the addition of new voices, alongside religious scholars and leaders. Many are well educated in Islam and Islamic studies or have expertise in other subjects, such as medicine, economics, education, and the environment. Some are also popular lay preachers, who, similar to Christian televangelists and their use of mass media and social media, have achieved great popularity and are recognized as making constructive contributions to building civil society and encouraging entrepreneurship and individual responsibility.

The question of who is an expert in Islamic law and qualified to issue fatwas has loomed large in the fight against religious extremism and terrorism. Two approaches have prevailed. Prominent Muslim religious scholars and leaders have emphasized the traditional methodology and teachings of their legal schools. This promotes a more conservative consistency in interpretation over more liberal or progressive interpretations. The 2004 Amman Message, created by the most highly recognized Sunni and Shia scholars, sought to counter, limit, and discredit "renegade" interpreters such as Osama bin Laden (Al Qaeda) and Abu Bakr al-Baghdadi (ISIS) because they lacked appropriate credentials to issue fatwas that contradicted authoritative opinions by qualified scholars. It recognized the validity of both Sunni and Shia law schools. It also emphasized that any jurist who issues fatwas must possess the traditional qualifications prescribed by the individual's school of Islamic law as well as adhere to its methodology. Although the Amman Message acknowledged that jurists could also use opinions from other schools, it explicitly rejected anyone's claim to engage in unlimited ijtihad or to create a new school of Islamic law.

There has been increasing recognition of the complexity of rendering legal opinions today, given the expertise one might need to address varied medical, economic, social, and scientific issues. Thus, in recent years fatwa councils and committees have been created that include not only legal scholars but also experts (scientists, physicians, lawyers, and others) who collectively engage in studying legal questions and issuing fatwas that reflect their consensus (ijma). One such body is the North American Fiqh Council, which brings together legal scholars from the United States and Canada, assuring that opinions are not overly localized. In addition, there are increasing efforts to add the voices of female legal scholars to assure that women's perspectives and concerns are heard. Organizations engaged in this kind of work include the Global Muslim Women's Shura Council as well as organizations such as Karamah, run by Muslim women lawyers, that raise attention to women's rights. In 2009, Musawah ("equality" in Arabic), developed from Malaysia's Sisters in Islam, brought together participants from fifty countries and launched a global movement focused primarily on reforms to assure equality and justice in the Muslim family. Progressive, pluralistic, and inclusive, Musawah has brought together broad, diverse groups of nongovernmental organizations (NGOs), activists, scholars, legal practitioners, policymakers, and grassroots women and men from around the world.

What Is a Shariah Court and How Does It Work?

A Shariah court is a court that uses Islamic law, rather than secular law, to adjudicate cases, usually related to family or criminal law and in jurisdictions that recognize Islamic law as state law. Today, the name may also be applied to federal courts in some countries, such as Pakistan's Federal Shariat Court, responsible for verifying that any legislation passed is compliant with Shariah in accordance with Pakistan's constitution. This role is similar to that of the Supreme Court of the United States, which judges whether laws are compliant with the US Constitution. In other countries, where the constitution recognizes Shariah as state law, secular federal courts, such as Egypt's Supreme Constitutional Court, typically determine whether legislation complies with Shariah. In such a case, because the judges' main training is in secular law, they are not considered experts in it.

In theory, the judge (qadi) presiding over the Shariah court should be a recognized expert in the Quran, Quranic exegesis, the Sunna (Muhammad's example), logic, Arabic language and grammar, and jurisprudence (*fiqh*) as well as Shariah. The judge's knowledge of jurisprudence is expected to include majority and minority opinions in his own law school as well as divergent opinions from other law schools. This breadth of knowledge is supposed to guarantee both consistency with the legal tradition and selection of the opinion most suited to the case and to the litigants. The judge is supposed to be guided in that selection by the quest for justice for the aggrieved party, not just the plaintiff, as well as for the broader community. Occasionally, in the event that a suitable opinion cannot be found, a judge might use independent reasoning (ijtihad) to determine his own opinion, particularly if following available opinions would not result in justice. While it is unclear how often (or possible) all of these parameters are actually met, they provide a vision of the ideal judge and how justice is to be enacted.

In many countries today, Shariah courts are limited to dealing with family law, such as divorce and inheritance matters. There are also instances of Shariah courts overseeing commercial law. In the limited set of countries where Shariah courts are part of the criminal justice system, Shariah courts typically operate alongside secular courts and have limited jurisdiction in the types of cases that can be tried there.

In the past, any person or law enforcement official could bring a potential criminal case to the court, without the use of a lawyer, but today this is typically done by the prosecutor. It is up to the judge to determine whether there is sufficient evidence to pursue the case. If so, the judge is then expected to hear evidence from both sides, consider surrounding circumstances for civil cases and mitigating circumstances for criminal cases, and render a decision to administer justice quickly and efficiently. If there is not sufficient evidence for the Shariah court to issue a judgment using Islamic law, which has high evidentiary burdens, but there is nevertheless enough evidence to suggest criminal activity, the judge can issue a verdict with a lighter sentence, based on a lesser offense, or turn the accused over to public security officials for trial under secular law.

If the case is heard in the Shariah court, the judge is responsible for assuring that the rules of evidence and procedure are followed. Historically, the harsh punishments on the books for some crimes were intended to express moral condemnation of certain acts and to serve as a deterrent. However, those punishments were rarely applied in practice. Instead, judges applied the "doubt canon," which they used to avoid criminal punishments in cases of doubt, a notion that they defined expansively, typically with respect to procedures. Historically, both the petitioner and the defendant represented themselves, although they sometimes had representatives to advocate for their interests. Most courts today operate with lawyers. The judge evaluates the evidence and the credibility and integrity of the witnesses to determine an appropriate outcome. There is no jury. Once the judge issues a ruling, that ruling becomes binding, along with any financial liability or punishment assigned.

Historically, although any potential criminal case had to be presented to the Shariah court to determine whether there was sufficient evidence for trial there, the Shariah court and its judge did not rule supreme. Classical Islamic law recognized three law enforcement agencies: (1) the judge of the Shariah court; (2) public security officials operating under the authority of the political ruler, such as police officers, military personnel, or other political appointees who served in the name of the ruler; and (3) the market inspector (*muhtasib*) who oversaw trade practices, maintained public transportation safety, and often investigated crimes or misdemeanors to maintain law and order. The system separated jurisdictions to provide checks and balances in order to prevent any one institution from wielding disproportionate power. In addition, private individuals could also bring concerns about an institution to the direct attention of the ruler, who could then investigate. Any institution or agent accused of corruption or abuse could be investigated by the political ruler and his tribunal (*mazalim* courts).

What Kinds of Cases Are Governed by Shariah Courts?

Historically, Shariah courts held jurisdiction over criminal cases, family law, and certain civil disputes, such as contracts, torts, and property rights. The courts served many functions that were seen as central to maintaining public order and protecting social cohesion. The courts were locations where important transactions, including sales of property, business contracts, and the contents of a deceased person's estate, were recorded. In addition, an individual could come to the Shariah court to request that a statement regarding his or her good character and reputation be recorded or to make a public record of an insult from or dispute with another person. These records could be utilized as protective measures in the event of future problems.

Shariah courts did not have jurisdiction over state matters, such as appointing political officials, tax collection, land tenure, traffic law, or market practices. Although they could hear corruption charges against state officials, such as police officers or tax collectors accused of abusing their power, they could not charge the ruler of the country. In some instances, the Shariah court had the right to hand down sentences, including capital and corporal punishments, imprisonment, and fines. Other cases were referred to the state courts for trial or sentencing following conviction. In all cases, it was the political authority, rather than the Shariah court judge, that was supposed to implement the sentence or perform an execution.

Islamic criminal law recognized three categories of crimes: (1) crimes against God that have specified punishments (*hudud*) listed in the Quran or other early texts, as interpreted by jurists; (2) crimes against persons, including personal injury and homicide, which could be punished either by retaliation in the form of corporal or capital punishment or by financial compensation to the victim or the victim's family in homicide cases; and (3) crimes against public order or state security, incurring a discretionary punishment (*tazir*) that typically could be administered by either the Shariah court judge or law enforcement officials acting on the ruler's behalf. Overall, Shariah courts did not rule alone, but alongside a state court system. Only with respect to accusations of hudud crimes (theft, illicit sexual activity, libel, alcohol consumption, and, in some cases, apostasy and banditry) did the Shariah court hold full power over trial and conviction, although state security officials carried out the punishments.

In practice, if there was sufficient evidence that a crime had been committed, but not enough to punish it as hudud (crimes with fixed punishments that have been codified), the Shariah court judge could still issue a discretionary punishment or refer the case to state security officials for sentencing. In the event of insufficient evidence, a case could also be dismissed.

Today, in many countries, Shariah courts operate alongside state courts. In the few countries that have Islamic criminal law, such as the Maldives and the northern Nigerian provinces, Shariah courts are limited to hearing hudud cases or, in Malaysia, minor misdemeanors. Exceptions are Iran and Saudi Arabia, where Shariah courts have broad powers. Much more commonly, in most countries, Shariah courts hold jurisdiction over charitable endowments (*waqf*) and personal status and family law matters, including marriage, divorce, inheritance, and child custody.

What Is the Difference between a Qadi and a Mufti?

A qadi is a judge in a Shariah court who issues judgments that are binding decisions. A mufti is an expert on Islamic law who serves outside of the court and issues advisory legal opinions (fatwas) that may or may not be related to court cases. Qadis often consulted muftis regarding difficult cases and complex points of law, although they were not required to. Historically, while a qadi served as a state employee, a mufti was traditionally a private individual.

The office of the qadi dates to the rule of Muhammad, by some accounts, or the second caliph, Umar, by other accounts. The ruler appointed qadis and set the parameters of their jurisdiction. However, the ruler generally did not determine how the qadi should rule or what law should be applied. Occasionally, in a case of strong public interest, the ruler might direct that a particular opinion within a law school should be considered the norm, but this was the exception rather than the rule.

Historically, qadis were expected to be deeply embedded in their local communities. They knew the members of the community and its customs and ways of life. Their authority was rooted in personal knowledge and experience, rather than simply due to appointment. Yet they were not allowed to use that personal knowledge and experience as a basis for judgment. Instead, they were bound by strict rules of procedure that in most schools of law forbade, among other things, ruling on the basis of personal knowledge. Qadis were expected to possess moral integrity and trustworthiness and to be personally and morally invested in their local communities. They spent only part of their time hearing court cases. They were also responsible for supervising other aspects of community life, including inspection and oversight of mosques and other public buildings, such as hospitals and soup kitchens, as well as charitable endowments (waqf). Qadis also served as guardians for orphans, the poor, and women who did not have male relatives. Because their skills as mediators were not limited to the courtroom, qadis often served in a less formal capacity to hear family or neighborly disputes and disagreements. The qadis' guiding principles were to be focused on maintaining justice and preserving relationships.

In the courtroom, the qadi was responsible for determining what type of crime had been committed and whether it was punishable by a fixed sentence (hudud), subject to the rulers' discretion (*tazir*), or whether it should be addressed by law enforcement or political authorities. In hearing a case, the qadi followed predetermined rules of procedure and evidence. If the case was particularly challenging or complex, a qadi had the option of requesting a fatwa from a mufti. The qadi was not necessarily expected to possess the same level of knowledge as a mufti or legal scholar. The mufti consulted did not have to be locally based. There are many instances in the historical record of a qadi seeking a fatwa from a distant mufti based on the mufti's reputation. In the Islamic West (al-Andalus, southern Spain), a qadi frequently consulted a council of muftis.

Historically, muftis were neither court officials nor state employees. They were private legal specialists known for their piety and advanced legal knowledge who issued legal opinions (fatwas) upon request. Anyone, from the ruler to the poorest of the poor, could request a fatwa. Muftis were not paid for their services; they were understood to fulfill a vital community function in which all parties had equal right and equal access to legal advice in keeping with the Shariah's overarching attention to the good of the entire society, rather than the interests of a specific class or the ruling elite. Muftis did not exercise any coercive, state, or military power. Because their services were provided voluntarily, muftis needed to have alternative sources of income and worked in other professions. Most of them came from the working and middle, rather than upper, classes.

The mufti's authority was rooted in his legal knowledge as demonstrated through practice, including legal writings, issuing fatwas, and winning scholarly legal debates, rather than degrees or diplomas. There was no specific school or institution that trained muftis. Rather, individuals often pursued legal learning with individual scholars who taught specific texts and held open circles for issuing fatwas and explaining their legal reasoning. They also went to the institutions established to train jurists as legal experts, such as al-Azhar in tenth-century Egypt and the Nizamiyya in eleventh-century Iran.

The rise and expansion of the Ottoman Empire ultimately led to the professionalization of the mufti's job, making him a state employee. This gave the state some leverage over muftis in terms of guiding and even demanding particular rulings. At the same time, the new financial incentive and increased local power essentially turned juridical knowledge into a commodity. From the thirteenth through the seventeenth centuries, juridical knowledge and positions came to be passed down from father to son, and by the eighteenth century these were a monopoly of certain families.

The European colonial era with its "modern" legal and bureaucratic systems challenged the traditional workings of the Shariah courts, shifting focus further away from local social practice to broader regional, national, and international connections. The subsequent codification and secularization of the law placed greater power in the hands of the state. Qadis lost much of their flexibility in considering the full parameters of court cases. Their jurisdiction was also limited in favor of the state's prerogative in making family law determinations and punishments more uniform and consistent. Muftis also lost much of their influence within the courts, although many remain respected as community and religious leaders.

What Is a Fatwa and How Does It Differ from a Court Sentence?

A fatwa is a private, nonbinding, or advisory legal opinion issued by a mufti (religious and legal scholar) in response to a request from any member of the community, a judge, or the state. It is based on a mufti's own reasoning about how Shariah principles are to be applied in a particular case. A court sentence, on the other hand, is a binding decision on a legal or criminal matter that is enforceable by the state.

Fatwas date to Muhammad's lifetime. His practice of issuing rulings on legal matters was continued after his death to keep the interpretation and implementation of Islamic law fresh and relevant in changing circumstances. In issuing a fatwa, the mufti's job was and is to state what the law is with respect to the known facts of a given situation. Although a fatwa is nonbinding on its own, it was often presented as evidence in court cases. It was up to plaintiffs or defendants to obtain a fatwa supporting their case, although a qadi could also request one. Individuals could seek multiple fatwas for their case in order to find the one that best upheld their interest as different law schools sometimes held very different opinions. Typically, only one fatwa was presented per side in a court case.

The qadi could accept or reject any fatwa, but he generally considered it admissible and important evidence as an authoritative statement of the law, comparable to the testimony of an expert in modern courts today. Fatwas were routinely upheld and applied. Only rarely was a fatwa dismissed, typically on the grounds that there was a more convincing fatwa issued by a mufti of higher caliber. Occasionally, a qadi might insert his own fatwa if he had sufficient reputation as a legal scholar. A disputant who did not present a fatwa in support of a claim generally did not fare well in court and either had to abandon the claim or settle for arbitration.

Fatwas are important resources for historians tracing the development of the law, while court cases provide information about how the law was put into practice by qadis. Records of court cases typically include the evidence presented, who the parties were, and the qadi's ruling on the case, but not the legal reasoning behind it. Fatwa collections, on the other hand, provide records of the legal precedents qadis investigated in determining those outcomes. Fatwas were typically edited to remove personal identifying information in order to keep the focus on the legal issues of the case. Fatwa collections also make it possible to determine when new issues were introduced and other issues passed out of relevance.

Today, fatwas are issued by many people, some of whom have training in the classical fields of Islamic law and some of whom do not. In the twentieth and twenty-first centuries, the lack of any centralized authorizing institutions of the type where muftis were historically trained has opened the door for people who are educated in other fields, such as engineering or philosophy, to insert their voices into religious legal interpretation. These voices have gained credence due to perceptions that those trained only in the classical fields of scholarship are out of touch with contemporary political, economic, social, and medical needs and concerns.

Fatwas are not generally binding for Sunnis, although they are influential. Shia, on the other hand, once they have pledged loyalty to a particular scholar, are obligated to follow that scholar's fatwas. Knowledge of those fatwas is thus a critical matter for foreign policy and national security. An example of a fatwa issued by a head of state, who was also a mufti, is the death sentence for blasphemy that Iran's Ayatollah Ruhollah Khomeini issued against Salman Rushdie in connection with his book *The Satanic Verses*. Shia Muslims outside of Iran were not obligated to follow this fatwa, not only because many Shia follow other ayatollahs but also because Khomeini had issued the fatwa as a head of state, limiting its relevance to Iranians. Nevertheless, it is an example that illustrates the potential impact and importance of a fatwa. Historically, the authority of a fatwa was understood to die with the scholar, although another scholar can renew the fatwa.

Some countries today are trying to exert greater control over the issuing of fatwas. Saudi Arabia permits fatwas to be issued only by the Council of Senior Scholars, composed of state employees, rather than private individuals. Egypt's Dar al Ifta, the authoritative official religious institution created in 1895 and charged with producing fatwas, has played a major role not only in Egypt but also internationally. In conjunction with Al Azhar University and the Grand Mufti of Egypt, it has sought to confront the "chaos of fatwas" it and others have seen as a major source of religious extremism and terrorism by standardizing and consolidating the power to issue fatwas. In other places, fatwas continue to be issued by individuals who are not state employees or where there is no oversight. There are a few female muftis who have been recognized as sufficiently learned to issue fatwas, including, most prominently, Sunni Egyptians Dr. Suad Saleh and Dr. Abla El-Kahlawy, and Shia Iranian scholars Nosrat Amin and Zohreh Sefati. Both Saleh and El-Kahlawy have their own call-in television programs during which they issue live fatwas in response to viewer questions.

What Are the Rules for Evidence and Testimony in a Shariah Court?

There are strict rules for evidence and testimony for Shariah courts under classical Islamic law. Standard rules of evidence for cases involving financial compensation and minor civil disputes included proving one's claim either by the witnesses' testimony or a defendant's confession. Early law schools considered the qadi's personal knowledge of a case sufficient evidence for issuing a decision, but after the eighth century, most did not or they severely qualified this basis for ruling.

Oath swearing could serve as corroborating, although not exclusive, evidence for a petitioner with a property or commercial claim. Refusal of a respondent to swear an oath denying a claim essentially served as an admission of guilt when there was firm evidence from the petitioner. However, if a petitioner could not produce sufficient evidence to prove a claim, the qadi would find for the defendant even if the respondent did not swear an oath denying the claim.

Circumstantial evidence was officially not permitted on its own. But, in practice, it was admissible, especially if it corroborated the defendant's known reputation, such as stolen goods being found in the defendant's possession. Reputation thus played an important role in establishing the credibility of witnesses or of tangible evidence.

Witnesses could be either male or female, but they had to be Muslim in order to testify in a Shariah court; the only cases heard in Shariah courts were under the jurisdiction of Islamic law, which applied only to Muslims. Cases involving non-Muslims could be tried and heard in secular courts or courts specifically designated for their religions and presided over by judges from those religions, such as the millet system under the Ottoman Empire. In the Shariah court, a minimum of two adult male witnesses was the baseline requirement for evidence to be considered sufficient. In some opinions, a stand-in for two witnesses could consist of a witness and a petitioner swearing an oath before the qadi or one male and two female witnesses (or four female witnesses in one minority school of law), or two female witnesses for cases involving issues exclusive to women. The differences in requirements of male and female witnesses were based on the view that women were less educated and more sheltered and that they had less experience in worldly affairs as well as the chance that they might be more subject to family pressures when testifying than were the men. In all cases, witnesses had to have a good reputation and provide their direct and concurrent testimonies to the qadi, although testimonies about the defendant's confession or what two other qualified witnesses stated outside of court were considered admissible. Testimonies had to be consistent with each other in both the essentials and the details in order to be considered valid evidence.

The testimony of a single witness was not considered sufficient evidence to issue a sentence. Thus, an accusation by a dying victim, the testimony of a single witness to a killing, or testimony that a witness saw someone attacking or striking a person later found dead were considered incomplete evidence. Insufficient or invalid evidence did not mean that the accused would escape without any punishment; it simply meant that the case fell outside of the jurisdiction of the Shariah court.

In the case of very serious crimes carrying harsh punishments, there were stricter standards for evidence and witnessing. The most serious offenses were hudud crimes—those carrying fixed penalties—and cases of homicide or wounding in which the victim or the victim's family demanded retaliation. For these cases, circumstantial evidence was not admissible. For allegations of sex crimes or homicide, four male witnesses were required. For all other crimes, a minimum of two male witnesses was required. The plaintiff could not be one of them. Secondhand testimony was not considered admissible evidence. Neither was the defendant's refusal to swear an oath or the qadi's personal knowledge of the situation. Testimonies and confessions had to be explicit in their wording, express the unlawfulness of the conduct witnessed or admitted, and use the specific terminology related to the crime, such as theft or *zina* (illicit sex). These parameters were required to assure that there was no doubt in the case—about its facts, about whether a crime had been committed, about what the crime was, or about whether the accused had willingly and willfully engaged in that conduct. Witnesses could withdraw their testimony at any point up until the execution of the punishment. Further rules were outlined in an elaborate set of rules and procedures that included a "doubt canon" that functioned like an expansive Islamic doctrine of presumed innocence and reasonable doubt.

The defendant's confession was only permissible in the Shariah court if the defendant confessed in the courtroom, without coercion, a total of four times. Confessions obtained under torture or coercion were not admissible as evidence. In addition, a defendant had the right to withdraw the confession at any time up until the moment before executing the punishment. This was true even in hudud cases.

Under classical Islamic law, the most difficult crime to prove was an accusation of illicit sex (zina). Quran 24:4 requires four adult male witnesses to the actual act of penetration in order to prove such a claim—a circumstance that was rarely, if ever, met. Alternatively, the confession of the accused four separate times in the courtroom without coercion was considered parallel evidence. In Maliki law alone, an unmarried woman's pregnancy could serve as presumptive evidence of illicit sex; this rule was tempered by the "sleeping fetus" doctrine that allowed a judge to avoid the punishment for divorced women on the theory that a woman could have been pregnant from a marriage for as long as five years after the divorce. Any person making an accusation of illicit sex who was unable to produce the requisite witnesses became liable to punishment of eighty lashes for false accusation.

The very strict rules of evidence in hudud cases left considerable space for accused parties to have their charges reduced to a lesser crime punishable at the qadi's discretion or by state security officials. It also meant that even in a case where the sentence had been issued, there was still space for the sentence to be nullified if a witness or the defendant withdrew testimony. Historically, this led European colonial officials to charge that too many guilty parties were getting away with crimes because the standards of evidence were too strict. This is very different from contemporary circumstances. Today, the standards of evidence and witnessing are often not observed in Muslim-majority countries that have revived Islamic criminal law, despite "Shariah" being reintroduced and implemented in some places. Reformers and legal historians have seized upon this as a deficiency requiring attention, particularly in cases of retaliation and hudud crimes, given the severity of the punishments, or in cases where a woman attempting to report rape can have her testimony used to accuse her of illicit sex (zina).

Does Islamic Law Permit Muslims to Lie or Conceal the Truth (Taqiyya)?

Criticisms leveled against Islam and Muslims by some today are that a Muslim's statements cannot be trusted because Muslims practice *taqiyya* and that taqiyya is a mainstream practice for infiltrating non-Muslim societies. These charges do not reflect the historical purpose and practice of taqiyya as a safeguard against persecution and/or death for religious belief.

Taqiyya, which literally means "caution" or "prudence," refers to the verbal denial of one's true religious belief or practice when faced with persecution or death. Because the genuine renunciation of one's faith—apostasy—is a serious matter, taqiyya has been used as a precautionary measure practiced in dire circumstances when a person's life or safety is at stake. It is not intended to justify lying or self-misrepresentation for the sake of convenience. It is also not a permissible practice with respect to legal testimony in court. Finally, it is never permissible if it results in harm to another person.

Historically, the practice of taqiyya can be traced to the early years of Muhammad's ministry in Mecca. Faced with persecution to the point of being killed, some early Muslims chose to hide their true religious status by publicly renouncing their beliefs as a matter of self-preservation. Once Muslims were in a position of relative power in Medina, taqiyya largely fell out of use among Sunnis until a conflict arose within the Abbasid Empire (750–1258 CE) over the nature of the Quran. The Caliph Mamun established an inquisition to determine individual beliefs about the nature of the Quran. Faced with torture and even death, some Muslims proclaimed adherence to Mamun's opinion, while maintaining their own private personal beliefs—an act of taqiyya. A similar situation occurred with respect to the Spanish Reconquista and the Inquisition when Muslims were given the choice of converting to Christianity or being killed or sent into exile. Many Muslims engaged in taqiyya to nominally accept Christianity in order to survive, but secretly they remained Muslims.

Taqiyya has been especially important to and associated with Shia Muslims who, from the death of Muhammad, experienced marginalization and persecution under Sunni-majority governments. Shia believed that Ali, the cousin and son-in-law of Muhammad, had a God-given right to succeed Muhammad as the leader or Imam of the Muslim community. Instead, Abu Bakr (followed by Umar and Uthman) was chosen as the caliph (successor) of Muhammad. Ali practiced taqiyya in that he outwardly accepted the rule of the first three caliphs, whom Shia have regarded as usurpers and heretics, until he was able to succeed Uthman. After Ali's death, Sunni caliphate rule was restored by the Umayyad and then Abbasid Dynasties, which were hostile to Shia belief in the Imam's political and religious leadership. During these times, Shia used taqiyya as a means of self-preservation, to hide the Imams during periods of danger and to shield Shia from persecution as a religious minority who were considered political dissidents.

In modern times, Shia and the Druze, who have distant Shia origins, have practiced taqiyya when faced with persecution or death as a religious minority or in opposition. However, in contrast to the past when, due to prevailing conditions of persecution, taqiyya was more commonly practiced, many Shia today emphasize its restriction to situations in which Shia face religious persecution or death.

Can the Decision of a Shariah Court Be Appealed?

Historically, there was no formal appeals process in the Western sense for Shariah courts. Courts were localized and served local communities. Qadis were seen to be invested in those communities and their customs and habits were responsible for assuring that the justice they administered was suitable for all the parties involved in a case and the community at large. However, qadis did not rule supreme in their communities. Capital sentences had to be reviewed by the ruler or regional governor before an execution could be carried out. A convicted person had the right to petition the ruler or governor to request a revision of the sentence. Grounds for requesting a revision included suspicion of bribery of involved officials, accusations of false testimony, or any other scenario that could raise doubt, however remote, about the guilt of the defendant. If the request was granted, a special investigator was appointed to review the matter and either issue a new decision or instruct the qadi to retry the case. Witnesses always retained the option of withdrawing their testimony up until the moment that the sentence was executed. Defendants had the same right with respect to a confession. Withdrawal of such testimony necessarily meant cancellation of the assigned sentence, although the case could be retried if sufficient evidence remained for a new trial. In addition, new qadis could validly refuse to implement the still-pending decisions of previous qadis whom they succeeded in the judgeship if they thought the previous qadi's opinions were at odds with the Quran or Sunna (Muhammad's example).

In traditional Muslim societies, personal conscience was expected to play an important role in decision making and acceptance of personal accountability. People's honor was tied to their honesty and their word was considered binding if sworn as an oath. There was thus a certain social pressure to confess any wrongdoing if asked to do so in court and to accept the punishment for the crime. Muslims were asked to privately repent and avoid confessions if not required to do so in court. Some Muslims believed that punishment for certain crimes in this life will excuse a person from being punished for the same in the Afterlife, thereby creating an incentive to accept a court's punishment. Social pressure to accept the decision of a court discouraged appealing a sentence since unwillingness to abide by the court's ruling might imply that a person was not a good Muslim.

Perhaps ironically, the parties most likely to be sentenced without the possibility of appeal were high-ranking government officials who were considered the personal servants of the ruler. In the Ottoman Empire, any member of the imperial household accused of a crime had to be tried by a special committee, typically in the presence of the sultan or the grand vizier (prime minister). The sultan usually issued the sentence himself, often with a supportive fatwa to show that he was not ruling arbitrarily but in accordance with Islamic law. Such sentences were not subject to appeal. If someone other than the sultan heard the case, the sultan had to ratify the sentence before it could be carried out.

Only in the nineteenth century did formal appeals processes begin to be introduced in some parts of the Muslim world. This went hand in hand with the bureaucratization of the justice system, in order to streamline judicial processes, and the establishment of the office of public prosecutor. (Previously, cases could be brought to court either by private individuals or by law enforcement, and the qadi served as both prosecutor and judge.) The resulting hierarchy inserted layers of courts, such as district and regional, between local-level courts and rulers. This enabled the process of appeal to higher courts. In many places, the ruler retained the obligation to review any capital or other severe sentences before they were carried out.

In the contemporary era, the reimplementation of Shariah in some countries has retained appeals processes introduced in the nineteenth century or under colonial rule. This may be a reflection of the sheer size of countries today, as well as the state's desire to retain power at the local and regional levels. In many countries, sentences issued at lower-level courts are reviewed by higher courts when serious punishments have been assigned. In addition, the ruler typically must also review all cases involving capital punishment or amputation. The timeframe for appeals processes is often much shorter than in Western countries where appeals can go on for years and even decades. There still remains an expectation that justice be administered in a timely manner under Islamic law, typically within months of the sentence, although this is now rarely carried out in practice.

The results of appeals processes vary by country and political circumstances. In Iran in the early years after the Revolution, the decisions of newly established revolutionary courts applying Islamic law were final and not subject to appeal. This was justified by the perceived need to protect the Revolution from dissidents. Today, appeals are possible, even if sentences are rarely overturned. In Nigeria, there are cases of serious punishments being overturned on appeal, although these tend to be decided along procedural lines, rather than on the basis of evidence. In addition, many Muslim-majority countries today allow or even require that an attorney represent defendants.

How Is Shariah Different from Other Legal Systems?

Because Islamic law was not a comprehensive system of law, despite arguments to the contrary, from earliest times rulers developed parallel systems of laws or regulations such as *siyasa Shariah* that supplemented religious law. They were supposed to be in harmony with and not contradictory to Islamic law. Religious scholars theoretically had the right to invalidate any of the ruler's edicts that contradicted Islamic law, but this rarely happened in practice.

An important historical example is the *qanun* (derived from the Greek *kanon* (meaning rule, edict, or decree) courts in the Ottoman Empire. The Ottoman sultan was the legislator of qanun, as opposed to Islamic law, which was the province of religious scholars (ulama). The Ottoman sultan Suleiman the Magnificent (r. 1520–1566 CE) was known as Suleiman Kanuni ("the Lawgiver") due to his code of laws.

Qanun in the Ottoman Empire was developed to address the administrative realities of ruling a vast territory containing a multiplicity of religious and ethnic groups, many of whom were not Muslim. The *kanunname* (literally "books of law"), issued first by Sultan Mehmed II (r. 1444–1446, 1451–1481 CE) and then added to most prominently by Selim I (r. 1512–1520 CE) and Suleiman the Magnificent (r. 1520–1566 CE), addressed fiscal and administrative matters, often based on customary practice. In fact, each administrative subdivision of a province had its own Book of Laws (kanunname).

The combination of Shariah and custom became particularly important with the spread of Islam to non-Arab regions. These regions often incorporated Islamic law into their customary practices (as did the Arab regions, although less consciously) rather than replacing them entirely with it. For example, before the arrival of Muslim traders and merchants, both Hinduism and indigenous religions were present among the Minangkabau of Indonesia. One vestige of this heritage is matriarchal lineage and inheritance, in contrast to Islamic inheritance law, which follows a patriarchal system. The Minangkabau developed a system that respects both traditions by dividing inheritance into "high" and "low" forms. "High" inheritance applies to property and assets belonging to the mother, which continued to be passed down matrilineally, while "low" inheritance of property and assets belonging to the father were assigned according to Islamic law. Similarly, in India there is a long history of adopting children, although some believe that Islamic law does not permit adoption. In fact, Islamic law encourages what we commonly call adoption and places a heavy emphasis on caring for orphans. But it does not support concealing the fact of the adoption or a child's lineage, if known. Indian Islamic religious courts have chosen to permit adoption and allow adopted children to inherit out of respect for local customs.

These examples demonstrate Islamic law's ability to work alongside or in conjunction with other legal systems. Today, however, many people question whether Islamic law is compatible with modern law. This doubt arises from the structural differences between the two systems of law. Modern law generally takes a "top-down" approach, with the state holding ultimate power at the top and reaching down to the individual. Ideally this is intended to render all parties to a case equal before the law, but critics have charged that this system can be manipulated by those in positions of state power or close to them. Modern law also uses a "winner-takes-all" model for litigation; one party clearly wins the case and the other party loses. The judge's ruling must then follow the requirements of the law for a given outcome, limiting the judge's discretion to the legal aspects of the case, regardless of the social impact of a sentence.

By contrast, Islamic law historically tended to operate at the grassroots level. The judge's main responsibility was to maintain the social order at the community level rather than uphold a centralized legal system. The judge was, therefore, given discretionary powers in order to meet local needs. That discretion was constrained by a chief judge or by the opinions of local jurist-experts. Critics of this system have charged that the perceived social interest was given greater consideration than the law, rendering questionable the judge's ability to issue justice. Concerns have also been expressed about the weakening of the state's power in such a decentralized system.

Some scholars have argued that it is impossible for modern secular and Islamic law to work together. Others see the potential for continuing the historical tradition of coexistence side by side or in combination with each other, allowing both Islamic principles and values and local customs and practices to work in parallel. This would allow for variations in the way the law is practiced in different locations as each community continues to develop its own responses to its specific issues and circumstances. This might also make possible a greater emphasis on restorative justice (rehabilitation) rather than retributive justice based on punishment, enabling the law's ability to adapt as it seeks to address the central concerns of fostering harmony and coherence of the community.

How Do Shariah Courts Compare to Secular Courts?

Like secular courts, Shariah courts are designed to hold individuals responsible for their actions and to assure that fines or punishments are assigned and carried out by a legal authority rather than by private individuals. Shariah courts generally have more limited jurisdiction than secular courts. While both may, in some instances, hear similar kinds of cases, such as homicide or personal injury, the standards for evidence, witnessing, and punishment are very different.

Historically, any criminal case had to be heard first in a Shariah court in order to determine whether the case was potentially connected to hudud (fixed punishment) crimes. If no such connection was found, the case could then be tried either as one carrying the potential for discretionary punishment in the Shariah court or left to state security officials. Cases related to personal status, such as marriage, divorce, child custody, or inheritance, fell to the Shariah court, while cases related to commercial transactions and state security were under the jurisdiction of secular courts. Some cases, such as homicide, could be heard in one, the other, or both, depending on the circumstances.

Traditionally, a Shariah court could hear a case only if it was brought by a plaintiff, whether the victim, the victim's family, or state security officials. Secular courts, on the other hand, had to respond to state institutions, including state security officials, in hearing cases. In criminal cases brought before the secular court, even if the victim or the victim's family did not wish to pursue the case, the state carried the obligation to see that the case came to trial. Issues related to state security, such as rebellions and public disturbances, fell under the jurisdiction of public security officials rather than the Shariah court judge. State security officials also held jurisdiction over homicides. Secular courts were permitted to consider circumstantial evidence, incomplete evidence, and the prior conviction history and reputation of the accused, while Shariah courts were bound by much stricter rules of evidence and witnessing, including being limited to hearing firsthand testimony, requiring multiple witnesses, and/or securing multiple, voluntary confessions. Secular courts were not bound by these procedural and evidentiary rules. Secular courts could consider confessions obtained under duress or even torture while Shariah courts could not. In order for a confession to be admissible in a Shariah court, it had to be freely given directly in the courtroom, typically multiple times, and had to specifically use the terminology related to hudud crimes or other infractions. In addition, confessions and testimony given in a Shariah court could be withdrawn at any time up until the execution of the sentence. These restrictions are not always observed in Shariah courts today. Confessions given in secular courts are not necessarily considered to be retractable, even if made under duress.

Shariah courts, because they ruled on issues of Islamic law, could hear only Muslim witnesses, while secular courts could hear the testimony of non-Muslims. Shariah courts were limited to the case at hand, while secular courts could consider the broader context of the case, including, for example, the personal history of a defendant as a repeat offender. Secular courts had the option of imprisoning a repeat offender for life and could even impose the death penalty in order to protect public security.

Shariah courts were permitted and in fact required to consider a wide range of mitigating circumstances with respect to hudud crimes, according to the doubt canon that raised issues of presumed innocence and reasonable doubt. Judges were required to avoid criminal punishments in cases of doubt. In order to be convicted, a person had to have had a choice about whether to commit the crime, had knowingly engaged in a criminal act, and had acted with criminal intent. Invalidation of any of these and other criteria meant that the judge could not convict a defendant of a hudud crime with a fixed punishment. Even if the defendant was found guilty of having committed a bad act, he or she would be liable only for discretionary punishment. In some cases, the judge could determine that the defendant was not culpable even if he did harm to another. Examples would include killing an attacker while engaged in self-defense or wounding someone while protecting one's family or property.

In both courts, the purpose of applying the law was to provide justice for victims and to consider the broader common good (maslahah) of the community. Shariah courts had a third objective to consider—rehabilitation of the offender, who was expected to reintegrate back into the community. Ultimately, justice was best fulfilled by restoring relationships broken by the offensive behavior. For this reason, Shariah courts often assigned indeterminate prison sentences. The purpose was to incarcerate the offender only for as long as required for him to express remorse for his crime, promise not to repeat it, and be judged to no longer represent a danger to society. Restoring the offender to the community was thus part of the goal of justice rather than simply punishment, based on the Quranic example of God assigning punishments for certain crimes "unless" or "until" the perpetrator repents (Q 5:34 and 39). This set the stage in some countries for consideration of justice that was restorative (emphasizing rehabilitation) rather than simply retributive (emphasizing punishment), particularly when juvenile offenders were concerned, although the state always retained the prerogative of punishment. For example, a juvenile offender might be placed under house arrest to be supervised by his parents while working to set right the damage caused by his delinquent behavior at a local business.

What Are the Strengths and Weaknesses of Shariah Courts?

Historically, the strengths of Shariah courts were their rootedness in the local community, flexibility in sentencing, and investment in justice and the common good (maslahah) of the entire society, not just the state or the ruling class. Rulings from the Shariah court were expected to consider the welfare not only of the immediate parties to the conflict but also of the community as a whole. Victims of crimes—or their families—had a voice in determining whether a case was brought to trial and what the sentence would be. Options for justice included retaliation, financial compensation, or forgiveness at the discretion of the victim or his or her family. This allowed those affected by a crime to be part of the procedure rather than outside it, to have a voice in deciding whether criminal charges would be brought, and to be included during the punishment phase. Ideally, this provided a strong sense of justice for the victim. In addition, because the law was not codified, judges were able to use their discretion in researching options for sentences that were most appropriate to the crime. No single interpreter of the law was understood to be infallible, so a multiplicity of perspectives could always be considered before choosing the one most appropriate for a given case. This flexibility further allowed for the law to adapt to new circumstances even as it retained continuity with the past. Finally, no one, including the judge, was considered to be above the law.

At the same time, there were also weaknesses in the Shariah courts, particularly from Western colonial perspectives. The flexibility of the judge in selecting the appropriate ruling meant that different judges could give different rulings on similar cases. From a Western perspective, accustomed to codified laws in which set punishments were assigned to specific crimes, this flexibility sometimes came across as arbitrariness. Some colonial administrators—for example, the British in India—were frustrated by the strict rules for evidence and witnessing that sometimes allowed perpetrators to get away with crimes they had clearly committed, although a case without sufficient evidence for trial in the Shariah court might be tried by a secular court or punished by state security officials. They also expressed concern about the personalized aspects of court proceedings in which victims and judges had stronger voices than the state. Many Western colonial officials consequently looked down on "kadijustiz" (qadi justice) as Max Weber famously described it. Colonial portrayals and critiques of "qadi justice" popularized the notion of Islamic judicial arbitrariness, arguing that it did not fully serve the interests of the state as a coercive power and placed too much power in the hands of an individual, rather than the depersonalized institutions of the state.

Although no one was considered to be above the law in the Shariah court, all persons were not considered equals before the law. Islamic law historically assigned people different values, such as for financial compensation, on the basis of gender, religion, and status as a free person or a slave. Some contemporary systems that reimplemented Shariah have reverted to this practice, although reformers argue against it as discriminatory and no longer relevant.

A weakness in Shariah courts in the eyes of reformers is that some judges fail to distinguish between Shariah as divine principles and Islamic law (fiqh, human-made law) as human interpretations of those principles, giving them equal weight in their considerations. Popular expectations of Shariah courts in terms of desired outcomes may reflect this failure to distinguish between the two, often at the expense of women. Because many judges are appointed today based on politics and networks rather than knowledge of the Islamic legal tradition, judges' understandings of Shariah and Islamic law in some countries can be superficial, literal, and lacking awareness of Shariah principles. Reformers have charged that the overall worldview of Shariah, including justice, liberation, and elimination of discrimination and oppression, has been lost, making a revision of the system based on principles, rather than punishments, critically necessary today.

Finally, there are some aspects of Shariah courts that can be considered both strengths and weaknesses. Shariah courts were known historically for their speed and efficiency in providing justice. In some places where crime and corruption are rampant, such as Nigeria, the promise of swift justice can be seen as a powerful deterrent and boost for community safety. In others where political dissent is punished as criminal activity, it threatens rapid execution of opposition figures. At the same time, Western-style procedures are often criticized for being too slow, detracting from a sense of timely justice.

How Have Shariah Courts Changed over Time?

Just as the societies in which they operate have changed over time, so Shariah courts have changed in terms of their jurisdiction, relationship to the state, and overall role in the community. In many cases, Shariah courts have continued to operate alongside secular courts.

Historically, Shariah courts were community based and were expected to uphold the interests of society as a whole rather than those of the ruling class. Rules of evidence and testimony had to be strictly observed. The qadi (judge) lived in the community he served so as to be rooted in community life, customs, and practices. In addition to serving in the court, he was expected to oversee buildings and organizations benefiting public welfare, serve as a legal guardian for those who did not have one, and arbitrate community and family disputes.

The qadi was not a political appointee of the ruler and was not an arm of state coercion or violence. Rather, the qadi's authority derived from his personal knowledge of both the law and the community, which permitted him to be flexible in applying the law based on the circumstances of the case and the parties involved, and on his willingness to consult expert jurists and maintain good relations with them. While the qadi might assign corporal or capital punishment, these sentences had to be approved by the ruler before being carried out as a function of the state. Historically, Shariah courts were central to community life but had no reach beyond that local level.

Today, the role of Shariah courts varies in many countries. In some, there are multiple levels of hierarchy in the court system. In certain countries, the jurisdiction of Shariah courts is limited to family law; in others, they may hear criminal cases as well. In many instances, the strict rules for evidence and witnessing are no longer implemented, making it easier for a person to be charged and convicted of crimes with serious punishments, particularly women accused of illicit sexual activity, as seen most notoriously in Pakistan. Although in the past confessions obtained under torture or duress were not admissible as evidence in Shariah courts, they are used in some places today.

Judges today are government employees and political appointees rather than local legal experts recognized for their depth of knowledge or personal piety. Although they are expected to rule on "Islamic law," they frequently lack knowledge of the historically accepted rules and methodologies for interpretation. Instead, they often rule according to political expediency and the demands of the state rather than the needs of the community as a whole. Judges are limited generally to their function in the courtroom as opposed to community oversight, although they may step in as legal guardians for those in need. In many countries, religious endowments are now under the purview of a government department rather than the qadi. In addition, qadis today typically do not enjoy the flexibility of the past as laws are generally codified and the qadi is expected to uphold the interests of the state.

The broad global acceptance of human rights standards since the 1948 Universal Declaration of Human Rights has brought an important change to the context in which Shariah courts operate. Many Muslim-majority countries are signatories to this Declaration as well as various other human rights treaties and conventions, such as the 1959 Declaration of the Rights of the Child and the 1981 Convention for the Elimination of All Forms of Discrimination against Women (CEDAW). Shariah courts with criminal law jurisdiction have sometimes been found in contempt of these standards if they have the capacity to assign corporal and capital punishments, particularly where such punishments have been applied beyond the crimes with which they are specifically associated in the Quran.

In some countries, such as post-revolutionary Iran, Shariah courts have been used to suppress political dissent. In others, such as Sudan under the presidency of Gaafar Muhammad an-Nimeiry, Shariah courts have issued capital and corporal punishments and life sentences to children under the age of eighteen. More convictions and implementations of capital and corporal punishments take place today than was the case historically, although it is not always clear in some places, such as Nigeria, whether designated punishments are actually implemented or are intended to serve as a deterrent.

On the basis of human rights standards, contemporary reformers have also challenged classical parameters of witnessing, particularly the valuing of a woman's testimony as only half that of a man's. In the past, because women were less likely than men to be educated and experienced in worldly affairs and also more likely to experience family pressure to testify in ways that were favorable to male family members, the testimony of two women together was portrayed as a safeguard for truthful testimony. Today, reformers argue that the education and experience gaps are no longer the same. Rather than basing the value of the testimony on sex, consideration should be given instead to the credibility of the witness.

Although supporters insist that Shariah courts are implementing "God's law," reformers note serious disconnects between historical and contemporary practices, particularly where contemporary interpretations of Islamic law are essentialized, literal, and absolutist. This is a special concern in places where state focus is on the implementation of hudud (fixed) punishments rather than the guiding principles and objectives (*maqasid*) of Shariah.

4

THE FIVE PILLARS OF ISLAM AND COMMUNITY LIFE

An important prophetic tradition maintains that "Islam was built upon five 'foundations.'" The Five Pillars (the profession of faith [*shahadah*], daily prayers [*salat*], almsgiving [*zakat*], the fast of Ramadan [*sawm*], and the pilgrimage to Mecca [Hajj]) blend the theological with the legal and represent the fundamental principles of personal and collective faith, worship, and social responsibility that unite all Muslims and distinguish Islam from other religions. Their centrality in Shariah is demonstrated by the agreement of both Sunni and Shia legal schools on the essential details of these duties.

The foundations or "pillars" of the faith hold a prominent place in Islamic legal literature, always appearing first in the opening chapters of legal works and constituting as much as one-quarter to one-third of their content. This pride of place not only symbolizes the role of the pillars as ways to fulfill an individual Muslim's relationship with God but also reinforces the sense of community among Muslims and provides the foundational support for other laws meant to regulate human affairs.

How Does a Person Become a Muslim in the Eyes of Islamic Law?

One can become a Muslim by simply professing a brief statement: "There is no god but God (Allah) and Muhammad is the messenger of God." This First Pillar, called the shahadah, which means witness or testimony, is repeated many times throughout the day in the Muslim call to prayer, demonstrating that faith is an ongoing process rather than a one-time event. The declaration of faith is not guided by extensive rules or procedures in the legal literature, other than the requirement that it be stated before two witnesses for the purpose of conversion. This makes the declaration a public statement of intent not only to adhere to the faith but also to be a member of the broader Muslim community. There are websites today that help to facilitate this process, such as by setting up conference calls for those living in non-Muslim-majority countries who do not have access to a local mosque.

The twofold statement in the shahadah reflects the two preeminent fundamentals of Islamic belief: belief in one true God and affirmation of the revelation of the Quran through Muhammad the Messenger. Belief in one true God, or absolute monotheism (*tawhid*), means that nothing—not money, ambition, or ego—except God deserves to be worshipped. If a Muslim values any person or thing more than God, he or she is committing idolatry (*shirk*), the one unforgivable sin in Islam. Quran 4:48 states, "God does not forgive anyone for associating something with Him, while He does forgive whomever He wishes to for anything else. Anyone who gives God associates [partners] has invented an awful sin." Islam's uncompromising belief in the oneness or unity of God (tawhid) is reflected in Islamic art. Because associating anything else with God is considered to be idolatry, Islamic religious art generally tends to avoid depicting human forms and to use calligraphy, geometric forms, and arabesque designs instead.

The second great fundamental of Islam centers on the critical importance of Muhammad, God's final messenger/ prophet. Like Jesus for Christians, Muhammad is the central role model for Muslims as the "living Quran," the embodiment of God's will in how he behaved and how he spoke. But, unlike Jesus, Muhammad is believed to be solely human, not divine. His life as an ideal husband, father, and friend provides extensive guidance for daily private life. He is also seen as the ideal political and military leader, diplomat, and judge, setting examples for the expected conduct of public officials. Muslims' focus on following Muhammad's example reflects the importance of practice and action. In this regard, we see Islam's emphasis on the law, in contrast to Christianity, which gives greater prominence to doctrines or dogma.

How and When Do Muslims Pray?

The Second Pillar of Islam is prayer (salat). Muslims worship in prayer five times throughout the day—at daybreak, noon, midafternoon, sunset, and evening—putting into practice what is expressed in the declaration of faith (shahadah) by demonstrating submission to and adoration of God. Prayer combines meditation, devotion, moral elevation, and physical exercise.

The purpose of prayer is to establish a connection and closeness between the worshipper and God, beginning and ending the day with God, along with remembering the Divine throughout the day. God is thus a part of daily life rather than being relegated to collective worship once a week. Prayers typically involve a time commitment of ten to fifteen minutes. Children grow into prayer gradually, learning from their parents and beginning the full prayer regimen at the age of ten.

The times for prayer and the ritual actions associated with them were not specified in the Quran. Muslims believe

Muhammad established them. Muslims can pray in any clean environment, independently or communally, in a mosque, at home, working or traveling, indoors or outside. A prayer carpet is typically used to assure clean space.

Although it is possible to pray individually, it is considered preferable and meritorious to pray with others as one body united in worshipping God. Group prayer illustrates and reinforces collective discipline, kinship, equality, and solidarity. Group prayer at the mosque is required only for the Friday noon prayer (*jumaa*), although many Shia in practice pray collectively on Thursday night instead. The Friday noon prayer is typically longer than the other prayers because it usually includes a sermon that relates the teachings of the Quran to contemporary life.

Many Muslim countries feature "calls to prayer" from a muezzin who helps to keep Muslims mindful of God amid daily distractions and concerns about work and family. The call is designed to reaffirm total dependence on God and to put worldly concerns within the perspective of death, the Last Judgment, and the afterlife. Often located high atop a mosque's minaret and aided by a megaphone, the muezzin calls out the invitation to prayer:

> God is most great [Allahu Akbar], God is most great, God is most great, I witness that there is no god but God [Allah]; I witness that there is no god but God. I witness that Muhammad is the messenger of God. I witness that Muhammad is the messenger of God. Come to prayer; come to prayer! Come to prosperity; come to prosperity! God is most great. God is most great. There is no god but God.

The Shia call to prayer adds phrases affirming Ali's place as a "friend of God" and calling the faithful additionally to good deeds.

As they prepare to pray, Muslims face Mecca, the holiest city in Islam and Muhammad's birthplace, located in present-day Saudi Arabia. The Grand Mosque in Mecca houses the Kaaba, a cube-shaped structure known as the House of God, which Muslims believe contains the original altar to God built by Abraham and Ishmael, considered the most sacred space in the Muslim world.

Regardless of their native language, Muslims pray their ritual prayers (salat) in Arabic, reciting passages from the Quran and glorifications of God that are accompanied by a series of movements—standing, bowing, kneeling, touching the ground with the forehead, and sitting. Worshippers begin by raising their hands to proclaim God's greatness ("Allahu Akbar"—God is most great), which reminds them of the exalted status of the One to whom they are praying and of the solemnity of their act of worship. Then, folding their hands over stomach or chest or leaving them at their sides, they stand upright and recite what has been described as the essential message of the Quran, the opening chapter, known as al-Fatihah:

> In the name of God, the Most Compassionate, the Most Merciful. Praise be to God, Lord of the Worlds; the Most Compassionate, the Most Merciful; Master of the Day of Judgment. You alone do we worship and from You alone do we seek aid. Show us the Straight Path, the way of those upon whom You have bestowed Your grace, not of those who have earned Your wrath or who go astray. (Quran 1:1–7)

Next, after reciting a self-selected Quran verse, Muslims bow and proclaim, "Glory to God in the Highest" three times. Returning to an upright position, they say, "God hears the one who praises Him" and "Our Lord, all praise belongs to you!" After repeating "Allahu Akbar" (God is most great), in an expression of ultimate submission, Muslims fall to their knees, place their hands flat on the ground, and bring their foreheads down between their hands to touch the ground. While in this bowing position, Muslims recite three times, "Glory to the Lord Most High!" After this, they stand up straight and repeat the entire cycle of prayer.

Prayer also includes sitting on one's heels and reciting what is known as "the witnessing," which contains the declaration of Muslim faith (shahadah) and then asking for God's blessings for Abraham, God's first prophet, and Muhammad, God's last prophet. Finally, prayer ends as worshippers turn their heads right and left and say, "May the peace, mercy, and blessings of God be upon you." While addressing fellow believers on the right and left, some Muslims also believe they are addressing their guardian angels, who remain over their shoulders as they pray. After the obligatory prayers, Muslims can make private petitions (*dua*) to God regarding their individual needs. There are recommended prayer texts in Arabic for such individual needs and problems, but worshippers can also address God in their own native language and words.

As with the other pillars, the daily prayers are intended to be a blessing rather than a burden. Thus, exceptions to the rule are possible when there are extenuating circumstances. When a Muslim is away on travel, for example, the five daily prayers can be collapsed to three time slots, allowing for two sets of prayers to be made at one time.

Is Charity Required by Islamic Law?

The Third Pillar of Islam, almsgiving (zakat), functions both as an integral religious ritual and as a substantive "wealth redistribution law" intended to support the less fortunate members of the Muslim community. While zakat is sometimes defined as a form of charity or donation, it is not a matter of individual choice but rather a formal duty incumbent on every Muslim. Zakat requires payment of 2.5 percent of one's total wealth, not just income, once a year. It is intended to discourage hoarding of capital, greed, and selfishness, and to remind Muslims that all that they have is a gift from God. In addition, by helping the poor meet their needs, ideally, zakat strengthens the security of the entire community, mitigating theft, vandalism, and other crimes by minimizing feelings of resentment and anger among the needy in society. This reflects the "purification" that is supposed to be inherent to zakat, as sharing with others is both psychologically and materially important for Muslims based on the belief that all things ultimately belong to God. As the trustees of earthly wealth, Muslims are accountable for how all things are treated and distributed.

Both men and women are required to pay zakat to Quranically specified beneficiaries. Quran 9:60, as well as Islamic law, stipulates that alms are to be used to support the poor, orphans, widows, and travelers; to free slaves and debtors; and to support those working in the "cause of God" (e.g., construction of mosques, religious schools, and hospitals). Quran 36:47 condemns the argument that people are poor because God wills it, placing the responsibility upon Muslims to recognize the needs of others: "Thus, when they are told, 'Give to others out of what God has provided for you as sustenance' the disbelievers say to those who believe, 'Why should we feed those that God could feed if He wanted?' Clearly, you are deeply misguided!" The forms of wealth subject to zakat include gold, silver, livestock, agricultural produce, articles of trade, currency, stocks and bonds, and other liquid assets. Today, zakat calculators are available online to help Muslims assess their wealth and the amount they owe.

For centuries, because zakat was formally viewed as a religious and moral duty, there was little difficulty in collecting it. It developed into an institutionalized, socioreligious duty expected of every Muslim who possessed a minimum amount of wealth, functioning as a form of social security in Muslim territories. Failure to pay zakat became a punishable offense. While it is still viewed as a religious obligation, zakat lost its prominent legal position in most Muslim states with the advent of colonialism and the institutionalization of secular tax systems. Some Muslim states (Jordan, Saudi Arabia, Malaysia, Pakistan, Kuwait, Libya, Iran, and Sudan) are now applying zakat as a tax, which may be seen as the beginning of a long process moving toward this historic ideal.

Zakat is intended to build the community, not place a burden upon it. Thus, exceptions can be made to payment of zakat, such as by delaying payment in the event of extenuating circumstances, such as drought conditions or natural disasters. There are also minimum thresholds beneath which Muslims are exempt from paying zakat and are to receive it instead. However, the ideal of charitable giving is so strong among many that even the poorest often try to make a symbolic offering.

When and Why Does Islamic Law Oblige Muslims to Fast?

Fasting is common in many religions, often used as a spiritual discipline designed to free people from a self-centered focus on their physical needs and appetites or as penance. The Fast of Ramadan, the Fourth Pillar of Islam, occurs once each year during the ninth month of the Islamic calendar. Ramadan, the only month specifically mentioned in the Quran, is the month in which the first revelation of the Quran came to Muhammad.

Islamic law requires that in Ramadan every Muslim whose health allows abstain from food, drink, and sexual activity from dawn to sunset. During the entire month, Muslims must emphasize religious reflection and prayer, performing good works and distributing alms to help the less fortunate. Fasting is gradually introduced to young children to help them prepare for the full fast when they reach puberty.

Before sunrise, Muslims awake to eat their first meal of the day, which must sustain them until sunset. The intent to fast must be present until the end of the day. Failure to maintain intent represents cause for an invalid fast. However, if a person forgets and eats while he should be fasting, a hadith (saying of Muhammad) declares that the fast is still valid if the eating was a mistake. If fasting was intentionally interrupted, the believer must make up for fasting days in their entirety.

At dusk, family and friends break the fast in the traditional manner established by Muhammad—with a glass of water and a few dates—followed by prayer. After prayer, they share in a bigger meal that often includes special foods only served during this time of year. Since Ramadan is a month devoted to achieving a deeper sense of interaction with God's revelation, many go to the mosque for evening prayer, followed by special prayers recited only during Ramadan. Some will recite the entire Quran (one-thirtieth each night of the month) as a special act of piety. In addition, public recitations of the Quran or Sufi chanting are heard during the evening. The fast ends on the twenty-seventh day of Ramadan when Muslims commemorate the "Night of Power," the time Muhammad first received God's revelation. The end of the fast is marked by celebration of the major Islamic holiday called Eid al-Fitr, literally, the Breaking of the Fast.

In Islamic law, the discipline of the month-long Ramadan fast is intended to stimulate Muslims' reflections on human frailty and dependence on God and thus to increase gratitude toward the Creator. Fasting also serves to increase self-control and self-discipline as well as compassion for those who often experience hunger so that one can identify more strongly with and help the less fortunate. Abstinence should also be accompanied by a conscious effort to avoid negative thinking and to embrace positive, proactive, ethical efforts to improve society and the members who live within it.

Exceptions are made for those unable to fast for either temporary or permanent reasons. Temporary reasons include issues such as illness, pregnancy, breastfeeding, or travel on a long and difficult journey. Permanent reasons include age and health conditions such as diabetes for which fasting would be detrimental. In modern times, exceptions to fasting may also apply to professional athletes in the middle of the sports season if their ability to perform or even overall health might be negatively affected by lack of water, in particular. In each case, it is up to individuals to follow their conscience. Those with temporary conditions can make up the fast at a later time once the condition has been resolved. Those exempted due to permanent conditions are to feed two hungry people each day in keeping with the spirit of caring for the less fortunate.

What Is the Hajj?

The Pilgrimage (or Hajj) to Mecca is the Fifth Pillar of Islam and occurs in the final month of the Islamic lunar calendar. It is required of every Muslim, both female and male, who is physically and financially capable, once in a lifetime. The Hajj is unique among the world's religious pilgrimages, bringing together the largest and most culturally diverse collection of humanity to worship in one place at one time. Every year, 1 million local pilgrims (residents and foreign workers in Saudi Arabia) join another 1.5 million pilgrims from virtually every nation—50 percent from Asia, 35 percent from the Arab world, 10 percent from Africa, and 5 percent from Europe and the Western Hemisphere. In the last four decades, the demographics of the Hajj have changed substantially, with the number of women soaring from one-third to one-half and increasing numbers of Asian, non-Arab, young, educated, and urban worshippers participating.

The Hajj is outstanding for its historical continuity, geographic focus, and doctrinal centrality. The complex and detailed laws and the many symbolic rituals, performed in unison by all pilgrims, focus on rejecting earthly luxuries and worldly concerns and directing the believer's heart, mind, and soul toward God. A Hajj that is properly performed is believed to absolve pilgrims of their previous sins. Critical to a valid pilgrimage is one's sincere intention to perform each ritual with care and attention in order to come closer to God.

In the initial rite of the Hajj, pilgrims circle the Kaaba seven times, moving in a counterclockwise direction. This is done at least twice, when entering Mecca and before departing. The circumambulation symbolically imitates the angels circling God's throne in adoration. The Kaaba is the cube-shaped "House of God" believed to have been built by Abraham and Ishmael and venerated as the spiritual center of Islam, the place that all Muslims face during their prayers.

An essential part of the pilgrimage is the massive procession of millions of pilgrims to the Plain of Arafat, where, from noon until sunset, pilgrims stand before God in repentance, seeking forgiveness for themselves and all Muslims throughout the world. Standing together on this plain, Muslims experience and reflect the underlying unity and equality of the worldwide Muslim community that transcends national, racial, economic, and sexual differences.

The pilgrimage concludes with the second major Islamic holiday, the Feast of the Sacrifice (Eid al-Adha), commemorating God's command to Abraham to sacrifice his son Ishmael (Isaac in Jewish and Christian traditions). God's permission to substitute a sheep for the boy is symbolized through the ritual sacrifice of animals, demonstrating pilgrims' willingness to sacrifice what is important to them. Historically, animals were a sign of a family's wealth and were essential for survival. The surplus of meat from more than 1 million animals (lamb, beef, and camel) is flash frozen, shipped overseas, and distributed to the poor around the world. Muslims internationally also participate vicariously in this experience of the Hajj by simultaneously making their own sacrifices at home. Thus, on a collective level, the Hajj celebrates the renewal and reunion of the *ummah*, the worldwide Islamic community.

5

WOMEN, GENDER, AND THE FAMILY

Muslim family law governs the rights and responsibilities of men and women in marriage, divorce, and inheritance. The Quran introduced important rights for women in marriage, divorce, and inheritance within a strong patriarchal society where men's superiority was taken for granted. The development of Islamic law and family laws, in particular, reflects a strong patriarchal heritage based upon a man's role as head of the family. The family unit was regarded as the foundation of society.

In modern times, the legal systems of most Muslim countries have been substantially informed by Western legal codes. However, family law remains for many an idealized connection to the Islamic past and, therefore, the most resistant and controversial to reform. Legal codes in Muslim countries have not always kept pace with substantial changes in the structure of the family or with women's expanding role resulting from modernization and globalization. Reformers have worked to reinterpret Islamic law to respond to contemporary realities, to protect and expand women's and children's rights and the public interest.

What Does Islamic Law Say about Marriage?

The Quran describes the ideal relationship between spouses as one of love and mercy (Quran 30:21), in which they are members of one another (Quran 3:195) and like each other's garment (Quran 2:187). Islamic law describes marriage as a protection of the family, especially children, a moral safeguard, and a social necessity. Marriage is the expected norm for all Muslims and is intended to strengthen and build the community.

Under Islamic law, marriage is a legal contractual relationship between a man and a woman that unites them as a couple and legitimates procreation. Marriage is also a much deeper relationship than a simple contract and is usually expected to last for a lifetime, providing emotional and psychological comfort and support as well as the foundation of a new family unit that brings two extended families together.

Both spouses have legal rights and responsibilities in marriage. The husband is responsible for providing a marriage gift (*mahr* or dower) for the wife, fulfilling his wife's sexual needs, begetting children, and providing food, clothing, housing, and other needs to the family at the level to which the wife was accustomed. The wife is responsible for fulfilling her husband's sexual needs, bearing children, and maintaining the integrity of the family. Traditionally, in accordance with prevailing gender dynamics, the wife was expected to care for the home and children, although this was not a legal requirement. Some jurists specifically stated that the wife was not obligated to do housework, cook, or clean. Today, changes in social context often lead to a reframing of these roles at the practical level, as many women work outside of the home and contribute to the family's financial support. While some reformists argue that this reality of shared responsibilities should lead to greater equality and balancing of power dynamics within the marriage, particularly with respect to access to divorce, current legislation generally does not reflect this. The 2004 Mudawana (Family Law) of Morocco has made some progress toward greater gender equality by recognizing both spouses as equally responsible for the family, but the husband remains the head of the family and the default legal guardian of the children.

Similar to marriage licenses in the United States, the marriage contract serves as a public record of the relationship and is legally binding. The required elements of the contract are the offer of marriage and its acceptance, specification of a marriage gift payable to the bride, and witnesses. The bride has the option of stipulating conditions in the contract, such as her right to complete her education or to live within a certain distance of her family. The bride's consent to the marriage is required in order for the contract to be valid, although the form of that consent varies in the legal literature based on age, status, and virginity of a woman.

In theory, a bride's lack of consent invalidates the contract, rendering the possibility of a forced marriage theoretically impossible. In practice, in many cultures, including Muslim-majority ones, the bride's male guardian negotiates the marriage contract. A woman may therefore feel pressured by family or social circumstances to accept a husband, particularly if he is recommended by her father. Historically, many jurists explained the male's guardian power to negotiate the marriage contract as a protection for women, who were assumed to have little experience with things like contract negotiations. In addition, a father was assumed to have his daughter's best interests at heart and thus to take care in choosing an appropriate husband for a lasting marriage. In practice, neither all male guardians nor all fathers fulfill these responsibilities and sometimes put their own interests ahead of the well-being of the bride. In some places today, particularly where women are more educated, women are participating more in screening potential husbands, particularly through the use of social media and dating websites that allow communication between the couple in a way that respects privacy norms.

Islamic law grants a woman independent ownership and control over her earnings, investments, inheritance, and other assets. The marriage gift, to which she is entitled, must be agreed upon by both partners. This stipulation is based on Quran 4:4, among others, which instructs men to "give women their bridal gift upon marriage." In the event that the marriage gift is not specified in the contract, the woman is legally entitled to a gift equivalent to what would be given to women of comparable educational status, social rank, and other considerations. The marriage gift becomes the personal property of the woman and is intended to provide financial security for her in the event of widowhood or divorce. This has been particularly important in places where women did not generally have independent wealth or income or did not work outside the home.

Historically, the marriage gift often represented a substantial amount in money, jewelry, or property, although it could also be something symbolic in value, such as a copy of the Quran. In practice, the gift is frequently divided into two portions—one given immediately when the contract is signed and the other deferred until the contract ends, whether by death or divorce. This practice has been observed since the eighth century and is common in many parts of the Muslim world today. Delaying the larger portion of the gift until the conclusion of the marriage is intended both to serve as a deterrent to divorce and to make marriage more accessible and affordable by requiring a smaller portion at the outset of the marriage—a rising concern in many Muslim countries that have large youth populations and high unemployment rates. Claiming the deferred portion of the gift is sometimes complicated in Western countries where the concept is not part of the legal landscape. Some women have successfully claimed their deferred gift under contract law or as a parallel to a prenuptial agreement, but these claims are not always successful in American courts, particularly where the amount is not specified in the contract.

In addition to a standard marriage (referred to as either *nikah* or *zawaj*), which is recognized everywhere, there are other forms of marriage that are accepted in some schools of Islamic law. The Shia schools accept temporary marriage (*nikah al-mutah*, literally "marriage of desire"). Carried over from pre-Islamic times, temporary marriage is a contractual relationship with a specified beginning and end date that is determined by the parties to the marriage. Parallel to the marriage gift in a standard marriage, a gift is given to the woman as part of the temporary marriage contract. Any children born of the temporary marriage are considered legitimate, the father is obligated to provide for them, and the children are considered legitimate heirs. However, in temporary marriage the husband is not responsible for providing for the wife financially or providing housing or food. Those who support temporary marriage argue that it satisfies sexual needs in a socially responsible and healthy manner by preventing fornication. Others view it with moral ambivalence and even negativity, as creating a stigma for the woman. Although Sunni Islamic law schools do not recognize temporary marriage, some Sunni scholars, particularly in the Gulf, have approved new forms of marriage, with similar characteristics. These are "travel" marriage (*misfar*) and "pleasure" marriage (*misyar*), which are understood from the outset to be temporary in nature—for the duration of a business trip or simply to legitimate sexual relations without incurring any obligation for the man to financially support the wife. In the eyes of many Sunnis, these structural similarities to Shia temporary marriage render it illegitimate.

Although there are opportunities for women to express agency and autonomy under the Islamic laws of marriage, many Muslim women are not aware of these rights or do not exercise them due to ignorance, family pressure, or local customs. Reformists and women's rights activists are working in many countries to redress these shortcomings through state laws and institutions. For example, in some countries today, including Iran and Egypt, state offices provide a standard marriage contract with printed conditions that the couple must negotiate before registering the contract. It is up to the couple to decide which conditions will apply to their marriage. Sample conditions include determining how marital property will be handled during the marriage and divided in the event of divorce, the wife's right to be paid for housework performed during the marriage in the event of divorce, and the wife's right to initiate divorce in the event of abuse, mistreatment, or failure to pay maintenance on the part of the husband. Simply having some printed options shows that this mechanism is legal and open to discussion and expansion.

Many women are not aware of their right to make a claim on property acquired during marriage. Morocco, Singapore, Malaysia, Turkey, and the Philippines are among the countries with legal provisions enabling Muslim women to make such a claim. Iran includes the right of the wife to claim half of the property acquired over the course of the marriage as one of the conditions on the standard state marriage contract. Stipulation of conditions is becoming more prevalent in the United States today, thanks to efforts to raise awareness by organizations such as the Islamic Society of North America, Karamah: Muslim

Women Lawyers for Human Rights, Muslim Women Living under Family Laws, Peaceful Families Project, the Fiqh Council of North America, and the Association of Muslim American Lawyers, among others.

Does Islamic Law Enable a Man to Have Multiple Wives?

In theory, Islamic law permits a man to have up to four wives. In practice, this permission is constrained by the Quranic requirement that the man treat them all equally (Q 4:3). This places the Shariah principles of justice, equality, and protection of and provision for the family at the heart of legislation governing polygyny, rather than male privilege.

Polygyny was a widespread practice throughout the ancient Near East and is mentioned in the Old Testament as well as in the Quran. In pre-Islamic Arabia, a man could have an unlimited number of wives. The Quranic specification of a maximum of four wives thus represented a limitation rather than a new permission. It was issued in the aftermath of the Battle of Uhud (625 CE) in which many Muslim men were killed, leaving a large number of widows and orphans without a male protector and provider. The "occasion of revelation" therefore was a context of addressing justice for widows and orphans. Quran 4:2–3 states, "Give orphans their property, do not replace their good things with bad, and do not consume their property with your own—a great sin. If you fear that you will not deal fairly with orphan girls, you may marry whichever women seem good to you, two, three or four. If you fear that you cannot be equitable [to them], then marry only one."

Although permission to marry more than one wife is clearly connected to concerns about protection of widows and eliminating exploitation of orphans and their property, historically, this passage was used in legal literature to uphold a man's right to have multiple wives. At the same time, the Quran itself placed limits on that right, making it clear that a man could have more than one wife only if he could treat them all justly (Quran 4:3). This emphasis on just treatment of wives is repeated in Quran 4:129, in which God warns men that they are never able to be fair and just between wives, no matter how much they desire to do so. Quran 33:4 further warns that God has not made two hearts in one body for any man, so that equal love for more than one woman at a time is not possible.

Based on these limitations and warnings against exploitation and unjust treatment of wives, some reformers have argued that Quranic permission to marry up to four wives is intended to be exceptional based on social circumstances rather than blanket permission for polygyny. Some have further argued that the Quranic intent over time was first limitation and then ultimately elimination of polygyny. These arguments are reflected in state laws in some countries. For example, Tunisia followed this reasoning in abolishing polygyny in 1956. Turkey outlawed polygyny in the Turkish Civil Code of 1926 and the ruling AK Party has effectively banned polygamists from entering or living in the country, although the practice still exists among Kurdish populations in the southeast of Turkey. To date, polygyny has been limited or restricted in half of the fifty-seven member countries of the Organization of Islamic Cooperation. Algeria, Indonesia, Egypt, Senegal, Bangladesh, Gambia, Jordan, Libya, Iran, Pakistan, and Malaysia have all enacted some form of restriction on polygyny, including notification and/or permission of the first wife, the possibility of divorce from the first wife if she is not in agreement, and requirement of documented proof of financial ability to provide for multiple households. In

2004, Morocco's family code strictly forbade polygyny unless a judge can certify that a husband is able to provide equally for his wives (and their children) and that the case is exceptional and warrants approval. In other countries in the Gulf (Saudi Arabia, Qatar, Kuwait, and the United Arab Emirates) polygyny is more common.

Does Islamic Law Allow Muslims to Marry Non-Muslims?

Islamic law regarding marriage reflects concerns about creating a harmonious marriage and family unit, and preserving the faith of children born into the union. Therefore, Muslim men can only marry non-Muslim women from among the "People of the Book," or those with a divinely revealed scripture, such as Jews and Christians (Quran 5:5). (In later centuries, this was extended to other religions including Hinduism and Buddhism.) As with marriage to a Muslim woman, a man marrying a woman from the People of the Book must offer her the marriage gift as part of the marriage contract. Muslim men are not permitted to marry women from faith traditions without a divinely revealed scripture.

According to classical Islamic law, a Muslim woman can only marry a Muslim man. This prescription reflects the patriarchal society in which Islamic law was originally developed. Women were expected to care for small children and oversee their earliest religious exposure and training, while men were recognized as the heads of the households and were responsible for the religious instruction of older children, serving as their guardians and overseeing their marriages. The concern was that children from a marriage between a Muslim woman and a non-Muslim man would be a "loss" to Islam because a non-Muslim father might not allow his children to be raised in the Muslim faith.

This tradition is being challenged today by a growing number of Muslims, particularly second-generation and indigenous communities in the United States and Europe. In some cases, the reasons are practical, such as a limited pool of potential Muslim marriage candidates. In others, issues related to compatibility are given a higher priority, and there is more acceptance than in earlier times of multicultural and multireligious relationships and family units. Nevertheless, there is still considerable family, social, and religious pressure to follow traditional marriage patterns, particularly in conservative communities.

Does Islamic Law Require or Encourage Arranged Marriages?

Muslim families around the world traditionally play a strong role in orchestrating the marriages of their children. However, arranged marriages are based on custom rather than a mandate of Islamic law. Islamic law requires the consent of the spouses in order for the marriage to be valid, although definitions of consent vary according to age and status. Some young Muslims reject the traditional arranged marriages of their parents and ancestors, while others embrace or accept this option, citing statistics of high divorce rates for non-arranged marriage and positing that arranged marriages are well thought out and based on common interests and backgrounds.

There are three main methods for arranging marriage: first, the parents plan the entire arrangement with no input from the children or interaction between future spouses; second, children tell their parents what they are looking for in a future spouse and the parents facilitate chaperoned interactions between likely candidates; and third, "joint-venture" arranged marriages, in which both parents and children are actively involved in the selection process, which often includes open courting or dating.

Partially as a result of the influence of Western culture, the desire to have more choice in selecting a future spouse has been growing among some young Muslims. For example, in major urban areas in Pakistan, especially among educated and high-income families, traditional marriages with no interaction between the future spouses are becoming less common. Arranged marriages are slightly higher in rural areas and among less-educated classes.

New practices for seeking spouses are also emerging, especially among Muslims in the West. While some parents and children still look abroad to Muslim-majority countries for spouses, others are using alternative methods, like meeting at family or community social events, exploring Muslim social networks at universities, or engaging in halal (permissible) dating accompanied by a chaperone. Still other venues have emerged, such as speed dating (an event where participants meet and talk for a few minutes with all the prospective partners and then make a list of those they are interested in dating) and marriage websites, social media, and personal advertisements. Young Muslims refer to these new practices as "assisted" arranged marriage.

Arranged marriages are not synonymous with forced marriages, which the Quran (4:1) and hadith (sayings of Muhammad) prohibit because any marriage that is forced or false in any way is not a proper marriage. Despite the Quran's prohibition of forced marriage, traditional Islamic law nevertheless allows a father to determine a husband for his daughter. Some Muslim countries have legislation requiring a woman's guardian to contract the marriage for her. This requirement has been viewed as a protective measure for both the woman and the family's honor. Other rationales for arranged marriages include ethnic customs and traditions that create strong social pressures on families to conform or face shame or community disapproval, as well as financial situations where girls are seen as an economic burden and are exchanged for goods or money or these arrangements are made to provide a secure future for daughters in poor families. Forced marriages are forbidden in eight Muslim countries: Saudi Arabia, Algeria, Iraq, Syria, Jordan, Morocco, the Philippines, and Malaysia, although the law is not always effectively enforced.

Is Child Marriage Sanctioned by Islamic Law?

Classical Islamic law permits a child's legal guardian to contract marriage for the child because a child below the age of majority has no legal capacity to enter any contract. However, the marriage may not be consummated before the child reaches a mature age. Once that mature age is reached, the child theoretically has the right to renounce the marriage, although, in practice, families often exert pressure on the child to accept it. Technically, the father or grandfather may contract a minor in marriage only if it is in the child's clear interest.

International human rights standards define child marriage as marriage of a person under the age of eighteen. By this definition, child marriage still exists to a significant extent in some parts of the world, particularly in developing countries in central Africa and Bangladesh, where more than 60 percent of all girls are married before they reach the age of 18. Although child marriage exists in parts of the Muslim world, many countries have set minimum ages for marriage. Age limitations differ from country to country but tend to range from sixteen to eighteen for females and seventeen to twenty-one for males. In some cases, the minimum age for marriage has been increased due to input from the medical profession about the negative physical and psychological toll that marriage and childbirth can bring for females at younger ages. In many countries, however, laws limiting child marriage are extremely difficult to enforce, especially in rural areas where historical, cultural, and economic factors supporting child marriage often outweigh legal restrictions.

Although these laws discourage child marriage, a variety of factors contribute to its resilience worldwide. Poverty is a huge motivator in some places as child brides are used to pay off a father's debts. In addition, local patriarchal custom and the belief that young brides are more likely to become dutiful wives is a motivator. In some countries, adults and families facilitate child marriage, believing that it will prevent socially and religiously unacceptable behaviors such as premarital sex.

❦

What Does Islamic Law Say about Divorce Rights for Men and Women?

Islamic law has always recognized the possibility of divorce under certain circumstances. Nevertheless, the Quran and Sunna (Muhammad's example) emphasize the undesirability of divorce and view it as a last resort. The Prophet Muhammad reportedly said, "Of all the permitted things, divorce (*talaq*) by the husband is the most abominable [detestable] with God."

Because the family is the foundation of Islamic society, Islamic law encourages Muslims to do all that they can to avert a divorce, including engaging mediators from both families. "If you fear a split between a man and a woman, send for an arbiter from his family and an arbiter from her family [thus the wife's interests are on an equal footing with her husband's]. If both want to be reconciled, God will arrange things between them" (Quran 4:35). The Quran also urges husbands seeking divorce to either "retain them [their wives] honorably or release them honorably" (Quran 65:2), so that divorce does not become a long process creating hardship for the wife.

Islamic law permits a man to divorce his wife at any time for any or no reason, while a wife's right to initiate divorce, whether by *khul*, which requires the husband's consent, or by *faskh*, which is pronounced by a judge, is more limited. Divorce is not intended to be arbitrary or the result of a moment of anger or frustration. The Quran calls for a declaration of divorce to be given three times by the husband in order for it to become binding (Quran 2:229–230). These declarations are to be spaced out by a month. Classical legal literature describes this time as an opportunity to work through problems, bring in mediators, and assure that the couple has ample time for reconciliation. In the event that the intent to divorce is pronounced a third time, the wife enters a waiting period to determine whether she is pregnant. She is not permitted to remarry until this period has ended so that paternity is clear.

Despite these Quranic guidelines, an abbreviated kind of divorce, known as the triple talaq, in which all three declarations of divorce are made simultaneously, became common in some places. Although it is considered a sinful abuse, some schools of Islamic law considered it legally valid at the same time that they discouraged it. Other schools permitted it to count as only a single talaq. The triple talaq is used most notoriously today in Saudi Arabia, even though it is theoretically illegal. It is not recognized at all in Algeria and Tunisia. Morocco requires that a court issue a triple talaq and Malaysia requires official notification and registration.

Classical Islamic legal literature discussed both direct and indirect statements of talaq divorces with varying conclusions as to their applicability. While all law schools agreed upon the validity of a direct declaration of divorce, others varied on indirect declarations. The ultimate question became one of intent—did the husband intend divorce or was he simply expressing dissatisfaction with some action on the part of his wife? Some schools of Islamic law, such as the Hanafis, were more lenient in their interpretations, requiring a clear statement by the husband in order to recognize the divorce. Others, such as the Hanbalis, were stricter in holding the husband accountable, believing that a matter as serious as divorce ought to preclude careless statements on the part of the husband. In many cases, though, the issue would only come to the attention of a judge if the wife sought counsel on her status. Divorce initiated by the wife but ratified (faskh) by a judge is limited to certain grounds that varied significantly by schools of law. Historically, these included insanity, impotence, sexual abandonment, infertility on the part of the husband, cruelty, prolonged absence, failure to pay maintenance, violation of conditions stipulated in the marriage contract, or the husband's imprisonment. Contemporary legislation has expanded these grounds in many countries today to include domestic violence, substance abuse (whether alcohol or drugs), and infectious disease, such as HIV, on the husband's part. Divorce pronounced by a judge preserves the woman's financial rights to maintenance during her waiting period and payment of any remaining portion of the marriage gift.

Divorce initiated by the wife as khul, on the other hand, requires the wife to offer financial compensation to the husband in parallel to the financial compensation a husband owed his wife if he initiated the divorce. Traditionally, this compensation was the marriage gift offered in the marriage contract, symbolizing the end of that contract. In addition, the wife waives any outstanding financial rights. The main requirement for khul is the husband's consent. Some men have used that consent as a bargaining chip, refusing to

initiate divorce themselves via talaq in order to pressure
the wife into seeking a khul divorce. This allows the man
to avoid financial obligations to the wife, who is essentially
trapped in the marriage unless she agrees to renounce those
rights. In addition, there have been cases of men demanding more than the marriage gift as compensation for the
divorce. In some instances, this has allowed men to benefit
financially from divorce, while in others it has served as a
roadblock to divorce as the amount demanded is beyond
what the woman can pay, particularly if she is asked to pay
the deferred portion of the marriage gift.

Because of abuses by husbands of divorce by khul,
Egypt passed legislation in 2000 giving a woman the right
to unilateral divorce by khul in exchange for renouncing
her financial rights, returning the marriage gift, going
through a three-month period of attempted reconciliation,
and making a public statement in court of her inability to
live with her husband. This placed the power of divorce in
the hands of the judge rather than requiring the husband's
consent and was intended to speed up divorce processes
that otherwise could drag on for years and even decades.
Other countries have followed this model to improve
women's right to divorce.

Abuses of divorce mechanisms by the husband have led
to stricter regulations surrounding divorce in most Muslim
countries today. Most importantly, many countries require
registration of both marriage and divorce with the courts
rather than leaving these matters to private arrangements.
This is intended to assure that both spouses have certainty as to their marital status. Algeria, Bangladesh, Iran,
Iraq, Jordan, Kuwait, Libya, Lebanon, Malaysia, Morocco,
Somalia, Syria, Tunisia, and Yemen require that divorces be
registered or notarized in court. In Indonesia, all divorces
must be court approved and the grounds for divorce are the
same for husband and wife. Some countries additionally

require hearings before a family judge. Arbitration is often advised and reconciliation between the husband and wife is frequently attempted before a divorce is officially granted. Reconciliation attempts are mandatory in Tunisia, Syria, Lebanon, and Algeria.

Failure to obtain divorce through the courts in countries that require it does not render the divorce religiously invalid, but privately conducted divorce is not recognized by the courts with respect to related issues, such as child custody or property rights. In the United States and Europe, only divorces obtained through the court are legally binding. In those countries where divorce does not have to be filed with the court, women who are uncertain about their status often seek the advice of a mufti. Recent cases have included questions such as whether notification of divorce via text or SMS qualified as official notification and whether a man changing his Facebook status from "Married" to "Single" constituted an indirect declaration of divorce.

How Does Islamic Law Treat Child Custody?

Islamic law determining child custody following divorce was formulated in a patriarchal society in which the father was understood to be the head of household and the legal guardian for children of marriageable age. Assigning custody to the father was considered appropriate to the social structure and a means of assuring financial support for the child. Mothers typically received custody only of young children, typically up until the age of seven or eight, unless they remarried, in which case custody reverted to the father.

Today, many countries have issued legislation that raises the minimum age for a father to automatically gain custody to between the ages of seven and twelve for boys and nine and eighteen for girls. In Morocco's Family Code, the mother has the right of custody until the age of puberty for her sons and until her daughters are married. In Pakistan and India, mothers have custody of their sons until the age of seven and puberty for daughters, while in Jordan the mother retains custody until puberty for both boys and girls.

In many countries today, when family courts or judges consider issues of divorce and custody, state laws allow decisions to be based on what is determined to be in the child's best interests. Consideration of the best interests of the child is a complex contemporary formulation that looks at the character of the parents, their relationships with the child and broader society, preferences of the child, and the financial means and living arrangements of both parents. For example, Tunisia and Turkey give equal rights of custody and guardianship to both parents and courts are instructed to make decisions considering the best interests of the child. The result is often that the mother retains custody and the father provides maintenance until the child becomes an adult.

Although a few countries allow the child to choose which parent gains custody, most still give strong preference to the father, based on influence from classical Islamic law and ongoing patriarchy. Nevertheless, mothers can and do petition for custody. In countries where mothers are unlikely to receive custody of their children, they are often reluctant to seek divorce for fear of losing contact with their children. A woman can lose custody of her child if she remarries, chooses to live too far from the father, or commits adultery. In many countries, non-Muslim mothers rarely get custody.

What Does Islamic Law Say about Inheritance?

Islamic inheritance law is complex and receives extensive coverage in the legal literature. The main parameters of inheritance, who is entitled to shares and in what proportions, are outlined in Quran 4:7–12. Portions are specified for both male and female relatives of the deceased. Islamic legal literature elaborated upon these verses, outlining any number of scenarios of heirs. Bequests could not exceed one-third of the total estate, with the rest to be split among the heirs.

The two main theological branches of Islam, Sunni and Shia, differ on how these rules are to be interpreted and applied. Sunnis believe that the Quran reformed the pre-Islamic system, while Shia believe that the Quran supplanted this older model. In both cases, women are guaranteed a share of inheritance—a right that was not given to women in the West until centuries later. Shia focus on keeping the inheritance within the nuclear family. This limitation on the number of heirs places daughters in a relatively advantageous position compared to the Sunni practice of extending inheritance benefits beyond the nuclear family. The inclusion of a larger number of heirs by Sunnis means smaller portions for everyone with a disproportionate impact on daughters.

It is often stated that the Quran assigns women only half of the share of men. This is not entirely accurate, as the amount of the share depends upon the relationship to the deceased. Some interpreters believe that this prescription must be followed literally. Others argue that it is necessary to understand the patriarchal context in which the Quran was revealed: Men were heads of household and were expected to provide financially for their families, which included wives, children, parents, and unmarried siblings. Women, on the other hand, regardless of their personal wealth, were not expected to make a financial contribution to household expenses—for themselves or anyone else. Men had a greater need for inheritance because of their financial obligations to care for others, while women were responsible only for themselves.

Today, Muslims live in a variety of contexts. Although many still believe that inheritance law is immutable, the reality of changed circumstances in many places, particularly where women work and contribute to household expenses, has led some reformists to argue that men and women should inherit in equal portions. Nongovernmental organizations and human rights activists have pushed particularly hard for equal inheritance rights between men and women. However, many Muslims continue to resist such change, believing it is a violation of Quranic prescriptions. Some other countries, such as Morocco and Egypt, have passed inheritance legislation to assure a more equitable situation for Muslim women.

Social pressures in many Muslim countries have often resulted in women essentially forfeiting their inheritance rights in favor of male relatives, whether due to ignorance of those rights or intimidation. Some individuals deliberately seek to keep property outside of official records in order to avoid giving women their allotted share, despite the fact that Islamic law limited such setting aside of property to a maximum of one-third for specific bequests. Some have even tried to argue that a woman can only inherit if no will is left and that the deceased may do away with this fixed inheritance through his will, although this claim has no support in either the Quran or Islamic legal literature. As Sheikh Mahmoud Abd al-Hafeet, an official at al-Azhar University, has noted, depriving women of inheritance violates all the principles of Islam and reflects pre-Islamic values of ignorance (al-Jahiliya) and the suppression of women.

Does Islamic Law Mandate Separation of the Sexes?

Many, though not all, Muslim societies practice social separation of men and women to varying degrees, in mosques, universities, schools, and clubs. Separation of the sexes is not unique to Islam; it also occurs in Greek and Russian Orthodox churches and Orthodox Jewish synagogues. In some Muslim-majority countries, Muslim women typically pray at home rather than in the mosque, or only attend the weekly congregational Friday prayer. In many mosques, men and women have separate areas for prayer, set apart by a wall, screen, or curtain intended to prevent distraction. However, many today believe that separation promotes inequality and deliberately excludes women from important social, educational, and religious spaces or implies that their presence and participation is less important than a man's. In contrast, during the Hajj (pilgrimage to Mecca), there is no segregation of the sexes and Islamic law itself stipulates that women not veil their faces during the pilgrimage. Integration of the sexes also occurs during festivities at Sufi saints' shrines.

The practice of separation of the sexes in Muslim-majority societies has both religious and cultural origins. Muhammad's community in Medina did not practice strict sexual segregation. The hadith are filled with female questioners presenting their situations to Muhammad. Both men and women attended the mosque together during Muhammad's lifetime. Muhammad's wives ultimately became a unique case—set apart from general society due to their special status described in Quran 33:32–33: "O wives of the Prophet! You are not like any of the other women. If you fear God, do not be complaisant in speech so that one in whose heart is a sickness may covet you, but speak honorably. Stay with dignity in your homes and do not display your finery as the pagans of old did." The Quran later tells Muhammad's wives to place a barrier between themselves and unrelated males. Muslim men are told, "And when you ask [his wives] for anything you want, ask them from before a screen. That makes for greater purity for your hearts and for theirs" (Quran 33:53).

There are many different interpretations of these Quran verses, reflecting tribal and regional cultures and customs in different countries. Many conservatives maintain that although these verses are addressed to the wives of the Prophet, they apply to all Muslim women, who should emulate the behavior of Muhammad's wives. Their argument is based not only on the wives' special status as the "Mothers of the Believers," but also on prophetic traditions (hadith) reflecting the patriarchal belief that women are a source of temptation (*fitnah*) for men.

By contrast, reform-minded scholars and social and political activists counter that the Quran was specifically addressing only the wives of the Prophet, not all of womankind. In support, they point out other unique attributes of Muhammad's wives that are not applied to all women, such as not being permitted to remarry after his death. In addition, personal status codes (family law) and national laws in many places, such as Pakistan, Indonesia, Morocco, Iran, and Egypt, even if they claim to be Islamic in inspiration, nevertheless reflect pre-Islamic or other cultural traditions and practices regarding acceptable and unacceptable interactions between members of the opposite sex. Because of the mix of influences and because they reject gender segregation as normative, these scholars and activists argue against gender segregation.

The reality in many locations today, from Egypt and Tunisia to Malaysia and Indonesia, is that men and women, especially in cities and towns, increasingly study and work together. In a modern, globalizing world in which two incomes are often necessary to maintain a household, women are increasingly pursuing education and joining the workforce, breaking down traditional notions of gendered space. Many believe that modesty requirements can be met through appropriate dress and modest interaction with unrelated males in professional and educational contexts. This holds true even in the religious realm. Women have come to play a more visible and important role in the mosque and society. Many women in some countries attend services and pray with men. They also interpret Islam, teach Quran classes, lead women in prayer, and even serve as qadis and muftis in some countries. In addition, women have served in a variety of public roles as elected officials, such as prime ministers, presidents, cabinet members, members of parliaments, and ambassadors in countries as diverse as Egypt, Senegal, Turkey, Bahrain, Kuwait, Iraq, Iran, Pakistan, Afghanistan, Bangladesh, Malaysia, and Indonesia.

Does Islamic Law Require Women and Men to Dress or Groom Themselves in Certain Ways?

A woman wearing a headscarf, popularly referred to as hijab, or a full-bearded man wearing a cap or turban are often the first images that come to mind when Westerners think about Muslims, but there is nothing in the Quran to mandate these modes of dress. The Quran does not explicitly require all Muslim women to cover their heads or faces. Neither does it call upon all men to grow beards or cover their heads. What the Quran does say is that both men and women should dress modestly and lower their gazes when meeting each other (Quran 24:30–31). This leaves responsibility for personal morality and conduct in the hands of the individual, applying the same standard to men and women.

The command to Muslim women to draw their scarves over their necklines was designed to mark them as respectable women who were not to be harassed. At the time, women who went out alone were often harassed by men. The purpose of the covering was to indicate that the woman was a pious and respectable individual, not someone who was publicly available. Rather than rendering her invisible, the veil was intended to serve as a visible marker of a woman's protected status.

What has come to be the traditional type of veiling focused on covering the head and sometimes the face was adopted from the surrounding Persian and Byzantine Empires as the Islamic Empire spread beyond Arabia and absorbed aspects of their neighbors' upper-class culture. In these societies, only upper- and middle-class women veiled—and did so to distinguish themselves from lower-class women and prostitutes. The veil thus served as a marker of wealth and prestige, available only to those who enjoyed male protection to the extent that a particular woman was kept "private" to an individual man. Veiling therefore served as a marker of a man's status and prestige rather than as a religious statement by a woman. Rising levels of urbanization among Muslims expanded the adoption of veiling by Muslim women, particularly due to the mingling of all classes at prayer and in the marketplace, as well as rising potential for contact with strangers.

Many Muslim women choose to cover their hair with the hijab as a sign of their personal commitment to religious values. In Western settings where the hijab or head scarf serves as a visible marker of a woman's Muslim identity, and often carries a stigma that sometimes provokes hate speech and even physical abuse, the choice to wear the veil is perceived as an act of courage and determination representing the struggle (jihad) to live a righteous life. At stake are issues related to personal identity, spiritual fulfillment, and the right to a choice of dress. In other places, veiling is a matter of compliance with a cultural norm or government regulation rather than an expression of independent agency.

A resurgence of "re-veiling" has occurred since the 1970s from Cairo to Jakarta, as young, urban, educated, middle-class working women have turned or returned to wearing Islamic dress. Contemporary Islamic fashions, which have become a profitable enterprise, also reflect new understandings of the status and role of women. Some Muslim women have started their own companies specializing in the design and marketing of fashionable and modest outfits featuring varied flowing garments and matching veils in a variety of colors and fabrics.

Those who choose to cover, in whatever form, offer multiple reasons behind their choice. Some say that it provides freedom from being judged based on physical appearance, enabling them to focus on spiritual, intellectual, and professional development, as well as personality. They see this as empowering because it pushes people to judge them based on who they are, not what they look like. It also frees them from competing with other women's looks as well as from being sex objects for men to reject or approve. Some see adoption of Islamic dress as a way to reconcile Islamic tradition with their modern lifestyle. In some cases, Islamic dress has also been used as a political statement of national pride and resistance to Western dominance (cultural as well as political) and authoritarian regimes.

Many young Muslim women have adopted Islamic dress to symbolize a return to their cultural roots and rejection of a Western imperialist tradition that they believe shows little respect for women, turning them into sexual objects available for public gaze and lacking in propriety and dignity. They disagree that "freedom" is represented by the ability to strip down to a tiny bikini on a public beach for public viewing and the use of women's bodies to sell everything from vacation sites to men's cologne to liquor. They argue instead that Islamic dress frees them from unrealistic and unhealthy obsessions about physical beauty and weight that plague many non-Muslim women. Women who wear Islamic dress find it strange or offensive for people to condemn their modest fashions as imprisoning and misogynist.

Others see the veil as a symbol of women's inferiority in Islam, of a society's backwardness and oppression in contrast to the individuality and freedom they perceive in Western dress. They see veiled women as victims of an abusive patriarchal culture or as uncritically submitting to the dictates of their religion. They perceive the burqa, which covers a woman's entire body and leaves only a small mesh screen for the eyes, as a means to control and segregate women, as occurred in Afghanistan under the Taliban. Both Muslim and non-Muslim critics of veiling stress the importance of individual freedom and self-expression. They believe that any person, religion, or culture that requires a mature woman to dress in a specific way infringes on her rights and freedom.

Some Muslim and Western governments have viewed the hijab as a sign of a dangerous form of political Islam or "fundamentalism" that is contrary to and threatens the principles and values of a secular government. In the past, secular Muslim governments in Tunisia and Turkey banned the hijab. Today in Europe, France has banned the hijab in schools; France, Belgium, the Netherlands, parts of Spain, Austria, and Switzerland have banned the niqab (full face veil) and France, parts of Spain, and Germany the burka (veil that covers face and body) in schools and government offices. The European Court of Justice, in cases of French and Belgian women who were fired from their jobs by employers for refusing to remove their hijabs, ruled that employers were allowed to ban the hijab. The European Court of Justice (ECJ) in March 2017 ruled that if a firm has an internal rule banning the wearing of "any political, philosophical or religious sign," this rule does not constitute "direct discrimination."

In the end, many of the debates are really about the perception of symbols and the question of individual choice: Should veiled women be able to speak for themselves and express what the veil means to them or must they be defined by outside observers projecting onto them things they may not personally believe or perceive? Many women who choose to veil complain that people simply assume that they are oppressed, regardless of their intelligence, strength of character, or personal achievements. Some note that women in other cultures and religions—Catholic nuns and Jewish, Russian, Greek, and Hindu women cover their heads but are not considered to be oppressed.

While Islamic law does not explicitly stipulate grooming regulations for Muslim men they, like Muslim women, are encouraged to attend to personal hygiene and dress modestly. Modest dress for men typically consists of loose-fitting clothing with sleeves and pants covering at least to the knee or a thobe or jallabiyya (which resemble a very long shirt). As with women's fashions, men's fashions include a variety of styles, colors, and fabrics. Regional distinctions are often apparent in specific types of collars and cuffs. Numerous traditions (hadith) indicate that Muhammad wore a beard and instructed his male followers not to cut their beards to a length of less than one fist-width, while keeping their mustaches neatly trimmed. Many Muslims do not accept this assertion and thus the different styles of beards vary greatly, from full beards that cover the entire jaw and cheeks to neatly trimmed goatees or a mustache. Many Muslim men choose not to wear beards at all.

Although it is not obligatory, many Muslim men wear some form of headdress: a prayer cap, traditional Arab head covering, fez, or turban. Some wear these out of religious conviction, others due to cultural custom or personal preference. In some cases, headwear indicates cultural or tribal identification. Turban colors can indicate the status of the wearer. Shia clerics in Iran wear turbans as a sign of their office, with black indicating descent from Muhammad and white indicating lack of such a connection.

6

GOVERNMENT, LAW, AND ORDER

Throughout history, while the example of Muhammad as head of state and Shariah principles have been reference points, diverse and competing models of government and law have existed. Although many changes occurred with the spread of the Islamic Empire and the rise and fall of governments, to this day an idealized vision of a united Muslim state governed by Islamic law and ruled by a single leader responsible for protecting citizens, providing security and marketplace justice, and promoting public welfare (*maslahah*) has remained a powerful influence.

Islamic law derived from Shariah is considered the central guide for all of a Muslim's actions and interactions, and Islam is seen as a comprehensive way of life that cannot separate religion and the state. There are many competing visions of how Islam, Islamic law, and the state are to relate in a modern state and how Muslims living in non-Muslim countries should understand their obligations.

Does Islamic Law Prescribe a Single Model of Government?

There is no single model for an Islamic state or empire. Diverse and competing models have existed throughout history along with various types of leadership, including caliphs, sultans, Imams, kings, and, more recently, ayatollahs, presidents, and prime ministers. The Quran does not provide a blueprint for Islamic government. Instead, in order to construct governments, Muslims have looked to the broad Shariah principles of the proper functions of the state, such as provision of security, public welfare (maslahah), and justice in the marketplace, and also to Muhammad's example as prophet and head of state. The lack of a singular model of government opens the door to a multiplicity of ways of fulfilling the objectives of Shariah.

During Muhammad's lifetime, his leadership of the Muslim community was clear. As recognized prophet and head of state, Muhammad could have chosen to be an authoritarian ruler. Instead, he followed the principles of consultation (*shura*) and achieving consensus (*ijma*) in the community, drawing upon recommendations, questions, and concerns from both women and men. Community participation was not limited to Muslims. Non-Muslim tribes, including Jewish tribes, were also included in governance and in a collective security arrangement known as the Pact or Constitution of Medina. Non-Muslims continued their own religious observances and followed their own religious laws, but at the same time they were united in the broader interests of the community for public welfare and security. This model of focusing on the common good while allowing for personal choice provides a flexible framework and broad political worldview that can be and has been reinterpreted over time to accommodate changes in societies and cultures.

Historically, this pattern played out in different ways, some more successful than others. States such as the Almohad Caliphate in North Africa (1121–1269) that tended toward extremely conservative religious and legal interpretations and political structures were often short-lived.

Other states, such as the Ottoman Empire (1299–1923) that ruled through a combination of Islamic and other customary types of law, permitted non-Muslim religious minorities within them to practice their religion freely and maintained flexibility and adaptability to changing circumstances. They tended to be longer-lived, although they experienced their own challenges. State and religious legal systems and institutions often existed side by side in Muslim societies in a variety of forms, from the Umayyad and Abbasid empires and sultanates of the Middle East to Timbuktu and the Malay archipelago. Almost all of them ultimately fell to European colonialism between the eighteenth and twentieth centuries.

European colonial rule and the threat of Westernization (Western political and cultural domination), which placed Muslim societies in positions of inferiority militarily, politically, culturally, and technologically, provided the spark for Islamic revivalist and reform movements. These reformers argued that the Muslims' defeat at the hands of European colonialists was due to their abandonment of the ideal of integrated religious and political authority. Recovery of power and prestige would require reuniting the religious and political aspects of public life and governance. The vision caught on at the popular level and many newly independent and newly formed states deliberately took on an Islamic character, including the Kingdom of Saudi Arabia, the Islamic Republic of Pakistan, Iran's post-revolutionary theocracy, and the Taliban's rule in Afghanistan. Although they all claim to be Islamic governments based on Islamic law, each of them took a different form. Other models temper the vision of a strict Islamic state through the use of human reason. One example is that proposed by Rashid al-Ghannushi, the leader of the Islamic movement al-Nahda (Renaissance) Party in Tunisia. Al-Ghannushi distinguishes between matters of religion, which are fixed by divine revelation, and the details of statecraft and governance, which belong to the sphere of reason, guided by Islamic principles. In sharp contrast, secular elites, a distinct minority in Muslim countries, have for many years wished to disestablish Islam from the public square in favor of making religious belief a matter of personal observance.

Is Leadership by a Caliph or Ayatollah Required in Islamic Law?

Shariah principles governing Islamic leadership focus on the functions the leader of the Muslim community is supposed to fulfill—providing justice and security, assuring care for marginalized persons, promoting the well-being of the community, and maintaining personal integrity—rather than a specific title or government system. These principles are all rooted in both Quranic values and Muhammad's example.

After Muhammad's death, one of the most pressing questions for the Muslim community involved who was to assume leadership and in what capacity. Muhammad was believed to be the last of the prophets, so no leader after him could credibly claim to receive revelation from God. This meant that no one could claim the same level of authority as a religious leader.

Leadership after Muhammad's lifetime initially followed two main tracks—the caliph model for Sunnis (the majority of Muslims) and the Imam model for Shia. For both Sunni and Shia, the development of leadership and governance relied upon a combination of the limited political prescriptions and guidance in the Quran, Muhammad's example, Arab tribal traditions, and the political systems and institutions of conquered lands, particularly the Persian and Byzantine empires. The spread of the Islamic

Empire over vast territories and the inclusion of a plurality of ethnicities, cultures, and religious groups over time led to ever-increasing complexity in governing systems and leadership. Islamic political theory was developed within this context, maintaining an idealized vision of a united and unified Muslim state and society under a single ruler who protects the state as governed by Islamic law.

Sunnis believe that the caliph, literally the successor to Muhammad, was to serve strictly as a political leader. Although the first four caliphs, known as the Rightly Guided Caliphs, issued opinions on matters of religion and law, their authority was based on their personal knowledge of and interaction with Muhammad rather than the office of the caliphate itself. Sunnis note that these caliphs were agreed upon by the consensus (ijma) of the community based on their qualifications rather than heredity. Some contemporary Sunnis therefore believe that this places democracy and the idea of a social contract between ruler and ruled solidly within the Islamic heritage.

In practice, many of the caliph's functions corresponded to the powers of rulers in other societies. The caliphate quickly transitioned from leadership by the most agreed upon member of the community to leadership by the one most able to seize and hold onto power, typically a military man. The original vision of the caliphate gave way to family-controlled dynasties and empires. By the eleventh century, the caliph had become a largely ceremonial role, while real power fell to the hands of military leaders, warlords, or provincial governors. Nevertheless, anyone wishing to wield power was expected to serve as the guardian of the faith and enforce—and abide by—Islamic law, rendering his function both political and religious. Although in theory any ruler who failed to uphold Islamic law could be disobeyed, in practice, unity of the Muslim community generally took priority, even at the cost of keeping an inept or corrupt ruler in power. Having a united community under the nominal leadership of a single individual was considered a public good that provided safety and security, even at the potential expense of justice.

That nominally unified Muslim state and society ruled by Islamic law was forcibly brought to an end with the collapse of the Abbasid Empire (750–1258) at the hands of Mongol invaders. A network of sultanates then emerged from Africa to Southeast Asia. By the sixteenth century there were three main contenders for power—the Safavid (Persian), Ottoman (in the Middle East), and Mughal (Indian subcontinent) empires—but from the eighteenth century on, the Ottoman sultan came to be regarded as the caliph of Islam by many Muslims around the world. The abolition of the caliphate in 1925 by Kemal Ataturk, along with the breakup of the Ottoman Empire in the aftermath of World War I, left Muslims without even a nominal caliph for the first time since Muhammad's death. For some, the vision of a united Muslim community under a single leader remained both an imagined past and a hoped-for future, and a number of organizations with political goals and global reach, often deemed extremist in the West, such as Hizb al-Tahrir and ISIS, have arisen with the goal of reestablishing the caliphate. Although Abu Bakr al-Baghdadi of ISIS has claimed the caliphate, the overwhelming majority of the world's Muslims reject him as unfit for the position as he has failed to fulfill the most basic Shariah objectives, including provision of security and public welfare.

Shia believe that the Imam was the rightful leader of the community, based on descent from the family of Muhammad. Although not prophets, the Imams were believed to possess the ability to interpret the Quran infallibly, thus making them legitimate legislators, as well as political and religious leaders. Shia trace the Imams through Muhammad's cousin and son-in-law, Ali (who

was married to Muhammad's daughter Fatima), and his
male descendants. Shia disagree as to the number and tra-
jectory of these descendants. However, all Shia believe
that there is no longer an Imam on earth, although some
believe that he is not dead but has entered into a mystical
existence from which he will return at some undetermined
time in the future. In theory, certain functions cannot legitimately be fulfilled in the absence of the Imam, including
authorization of jihad as military action. In practice, leadership of the Shia community has fallen to its foremost
religious and legal scholars, the highest level of which is
an ayatollah. Historically, this leadership did not include
political leadership of the community. Ayatollah Khomeini
melded political and religious leadership in Iran during
the 1979 Revolution in order to place the jurist (*faqih*) in
the Imam's place during his absence, although not all Shia
follow this model.

Do Most Muslims Want to Return to a Caliphate?

For many Muslims, the caliphate is a powerful symbol that
represents a past ideal society in which the entire Muslim
community was united under a single leader and was a
global power. The Abbasid Empire (750–1258), the Golden
Age of Islam, was a time filled with discovery in science,
medicine, mathematics, astronomy, chemistry, zoology,
cartography, and geography; strong international trade and
commerce; and architectural, artistic, and literary achieve-
ment. Baghdad's House of Wisdom (Bayt al-Hikmah) was
home to the largest collection of books in the world, including Greek, Syriac, Persian, and Indian texts, and served as
a hub of scholarship for Arabs and Europeans, Muslims,
Christians, and Jews alike. The destruction of the Abbasid
Empire at the hands of Mongol invaders marked the end of
this Golden Age, an era Muslims look to with nostalgia as

a time when their civilization was powerful, wealthy, and a symbol of refinement and culture. When Muslims talk about returning to a caliphate, it is often this image that is in mind.

Yet there is also the contending image of the "caliphate" established by ISIS, with Abu Bakr al-Baghdadi as its caliph. Al-Baghdadi clearly recognized the popular appeal of the idea of the caliphate and has tried to attract pledges of loyalty from Muslims around the world. While a small minority has responded positively, the overwhelming majority has not and has roundly rejected al-Baghdadi, his caliphate, and ISIS in general. A 2006 Gallup Poll found two-thirds of Muslims living in Egypt, Morocco, Indonesia, and Pakistan in favor of unifying all Islamic countries into a new caliphate, but this did not translate into support for ISIS. A November 2015 Pew Research Poll found that Muslim populations throughout the world have an overwhelmingly negative view of ISIS, ranging from a high of 100 percent negative in Lebanon, 94 percent in Jordan, and 84 percent in the Palestinian territories to 64 percent negative in Burkina Faso and Malaysia. No country registered more than 14 percent (Nigeria) of the population with a favorable view. What this shows is that the idea of religious unity remains alive, but the current available options are not satisfactory in terms of form or ideology.

Why Don't Muslims Practice Separation of Religion and State?

Muslims often describe Islam as "a comprehensive way of life," in which religious belief guides a Muslim's actions and interactions. The primary act of faith for the Muslim is striving to implement God's will in both private and public life. Shariah provides the guiding principles for appropriate behavior, while Islamic law was developed to enforce it. Throughout history, being a Muslim has meant not only being a member of the Muslim faith community (*ummah*), but also living in an Islamic state governed by Islamic law (in theory if not always in practice). The centrality of the law for Muslims is comparable to the centrality of the law for Jews; it differs from the Christian idea of rendering unto Caesar what is Caesar's and rendering unto God what is God's. For many Muslims, religion and state cannot legitimately be separated.

The interconnection of religion, state, and society is stressed in many places in the Quran, which teaches that the earth was given by God as a trust to humankind (Quran 2:30, 6:165); as God's representatives on earth Muslims have a divine mandate to establish God's rule by the creation of a just society. The Muslim community is necessarily a political entity. Quran 49:13, for example, teaches that God "made you into nations and tribes." Muslims, like Jews and Christians before them, have been called into a relationship with God to form a community of believers. By creating a moral social order they will stand as an example to other nations (Quran 2:143). "You are the best community evolved for mankind, enjoining what is right and forbidding what is wrong" (Quran 3:110).

The idealized vision of the Islamic state was historically that of a community ruled by Islamic law (nomocracy), and not a theocracy or autocracy governed by the clergy or the ruler. The role of the state was to provide security and order, enabling Muslims to carry out their religious duties, to do good and reject evil. Rules and judgments were to be based on classical Islamic law rather than created by new legislation. Finally, a balance of powers was distributed among three entities: the caliph as the guardian and defender of the community and the faith; the *ulama* (religious scholars) as dispensers of religious and legal advice; and the qadis (judges) as adjudicators of disputes in accordance with Islamic law. Over time, many Muslims came to believe that a perfect state based on this ideal blueprint had actually existed in the past and should be restored.

In reality, while some of the concepts of the idealized state have existed in different places at different points in time, there is no one single actual historical model upon which all Muslims agree. Rather, there are competing visions of the precise nature of the relationship between Islam, Islamic law, and the state, as evidenced by the diverse existing forms of government throughout the Muslim world. These include a variety of self-proclaimed Islamic governments, such as Saudi Arabia's Wahhabi monarchy, Iran's clergy-run state, Sudan's and Pakistan's Islamic Republics, and the Taliban's Afghanistan. Monarchies like Morocco, Jordan, and most of the Gulf States have parliaments, while Muslim countries from Senegal to Indonesia have parliamentary forms of elected government.

For some, an Islamic state means having Islam as the official state religion, a Muslim as the ruler, and no law that contradicts Shariah. Others reject any secular aspect to the state and insist on an idealized vision of a "pure" Islamic state, although whether this state is to come about gradually, as projected by the Muslim Brotherhood, or immediately, as projected by Hizb al-Tahrir and ISIS, is open to debate. Still other Muslims believe that Islam can be a broad inspiration to state and society, but that the contemporary realities of globalization, including increasing diversification of national populations, requires a more secularly based approach in which religion should not be the determining characteristic of the political or legal system. They point to the historical practice of the permissibility of living in territories not governed by Islamic law as long as Muslims are free to practice their religion there.

Thus, the critical legal determining factor is freedom of religion rather than rule by Islamic law.

How Does Islamic Law Relate to Civil Law?

In theory, Islamic law regulates every aspect of a Muslim's life. In practice, however, the authority of Islamic law has always been accompanied or limited by other legal systems. Shariah courts have usually operated alongside other nonreligious legal institutions and regulations that are typically based on the customary law of the location. From early Muslim dynasties (Umayyad and Abbasid) that ruled during the formative years of Islamic law, sultanates from Timbuktu to Indonesia, and the Safavid, Mughal, and Ottoman empires, Islamic law has existed alongside and interacted with other legal systems such as *siyasa Shariah* and other institutions. Since the rise of the industrial revolution and the colonial era, European codes of law have also served as sources of both inspiration and contention.

Generally speaking, Sunni Muslims have recommended obedience to civil authority, believing that the absence of law and order leads to chaos (*fitnah*), which is not in the interest of public welfare (maslahah) or security. Therefore, Sunni Muslims historically favored the acceptance of an imperfect civil authority or even an impious ruler over the dangers of chaos and lawlessness. The desire for stability led to theological justifications for the legitimacy of and obedience to government.

Shia Muslims, in contrast, have held that all governments, in the absence of the Imam, are usurpers. However, although they denied the legitimacy of what they regarded as unjust governments, they nevertheless justified dealing with governments and having limited participation in public affairs as a matter of necessity. Thus, while Sunnis legitimated government power, Shia gave de facto recognition to political authority but not de jure legitimation.

In general, Muslims today both in Muslim countries and in the West are expected to observe civil law in the countries in which they reside. However, just as Christians, Jews, and Muslims in the Civil Rights movement in the United States in the 1950s and 1960s felt compelled to commit acts of civil disobedience in the face of unjust governments, laws, or practices, so too in the Arab Spring 2011–2013, hundreds of thousands in the Middle East rose up in protest against oppressive authoritarian governments in Egypt, Tunisia, Libya, Syria, and elsewhere, out of the belief that their obedience to a government and its civil laws is justified by the legitimacy of the government, evidenced by their just laws and regulations.

Is Islamic Law Compatible with Pluralism and Democracy?

The absence of democracy in many Muslim countries often leads to questions about whether Arab and/or Muslim culture or the teachings of Islam by their nature are antithetical to democracy. The religious record asserts Muhammad's example in consulting (shura) with advisors, female and male, Muslim and non-Muslim alike, in order to achieve consensus (ijma). Thus proponents of pluralism and democracy argue that these principles are the foundation of the "true" nature of Islamic rule. A majority in many Muslim countries contend that Islam is fully capable of accommodating and supporting democracy while still giving a role to Shariah. They cite the principles of consultation (shura) between ruler and ruled, community consensus (ijma), public interest (maslahah), and ijtihad (the use of human reason to reinterpret Islamic principles and values) in support. These principles are seen as validating and supporting parliamentary forms of government.

Four major attitudes exist toward Islam and democratization today: (1) There are those who espouse the ideas of democracy, many of whom claim that it is compatible with Islam, including many protestors who toppled Arab dictators during the Arab Spring. The majority of those who support democracy believe that there can be a public role for Islam within democracy. (2) Some accept democratic procedures such as elections but voice religious or moral objections to aspects of Western democracy and desire some limits to ensure conformity to Shariah; among these is the prominent Sunni Shaykh Yusuf al-Qaradawi. (3) Some reject democracy as a Western construct, ranging from monarchs in the Gulf to Muslim extremist organizations such as Al Qaeda and ISIS, who claim that Islam has its own mechanisms and institutions that do not recognize democracy. (4) A minority believe that democracy can only fully be realized if Muslim societies restrict religion to private life.

These attitudes reflect the complexity of the interplay between religion, history, and politics, highlighting the importance of looking beyond simplistic assertions of religion as the source of opposition to democracy in Muslim societies today. Most modern Muslim states were carved out by European powers and are only a few decades old in contrast to the West, which had centuries to complete its transformation from monarchies and principalities to modern democratic states, a transformation often marked by revolutions and civil wars. The Muslim world further experienced several centuries of struggle against European colonial rule that resulted in the emergence of authoritarian regimes, often ruled by monarchs as well as military and ex-military men. These nondemocratic regimes have been supported by Europe and, later, America, which tolerated their authoritarian ways in exchange for their allegiance during the Cold War and Western access to oil. These rulers often use—and abuse—religion to claim legitimacy for themselves and their policies. Moreover, they use the threat of "Islamic extremism" to justify suppression of any opposition, both secular and Islamic, to their undemocratic rule.

Not surprisingly, these authoritarian Muslim rulers have been plagued with issues of identity, legitimacy, human rights, and corruption. The artificial nature of many modern states and the weak legitimacy of their rulers have produced societies in which state power relies heavily on the military and police and remains opposed to democratization, civil society, independent political parties, trade unions, a free press, and freedom of speech. Government opposition to democracy, pluralism, and human rights is thus rooted in historical and political realities rather than religion per se.

Today, polls by Gallup and PEW report that a majority of Muslims wish for greater political participation, the rule of law, government accountability, freedoms, and human rights, despite different visions of how these goals should be achieved. Just as the modern democracies of the West accommodate religious diversity, many Muslims believe that they too can develop democratic states that are responsive to indigenous values. These polls reveal the desire in the Muslim world today for greater democratization as well as Shariah. When asked what they admire about the West, the top four spontaneous responses for majorities of Muslims were (1) technology; (2) education; (3) the West's values of hard work, self-responsibility, rule of law, and cooperation; and (4) fair political systems, democracy, respect for human rights, freedom of speech, and gender equality.

In general, many Muslims see no contradiction between democratic values and religious principles. Muslims want neither a theocracy nor a secular democracy and would opt for a third model in which democratic institutions and values coexist with the religious principles and values of Shariah. Both men and women support a role for Shariah as a source of legislation, but most do not want religious leaders directly in charge of drafting legislation.

Although both Islamic and secular movements for democracy tend to be ignored, discouraged, or suppressed by the rulers of authoritarian states, nevertheless, in recent years, competitive elections have occurred in countries like Morocco, Egypt, Tunisia, Nigeria, Indonesia, Pakistan, Bangladesh, Malaysia, Turkey, and Senegal.

7

FREEDOM AND
HUMAN RIGHTS

Muslim countries and societies face major human rights challenges today, especially for those living under patriarchal societies and authoritarian rule. These include equal rights for women; freedom of religion, speech, and expression; and freedom of the press. Major polls report that majorities of Muslims strongly favor these basic freedoms.

While Shariah has many precedents for individual rights, including the right to life, property, and freedom of religion, the duties and obligations of both the ruled and the ruler are also contingent upon preserving collective rights such as security and the common good (*maslahah*). Classical Islamic law developed in patriarchal societies in which religious and governmental authorities were given broad responsibility for preserving and protecting the community.

Today, debates abound over limiting speech criticizing Islam or religious figures, about controlling freedom of speech in multireligious societies, and even over controlling criticism of and derogatory statements about governments. Controversies continue over allowing religious conversion or the building or repair of churches. Amid contentious politics in some countries, ultra-conservative voices as well as religious extremists misuse the traditional crimes of blasphemy and apostasy to condemn and silence religious minorities as well as other Muslims, intellectuals, and religious leaders with whom they disagree. In addition, extremist organizations and individuals in some Muslim countries target and attack Christians and other religious minorities as well as Muslims who are not considered sufficiently orthodox.

Muslim reformers seek ways to move beyond medieval interpretations of Islamic law to reforms that address contemporary needs. They point to more than 100 Quranic verses promoting religious freedom and emphasize drawing on these and Muhammad's example. Their tools for reform include Shariah's emphasis on protecting the People of the Book, the requirement that there be no compulsion in religion, the historic technique of *ijtihad* (interpretation), and establishing justice, one of the principal goals of Shariah (*maqasid al-Shariah*).

Does Islamic Law Protect Human Rights?

The United Nations' 1948 Universal Declaration of Human Rights (UDHR), which was signed by every Muslim country except Saudi Arabia, articulates a set of inalienable, fundamental rights to which every human being is equally and personally entitled. Members of the Commission on Human Rights, which formulated the declaration, were predominantly from Western countries; there was no Muslim representation. While most Muslim countries signed the declaration, subsequent Muslim declarations, which also demonstrate the degree of progress internationally that has been made to ensure these rights, reflect the thinking and concerns of other Muslim countries about the compatibility of some UDHR provisions with Islam.

Shariah has many precedents for individual rights, including the right to life, property, and freedom of religion. However, the duties and obligations of both the ruled and the ruler, such as security and the common good (maslahah), are subordinated to collective rights. While Islam guarantees certain individual freedoms, they are not absolute; broader social consequences must be considered. To protect the community's identity and security, Islamic law set boundaries on some individual rights—for example, curtailing freedom of speech and religion by prohibiting apostasy and blasphemy. These behaviors were understood not as private, personal matters of conscience but as public actions with public consequences for community cohesion and safety.

The Cairo Declaration on Human Rights (1948) reflected this understanding. While the declaration states that safeguarding fundamental rights and freedoms is both an individual and a collective duty, at the same time, Articles 1 and 22 set boundaries on these freedoms, namely, that they must not contradict Shariah and should not be used to denigrate or weaken religion, undermine moral or ethical values, or disintegrate, harm, or corrupt society. Criticizing government policies and exercising freedom of conscience are permitted if the goal is to engage issues constructively, not to cause chaos, which is considered a social ill. Asserting one's own individual rights cannot come at the expense of the rights of others, particularly when issues such as public security and the common good are concerned.

The Universal Declaration and the Cairo Declaration were followed in 1953 by the ratification of the European Convention on Human Rights (ECHR), which affirmed freedom of thought, conscience, and religion in Article 9. However, these freedoms were tempered or limited by restrictions deemed "in accordance with the law" and "necessary in a democratic society." Article 9 was put to the test in 2004 in the European Court of Human Rights in a case brought against Turkey by a medical student who challenged the Turkish ban on the headscarf in universities and other state and educational institutions. The Court upheld the Turkish law, citing limits to the guaranteed freedom of religion.

The Universal Islamic Declaration of Human Rights was ratified in 1981 as a counterpart to the original 1948 UDHR. In 1990, the Organization of the Islamic Conference (which represents fifty-seven Muslim countries) issued a human rights declaration that combined elements of international and Islamic law, but subjected the freedoms of the 1948 UDHR to Shariah. Some scholars have argued that the 1990 declaration was not so much about Shariah as it was about maintaining the power of autocratic governments, since it did not require freedom of religion, association, or the press. In addition, the discourse on women was shifted from equal rights to complementarity of rights and roles for women and men that retained gender-based distinctions. While conservatives argued that this was in keeping with classical Islamic law, reformists countered that denying full equality to all persons is un-Islamic. Maintaining that the interpretation of the Quran was formed by and responded to historical cultural contexts in which patriarchy was the norm, they called for reinterpretation of the Quran to respond to modern realities, and thus for recognition of the need for women's full participation in society. Major polls by the Gallup Organization, PEW, and others in recent years report that majorities of Muslims believe that women should have equal rights. They also report majorities of Muslims in favor of basic freedoms like self-determination, human rights, and freedom of speech.

Does Islamic Law Accept Slavery?

Slavery existed in pre-Islamic Arabia and the practice carried over into Muslim societies. The experiences of slaves varied according to owner, location, and time period. Some slaves had opportunities to rise to power and wealth within existing political institutions; many others lived sequestered lives of limited or no autonomy.

The Quran addresses slaves in many verses, outlining both rights and protections for them. Slaves had the right to life, bodily integrity, property ownership, and inheritance. Owners were not permitted to kill or seriously injure their slaves and were subject to punishment themselves if they did.

Islamic law discusses rights and responsibilities of both masters and slaves. In the eyes of the law, slaves were considered minors in need of a legal guardian to represent them, for example, in contracting marriage. They were also considered to be of lesser value than a free person with respect to the amount of monetary compensation assigned to them for bodily harm or murder. Nevertheless, slaves held some degree of autonomy and could be employed by other parties for paid wages, which some used to buy their freedom. Sometimes, slaves were given their freedom in reward for exceptional or lengthy service. External parties, such as the family of a previously free person who had been captured, could also purchase a slave's freedom.

Slavery existed in various forms throughout Islamic history and civilizations. Some slaves were captured in war or battle while others were purchased in slave markets or from other slave owners. Still others such as the Janissaries, who served as an elite infantry corps in the Ottoman Empire, were conscripted from conquered populations. Although the Janissaries were slaves, they were paid—and rewarded—for their work, and they sometimes even engaged in protests for better wages. Some slaves served in high positions in the ruler's court and some like the Mamluks of Egypt even established their own dynasties. Yet other slaves experienced hardships. A man had the right to sexual intercourse with his female slave, although he did not have this right with a female slave belonging to his wife. One of the most scandalous stories in early Islamic history was the capture and selling into slavery of some of Muhammad's own extended family following an uprising against the Umayyad caliph led by his grandson, Husayn. Husayn's martyrdom and the subsequent enslavement of the women and children in his band of followers became the tragic foundational identity story for Shia Muslims.

Although slavery was accepted historically as a social reality, the formal freeing of slaves (manumission) was considered an important charitable act, based on Muhammad's example. One of his most famous manumitted slaves was a black man named Bilal who became an important voice in the early Muslim community not only as an example of acceptance of people from all races and backgrounds but also due to the beauty of his voice in issuing the call to prayer. Judges could require a convicted party to free slaves as compensation. Some sins could be atoned for by freeing slaves. A slave woman who bore a child to the master was to be freed upon the master's death, as was the child, who was considered a legitimate heir to the father's estate. A slave who bore a child to the master could not be sold.

Some Islamic scholars have argued that although the Quran acknowledged slavery, this is descriptive (describing how things were) rather than prescriptive (how things ought to be) and that the Quranic intent over time was toward abolition of slavery. The formal institution of slavery was largely abolished in the Muslim world in the nineteenth and twentieth centuries, although it continues to be practiced in a few places. In recent times, ISIS has reintroduced both slaves and slave markets. Some reformers have argued that new contemporary forms of slavery exist throughout the world today in the forms of human and sex trafficking, forced migrant labor, bonded labor, child labor, and even corporate and technological slavery. They believe these issues need to be addressed as a matter of justice and preservation of life and the public interest (maslahah).

Does Islamic Law Protect Freedom of Speech?

Islamic law considers freedom of speech and expression to be an individual right, but one that is tempered by responsibility toward the broader community. A Muslim has the inherent right to express his or her individual conscience and opinion within the parameters of preserving the common good (maslahah), public security, and communal identity. Historically, in the name of preserving respect for religion and community cohesion, Islamic law set limits or restrictions on freedom of speech by prohibiting blasphemy and defamation, and criminalizing statements designed to offend religious sensibilities. At a time when religious identity was central to community cohesion, this was seen as a matter of public security, not personal conscience per se. Historically, as with all freedoms, the rights of the individual were subordinate to the needs of the community. The responsibility for assuring those rights—and enforcing their limits—was a matter of law, not vigilantism.

Today, issues related to freedom of speech tend to be framed within the parameters established by Article 22(a) of the 1948 Cairo Declaration on Human Rights in Islam, which states that freedom of speech is allowed, provided that such expression is not contrary to Shariah principles. Article 22(c) clarifies that freedom of speech "may not be exploited or misused in such a way as may violate sanctities and the dignity of Prophets, undermine moral and ethical values or disintegrate, corrupt or harm society or weaken its faith."

In recent years freedom of speech and expression issues arose in the West in the context of the portrayal of the Prophet Muhammad in the Danish cartoon crisis of 2005 and the French satirical magazine *Charlie Hebdo* in 2011 and 2015. The depiction of Muhammad wearing a turban shaped like a bomb with a burning fuse in the Danish cartoons was widely denounced by Muslims as unacceptably intolerant and provocative, reflecting prejudice and discrimination against Islam and Muslims. Not only did many Muslims see these portrayals to be personally offensive, but they also questioned whether they represented a form of hate speech that would have been unacceptable if targeting other religious groups. While some protests in Europe, the Middle East, and Asia turned violent, many Muslims chose to engage in nonviolent protest and action, boycotting Danish goods and working to educate the public about why the cartoons were so offensive to Muslims.

In 2006, *Charlie Hebdo* reprinted the controversial Danish cartoons, a decision criticized by French President Jacques Chirac as "overt provocation." In 2011, the magazine's offices were destroyed by a bomb after it published another caricature. In January 2015, two Muslim gunmen claiming affiliation with Al Qaeda in Yemen forced their way into *Charlie Hebdo*'s Paris headquarters and killed twelve people, including four staff cartoonists and a Muslim police officer who tried to stop them. Several related attacks followed in which five more individuals were killed.

Reactions in France and globally reflected outrage at the attacks, which occurred during a wave of ISIS terrorist attacks in Europe, and an affirmation of freedom of speech and of the press. Millions of French citizens, including French Muslims, marched across France, and world leaders gathered in Paris to march in solidarity with the victims. Major Muslim organizations around the world condemned the attacks.

In many Muslim countries today the main debates about freedom of speech involve two central issues: (1) whether and to what degree freedom of speech should be limited with respect to derogatory (blasphemous) statements about religion and religious figures, and (2) whether universal freedoms of speech and expression should limit the powers of Muslim governments. Reformists particularly question the degree to which authoritarian regimes can apply traditional religious laws or practices to limit freedom of speech and religion in contemporary multireligious Muslim societies.

Does Islamic Law Protect Freedom of Religion?

Islamic law contains both protections for and limitations on religious freedom. There are more than 100 Quranic verses that not only affirm freedom of religion and conscience but also honor other prophetic messengers; Quran 28:46 states "We have always sent messengers to people." The Quran recognizes all the biblical prophets and the truth of God's other revelations to Moses and Jesus (the Torah, the Psalms, and the Gospels) such as Quran 4:163–164. Quran 5:44–47 states that judgment within each religion is to be made according to its revelation and that people should fear God, not the judgment of other people. While the Quran identifies as the People of the Book Jews, Christians, and Sabaeans (Quran 5:70), the definition of protected religious minorities was expanded over time to include other religious groups, including Magis, Samaritans, Zoroastrians, Hindus, and Buddhists. Quran 2:256 commands, "There is to be no compulsion in religion," making it clear that religious affiliation is intended to be a personal choice rather than something enforced by a state. Thus, many Muslim reformers believe that no one should be forcibly converted to Islam—or prevented from leaving Islam. While the

Quran contains warnings against unbelief and threatens punishment for it in the Afterlife, there is disagreement as to whether unbelief is to be punished during this lifetime or simply left to God.

Examples from the early Muslim community support the potential for people of different religious faiths to come together as a single community that respects freedom of religion yet upholds public safety and the common good (maslahah). One of the most important examples is the Constitution or Pact of Medina, a collective security arrangement between Muhammad and both Muslims and non-Muslims, including Jews and polytheists, that permitted each religious group to continue to practice their own religion, yet work together for public safety and well-being (maslahah). Additional support can be found in the conquests of the early Muslim community in which People of the Book (Jews and Christians initially, but later extended to other religious communities) were permitted to continue to practice their religion. In place of serving in the military, members of these communities paid a special tax, called the *jizya*. In some cases, otherwise persecuted religious minorities, both Christians and Jews, fared better under Muslim rule than they did under Christian rule. Many Muslim reformers today point to these examples of Muslim-led multireligious states as a model for a contemporary Islamic state to embrace religious pluralism.

At the same time, Islamic history and law also contain examples of limits and restrictions on religious freedom. While some Muslim rulers permitted the construction and repair of churches and synagogues, others were less tolerant. The Covenant of Umar was used in some places, particularly during the Middle Ages, to assign distinctive manners of dress and behavior to minority religious groups, as well as to forbid construction of churches and synagogues. Despite its later inclusion in the theory of Islamic jurisprudence, this covenant was in fact often disregarded, and scholars have challenged its historical authenticity, maintaining that it could not possibly have originated during the rule of the Caliph Umar, as claimed.

Today, while churches exist in many Muslim countries, in some countries the building and repair of churches are controlled or limited by governments. In Saudi Arabia, churches and clergy are banned and Christians have limited freedom to gather for common prayer or sacraments.

Historically, apostasy was sometimes punishable by death in Judaism, Christianity, and Islam. While it is no longer the case in Judaism and Christianity, in many countries in the Middle East–North Africa, apostasy remains a crime and in some it is a capital offense punishable by death. Many conservative Muslim religious leaders today believe that the legal repercussions of apostasy should be retained, even where it is a religious issue only. Some believe that religious minorities should not be permitted to express their own beliefs when they conflict with Islam. In some places, such as Egypt, Pakistan, and Nigeria, Christians have also at times suffered persecution and violent attacks by religious extremists. Muslim reformers today maintain that apostasy in the past was seen as the equivalent of the serious political act of treason, which explains why it was harshly punished. Some major religious leaders, including two former grand muftis of Egypt, Sheikh Ali Gomaa and Shaykh Muhammad Sayyid Tantawi, argue that people are free to either embrace or reject faith and that this choice is up to the individual with only God serving as judge in the Afterlife. Charges of treason are only applicable to those who attack Islam, not those who simply change their faith or believe in a faith other than Islam.

Contemporary reformers, emphasizing the importance of religious freedom and religious pluralism, have returned to the Quran as the single, authoritative source that all

Muslims agree is the starting point for conversation. They point to verses such as Quran 49:13, which states that God deliberately made human beings into different nations and tribes so that we might come to know one another. Similarly, Quran 30:22 asserts diversity as a deliberate choice of God's creation, while Quran 2:148 affirms that scripture comes from God and that each community has its own direction. Thus, all communities should "race to do good deeds" so that God can bring them together. Quran 5:48 declares that God has assigned a law and a path to each religion in order to test its followers. Therefore, all are to do good, knowing that they will return to God and that God will clarify matters for everyone. The same chapter (Quran 5:69) confirms that those members of each faith tradition who follow its teachings will go to Paradise in the Afterlife. In light of all of these verses, reformist scholars argue that religious pluralism is a Quranic mandate. Since God is to be the judge of right and wrong, people should not invest time in fighting about differences in belief, but rather they should compete with each other in doing good works. In addition, contemporary reformers call upon people to learn to handle their differences through dialogue and working together, so that diversity and unity can exist simultaneously within a single nation.

What Are Blasphemy Laws and How Are They Enforced?

Blasphemy refers to words or actions that insult or vilify God, Muhammad, and/or other persons, such as Muhammad's wives or Companions or other prophets. The hadith (traditions of Muhammad) forbid blasphemy, as did the majority of classical jurists who considered it a capital offense. Judges nevertheless had considerable discretion in determining when and how it was to be punished. Historically, capital punishment for blasphemy was rare.

Today, many Muslim countries, secular as well as Islamic, because of the potential for social unrest, have laws making blasphemy a criminal offense. Though rarely enforced in many countries, blasphemy laws exist in Egypt, Sudan, Nigeria, Saudi Arabia, Iran, Pakistan, Afghanistan, Bangladesh, Malaysia, and Indonesia. In recent years, a number of Muslim-majority countries, as well as the fifty-seven-member Organization of Islamic Cooperation (OIC, formerly the Organization of the Islamic Conference), have argued that blasphemy was a form of hate speech and that its prohibition should be recognized as a binding international human rights norm supported by the United Nations. Several nonbinding resolutions condemning "defamation of religion" were voted on and accepted by the UN.

In 2011, the UN Human Rights Council and OIC found a compromise. The "defamation of religions" resolution was replaced by a resolution, supported by OIC member countries, the United States, and European countries, that called upon all countries to take concrete steps to protect religious freedom, prohibit discrimination and hate crimes, and counter offensive expression through dialogue, education, and public debate rather than the criminalization of speech.

Blasphemy laws have sometimes been abused by individuals and vigilante groups to accuse and target intellectuals, religious leaders, and politicians whose opinions are disputed, as well as to injure or kill victims and desecrate or destroy churches and occasionally mosques. For example, on August 1, 2009, after several days of rioting and violence in Pakistan over allegations that Christians had desecrated the Quran, an estimated crowd of 1,000 people stormed a Christian neighborhood, killed nine people, and burned and looted dozens of houses. Upon investigation, the Human Rights Commission of Pakistan reported that the riots had been planned and were even announced in some mosques the day before at the Friday congregational prayer. The Pakistani government and National Assembly quickly condemned these actions as contrary to Pakistan's constitutional tradition and reiterated the nation's commitment to ensuring protection of religious minorities as equal citizens. Many Christians and Muslims called for repealing Pakistan's blasphemy laws in the aftermath of this incident, but the laws remain on the books, despite a 2014 poll showing that 68 percent of Pakistanis support repealing them.

How Does Islamic Law View Proselytizing?

Islamic law and the legal systems in Muslim countries have had diverse attitudes toward proselytizing. Throughout history, Muslim-majority countries and empires, such as the Ottoman and Mughal empires, permitted other religions to maintain their own practices, leaders, and even laws. This was in keeping with Quran verses recognizing freedom of religion, freedom of conscience, and the potential for members of other faith traditions to go to Paradise in the Afterlife. At the same time, public preaching and attempted conversions of Muslims to other faith traditions have not always been allowed, due to conservative and fundamentalist opposition and political concerns about security and social stability. Thus, while allowing individual adherents to maintain their faith traditions and practices, albeit often with preference for their keeping a low public profile, many countries took a more cautious approach toward missionaries. When European colonial powers sent missionaries to the Ottoman Empire in the nineteenth century, Muslim religious authorities generally tolerated their work in education and social services provided that they did not evangelize Muslims. Although missionaries only began aggressively trying to convert Muslims in the 1880s, their proselytizing efforts left a legacy of suspicion in some places that has remained until today.

The rejection of non-Muslims who proselytize is for the most part based less on Islamic law than on memories and resentment of past European colonial experience and, more recently, suspicion of American fundamentalist and evangelical missionaries. In many places that experienced colonialism, Christian evangelism served as a vehicle for Western imperialism and a threat to Muslim identity and culture. In some countries where Islam is the state religion, the status of proselytization in civil law can be unrelated to traditional Islamic jurisprudence. For example, in Algeria, individuals have the right to convert out of Islam: apostasy and conversion are not crimes. However, preaching religions other than Islam carries a fine or a prison sentence because it threatens social stability. Even in secular countries, government and public sensitivities about proselytizing remain. For example, following the American-led invasion of Iraq in 2003 and natural disasters including earthquakes and the tsunami that struck off the coast of Indonesia in 2004, some humanitarian institutions, including hospitals, medical and dental centers, schools, and women's centers, were established with funding from evangelical Christian organizations as well as the US government. This led to fears and rumors that receiving humanitarian aid would be contingent upon being subjected to proselytizing.

Public concerns about proselytizing today include not only non-Muslim missionary activity but also extremist Muslim organizations preaching militant theologies of violence and hatred, as well as Muslim groups, Sunni, Shia, and Sufi alike, not considered to be sufficiently orthodox. Since the September 11, 2001, terrorist attacks in the United States, some countries, including Saudi Arabia, have formally banned the preaching of extremist ideology and asserted stronger government control over mosques.

What Were the Status, Rights, and Responsibilities of Non-Muslims (Dhimmi) in Muslim States in the Past?

While the Quran repeatedly assures that non-Muslims are free to practice their faith as long as they do not interfere with the right of others to do the same, the status, rights, and responsibilities of non-Muslims (*dhimmi*) in Muslim societies and in Islamic law have varied throughout history.

The earliest example of non-Muslims living in a Muslim state dates to the lifetime of Muhammad. His migration (*hijra*) to Medina in 622 CE to serve as head of a multireligious state resulted in the Constitution or Pact of Medina, a collective security arrangement that brought Muslims and non-Muslims into a cooperative, protective relationship with each other. Religious freedom and internal autonomy were given in exchange for political loyalty. The guiding Shariah principle of this arrangement, underscored by Quran 3:28, 29:46, and 60:8–9, is that believers should treat unbelievers decently and equitably as long as the unbelievers do not behave aggressively. This principle was later followed by the second Caliph Umar who, after conquering Jerusalem, guaranteed personal and property rights and safety for the Christian inhabitants and permitted Jews to return to worship and live. Judaism's Golden Age occurred under Muslim rule in al-Andalus (modern-day Spain). Although attention is also often given to the contentious historical Covenant or Pact of Umar, which is the source of what many today point to as discriminatory laws against Jews and Christians, such as having to dress differently from Muslims, many scholars argue that the intent of the pact was to establish legal parameters allowing for peaceful coexistence to occur.

While the Quran provided certain guidelines for interaction with non-Muslims, their actual situation was conditioned by the political, economic, and social circumstances prevailing in various Islamic territories and by their relations with the major non-Muslim powers of the day. As a matter of state policy, Muslim territories often associated non-Muslim communities enjoying protection from an external entity with that entity, sometimes offering greater benefits and protections if the relationship was good and sometimes viewing them with greater suspicion if the relationship was hostile.

Under Islamic empires, non-Muslims were typically guaranteed the rights to life, security, property, and freedom of movement and religious practice, and they were exempted from military service in exchange for payment of a head tax (jizya), based on Quran 9:29. Persons within this arrangement were known as dhimmi, literally, protected. The connection to exemption from military service was made clear by the fact that only free, sane, adult males paid the jizya; women, children, slaves, the elderly, the handicapped, and non-Muslim religious leaders, such as monks—all of whom were exempt from military service—were exempted from the tax. The tax was sometimes described as a sign that the Islamic state and its authority were accepted, although it was also sometimes described as a sign of humiliation. In the event that the state failed to protect its non-Muslim subjects, the state was required to pay back the jizya.

During the modernization period in the Ottoman Empire, known as the Tanzimat (1839–1876 CE), non-Muslims received legal equality with Muslims and the jizya tax was replaced by either conscription into the military or payment of an exemption tax. For example, under the Ottoman millet system, leaders of the Greek Orthodox and Armenian Christians, as well as Jews, had oversight over both their communities and their own religious, legal, educational, social, and charitable institutions.

Other Muslim countries maintained the legal concept of dhimmis which, by twenty-first-century standards, translates into second-class citizenship and a limited form of pluralism and tolerance.

What Are the Status, Rights, and Responsibilities of Non-Muslims in Muslim States Today?

The status and rights of non-Muslims and their persecution in Muslim states today have become major human rights issues. Many, although not all, Muslim countries constitutionally guarantee non-Muslims citizenship and religious freedom, although the degree of freedom varies from country to country. Moreover, militant religious extremists and terrorist groups like Al Qaeda, ISIS, and Boko Haram have attacked, murdered, and terrorized non-Muslims (Christians, Jews, Bahai, Yazidis, and Ahmadis) and often Muslims who do not cooperate in Egypt, Sudan, Iraq, Syria, Nigeria, Pakistan, and elsewhere. Villages, churches, and mosques have been destroyed in some countries,

Human rights abuses raise concerns about the freedoms, political rights, civil liberties, and security of non-Muslims living in many Muslim states and whether Muslim governments and religious leaders are doing enough to address them. At the same time, many Muslims today recognize that contemporary global realities, including immigration and the increasingly globalized economy and workplace, necessitate learning to live with the religious "Other." Just as Muslims living in non-Muslim countries are often concerned with their rights and civil liberties as minorities, so some consider the rights and status of non-Muslim minorities living in Muslim countries to be a parallel issue.

Contemporary Muslim reformers argue that adoption of pluralism at both the individual and state levels would open the door to healthier civic discourse and relations as well as for the possibility of genuine dialogue and dissent, not only between religions, but also within them, while precluding the possibility of violence.

Reformist Muslims further call for full citizenship for non-Muslims on the basis of the Quran's assertion of the equality of all humanity, God's deliberate creation of diversity as an opportunity for people to come together to know each other (Quran 49:13), and God's intentional revelation of different religious traditions (Quran 5:48 and 2:148). In their eyes, dhimmi status should focus on establishing a formal relationship, rather than assigning dhimmis secondary status. Rather than engaging in conflict with each other, the projected goal is for all people to live and work together for the common good (maslahah), justice, and peace. Two of the most important tools for doing this are the goals (maqasid) of Shariah, which include establishing justice, cooperation, and mutual support in society, and ijtihad, or reinterpretation, which allows for moving beyond classical or medieval interpretations of Islamic law in favor of readings that are more appropriate for contemporary circumstances. Nevertheless, even reformers in some countries uphold the ideal of Islam as the state religion and Shariah as either "a" or "the" source of legislation, with the result that only a Muslim could serve as head of state or in high positions in the military and judiciary. That does not preclude non-Muslims from holding other offices. Jordan and Iran guarantee a certain number of seats in parliament to non-Muslims.

Concerns about human rights violations against and persecution of religious minorities throughout the Muslim world led to a major conference in Morocco in 2016, attended by more than 250 Muslim religious leaders, heads of state, and scholars from around the world. The conference concluded with the Marrakesh Declaration, calling for Muslim leaders to be accountable for their treatment of minorities and for them to engage the principles of justice and ethics outlined in the Constitution of Medina. The declaration was well received, although how and when it is to be implemented and enforced is yet to be determined.

What Are the Status, Rights, and Responsibilities of Muslims in Non-Muslim States Today?

While much of the Islamic legal tradition called upon Muslims to live in an Islamic state whenever possible, the situation has changed dramatically in the late twentieth century because of the desire for greater educational and employment opportunities and the need to escape political repression or failed economies. These factors plus the higher birth rates of Muslims have resulted in Islam becoming the second or third largest religion in the United States and many European countries, although they remain small minorities of the overall population, accounting for less than 8 percent of the population throughout Europe and about 1 percent in the United States.

In the first decades of the twenty-first century, globalization as well as mass migration of refugees from the political violence, atrocities, and destruction perpetrated by militant groups like Al Qaeda and especially ISIS have seen increasing numbers of Muslims emigrating from their homelands to the West. At the same time, in recent years the rise of far-right political parties and movements has resulted in an exponential growth of xenophobia and Islamophobia (anti-Islam and anti-Muslim bias, discrimination, hate speech, and hate crimes) in the West, in places ranging from the United States and Canada to Europe and Australia. Far-right politicians, pundits, media, and religious leaders and organizations warn of a demographic and domestic terrorist threat and question the loyalty of all Muslims. They condemn the religion of Islam as inherently evil or dangerous, the source of a clash of civilizations, and accuse Muslims of attempting to implement Shariah and undermine Western legal systems.

Muslim scholars and reformers note that the central issue for Muslims lies in whether they live as good Muslims wherever they are, not whether they live in an Islamic state. Mainstream Muslims in the West focus on the common shared aspirations and values of Muslims and non-Muslims and the equality of all citizens alike amid a diversity of ethnic and religious groups. Muslim reformers cite Shariah principles of the common good (maslahah), social justice, and protection of life and property that enable Muslims to participate in the community in which they live, regardless of its religious or secular nature, as loyal and contributing citizens politically, economically, and socially.

Many cite Shariah principles and values that require a good Muslim to be religiously observant, working to build strong communities, supporting the less fortunate, engaging in fair and ethical business practices, and setting a positive example through one's own character and dedication to the faith. Engaging in criminal activity, violence, or extremist behavior are reprehensible actions that create a bad name not only for individuals but also for the religion and the religious community as a whole.

Many Muslim religious and civic leaders and organizations have called upon Muslims to play a leading role in establishing a constructive approach to inter-religious cooperation and bridge-building based on common values and purpose as well as education.

8

WAR, PEACE, AND THE COMMON GOOD

In the twentieth and twenty-first centuries, visions of Islamic societies and claims to Islamic authenticity and legitimacy have expanded in many directions. At times, these calls for construction of societies are based on Islam and Shariah; at others, they call for defending the Muslim community from aggression, whether political or cultural. Since the late twentieth century, Islam has been a significant factor in the politics of mainstream and extremist rulers, activists, and both nonviolent and terrorist movements. In many cases, reference is made to jihad, sometimes in the form of nonviolent civil resistance and sometimes as violence.

Understanding jihad's power to inspire, past and present, as well as how it has been used and abused continues to be an important issue. Are there criteria in Islam and Islamic law that define a just war, limit the use of force, demand proportionality in violence, and require the safety and security of noncombatants? Do jihad and Islamic legal guidelines support the actions of terrorist movements like Al Qaeda and ISIS, or speak to the permissibility of suicide bombings? Can Islamic law influence peaceful relations with the non-Muslim world?

Does Islamic Law Permit Peaceful Relations with Non-Muslims?

Islamic law covers the spectrum of possible relationships between Muslims and non-Muslim communities, ranging from peace to war, based on the context and circumstances. Islam began as a minority religion surrounded by other religious communities, including polytheists, Jews, and Christians. The revelation of Islam did not come with prescriptions for violence or warfare between Muslims and non-Muslims. In fact, for the first twelve years of Muhammad's ministry in Mecca (610–622 CE), violence was strictly prohibited by more than seventy Quran verses.

Although peace was expected—and desired—to be the normal state of affairs, the reality was that war sometimes entered the picture. Violence in the form of self-defense and defense of the community became permitted and even recommended after the migration to Medina in 622 CE, when Muhammad became head of a multireligious state that was capable of defending itself. That defense was outlined in the Constitution or Pact of Medina, a collective security arrangement that included non-Muslim tribes, specifically polytheists and Jews. According to this arrangement, an attack on any member of the pact was considered an attack on all of them. All tribes were then obligated to rise in collective defense of the attacked party. Other methods of building alliances and relationships included establishing parameters for commerce and trade agreements, intermarriage between tribes, and formal treaties, such as the Treaty of al-Hudaybiyya, which brought an end to armed conflict with both sides receiving benefits and making concessions.

There are many verses in the Quran, from both the Meccan and Medinan periods, that call for peaceful and cooperative relations with People of the Book (those with a revealed scripture), specifically mentioning Christians and

Jews. Many of these verses place Islam within a long line of prophets beginning with Adam and continuing through biblical figures including Abraham, Moses, Joseph, and David up through John the Baptist and Jesus. The Quran also explicitly confirms the truth of the Torah, Psalms, and Gospels as revelations from God (Quran 3:3–4, 5:45–47), calls upon Muslims to respect the People of the Book as those sharing a common faith in God (Quran 3:64, 29:46), and assures that Jews and Christians who follow the teachings of their faith will go to Heaven (Quran 5:69). Quran 5:48 addresses Muslims, Christians, and Jews alike: "We have assigned a law and a path to each of you. If God had so willed, He would have made you one community, but He wanted to test you through that which He has given you, so race to do good: you will all return to God and He will make clear to you the matters you differed about." Similarly, Quran 49:13 declares, "People, We created you all from a single man and a single woman, and made you into races and tribes so that you should come to know one another. In God's eyes, the most honored of you are the ones most mindful of Him: God is all knowing, all aware." The fact that these messages and guidance were repeated in both Mecca and Medina means that peaceful coexistence, cooperation, and religious pluralism are the overall guiding principles (Shariah) that span the full history of Muhammad's ministry.

Islamic law recognized three broad categories of relationships, often referred to as "Abodes" or "Houses"—Dar al-Islam (the abode of Islam), Dar al-Harb (the abode of war), and Dar al-Sulh (the abode of the treaty). The abode of Islam was those territories controlled by a Muslim ruler and presumed to abide by Islamic law. The abode of war applied to other parties with whom Muslims were in conflict. The abode of the treaty referred to entities with which Muslims held alliances or treaty relationships governing interactions between them. Within those territories covered by the treaty, the rights of all subjects were protected, including the lives and property of non-Muslims and their clients living or traveling there. Treaty partners were required to do the same for Muslims and their clients. The territories classified as the abode of war were those that refused to provide such protection to Muslims and their clients.

Treaties or alliances were typically undertaken for ten years at a time but were renewable. This suggested that relationships are subject to renegotiation based upon changing circumstances, but that regulated and mutually agreeable relationships are the best means for assuring peace and cooperation between nations. The abode of the treaty established the historical precedent for contemporary international alliances and treaties to which Muslim nations are signatories along with non-Muslim nations.

Does Islamic Law Have a Theory of Just War?

Once permission was given to Muslims to engage in defensive violence, questions quickly emerged as to what constituted proper behavior in war. Muslim jurists invested great effort in consulting the Quran and Sunna (Muhammad's example), detailing guidelines and legal regulations regarding the authority to declare war; the conduct of war, including notice to the enemy before launching an attack and offering the alternative of paying a yearly tribute; determining who is to fight and who is exempted; how fighting should be conducted; when and how hostilities must cease; and how prisoners should be treated.

Most important, as in modern just war theories, strong emphasis is given to controls reflected in Quran verses such as Quran 2:190, which makes it clear that Muslims should not initiate violence but are expected to respond to violence inflicted upon them. The concept of sanctuary is to be respected unless the enemy has refused to acknowledge sanctuary for Muslims, in which case fighting back is permitted (Quran 2:191). The enemy's wish to end fighting must be respected. "If they cease hostilities, there can be no [further] hostility, except towards aggressors" (Quran 2:193). Warfare and the response to violence and aggression must be proportional: "Whoever transgresses against you, respond in kind" (Quran 2:194). Forbidden acts include treachery, torture, and mutilation. Finally, violence should not be sought for the sake of personal gain (Quran 4:94).

From the earliest times, Islamic law forbade killing noncombatants as well as women and children; farmers; slaves; the handicapped, elderly, and chronically ill; and monks and rabbis, who were given the promise of immunity unless they took part in the fighting. The legal reasoning behind these various prohibitions lay in questions of legal agency and capacity. Women and children were understood to fall under legal guardianship of the male head of household and thus could not be held responsible for his actions, in addition to being considered legal minors with respect to agency. Slaves by the nature of the condition of slavery could not exercise agency of choice. The handicapped, elderly, and chronically ill were assumed to be unable to care for themselves, so they were not capable of being soldiers. Farmers were crucial to ongoing life after the conflict because of their role in raising food. Monks and rabbis were understood to fulfill a vital community function of religious, albeit non-Muslim, leadership. These restrictions thus reflected not only exemption of those lacking the potential for engaging in armed combat but also forward thinking about life after the conflict—a significant point as it assumes that the conflict will end.

The Shariah principles of minimizing harm to human life and property are reflected in prohibitions against burning crops and beehives, uprooting trees and plants, killing animals not used for battle purposes, and poisoning water supplies. Loss of life or damage to property behind enemy lines was only permissible if it was essential for the enemy's defeat and if victory over the enemy was proximate. However, like the fighting itself, such damage and loss of life had to be proportionate to the battle being fought. Finally, after the enemy had surrendered, major assaults and use of force were not permitted and all warring acts were to cease immediately. Those who were not to be taken as prisoners include the elderly, handicapped, chronically ill, monks, and rabbis. Women and children could be held captive, but jurists universally agreed they should not be harmed.

Many Quran verses underscore that peace, not violence and warfare, is the norm. Permission to fight the enemy if they attack is balanced by a strong mandate for making peace: "If your enemy inclines toward peace, then you too should seek peace and put your trust in God" (Quran 8:61) and "Had God wished, He would have made them dominate you, and so if they leave you alone and do not fight you and offer you peace, then God allows you no way against them" (Quran 4:90).

What Does Jihad Mean?

Although the term "jihad" has been used and abused throughout history to justify and legitimate both holy and unholy wars, ranging from political resistance and liberation struggles to extremism and terrorism, there is no one single definition of jihad. The term carries a multiplicity of meanings—religious, legal, and political—depending on historical contexts and developments. Jihad is a central concept in Muslim belief and Islamic law, but it is not one of the Five Pillars, although some legal and religious scholars refer to it as the unofficial Sixth Pillar of Islam.

Jihad literally means struggle, striving, or exertion. It is often connected to the phrase "in the path of God" and the word for patience or steadfastness (*sabr*). It does not mean killing (*qital*) or war (*harb*). In fact, there is no word or phrase in the Quran that means "holy war." Fighting and killing are never described in the Quran as being "in the path of God."

Historically, there have been two broad meanings of jihad, referred to as the greater or inner jihad, and the lesser or outer jihad. This distinction was based on traditions from Muhammad that made it clear that war was the lesser of the Muslim's obligations and that not every person was obligated to fight in the physical defense of the Muslim community. In one famous tradition, a young man came to Muhammad asking to join in the fighting. Muhammad informed him that his jihad was to return home to care for his parents who were dependent upon him. In another tradition, Muhammad, hearing Muslims returning from the battlefront congratulating themselves on having fulfilled their jihad in defense of the community, informed them that they were returning from the lesser jihad; they were now to undertake the greater jihad of working toward self-improvement.

The greater or inner jihad is defined as striving to live a righteous life, follow the teachings of Islam, and avoid greed, selfishness, egotism, and evil. The lesser or outer jihad involves defending Islam and the Muslim community. Such defense may take military form, but it does not have to. Other methods of defense include jihad of the hand (working to address oppression and injustice by seeking to change circumstances), jihad of the tongue (speaking out against oppression or injustice), jihad of the pen (writing), and jihad of the heart (combating evil inclinations within oneself). Many Muslims today embrace these latter definitions as a call to civic activism—"civilian jihad."

The earliest verses of the Quran using the term jihad refer to pious actions, such as striving to lead a moral life and to improve one's community, as well as focusing on charitable acts and prayer. For the first twelve years of revelation (610–622 CE), violence and fighting in any capacity was prohibited for Muslims, even in the case of self-defense. There are more than 70 Quran verses insisting upon non-violence during this time.

Permission to fight in defense of the community was given only after the emigration (*hijra*) to Medina when Muhammad took over as head of state. Fighting became permissible for the Muslims who had been driven from their homes for the sake of their faith. Quran 22:39–40 states: "Leave is given to those who fight because they were wronged—surely God is able to help them—who were expelled from their homes wrongfully for saying, 'Our Lord is God.'" Even then, these verses limited fighting to situations where the community was either under attack or under the imminent threat of attack. The defensive nature of jihad following attack is also clearly emphasized in Quran 2:190, "And fight in the way of God with those who fight you, but aggress not: God loves not the aggressors." Moreover, such fighting is not unlimited; the passage continues with the command that if the enemy stops fighting, Muslims must also stop fighting (Quran 2:192). Additional guidelines for defensive fighting were given at other critical points throughout the years.

Like other religious scriptures, the Quran was revealed in a specific social and political context. Understanding that context is critical to its interpretation. The world of the Quran, like much of the ancient world, was filled with tribal raiding, warfare, conquest, and booty. Fighting and warfare were the primary ways to guarantee security and freedom, future prosperity, and territorial expansion. Muhammad and his followers lived in a violent setting where war (harb) was often the regular state of affairs until a peace treaty was established with other tribes. The broader Near East that surrounded Arabia was itself divided between two warring superpowers, the Byzantine (Eastern Roman) and the Sasanian (Persian) empires.

Many Quran passages regarding fighting were revealed in response to these political realities and the need to survive and thrive in defensive as well as offensive conflicts. Because the enemies that the early Muslims feared were non-Muslims, Quranic injunctions often speak of conflicts and fighting between Muslims and non-Muslims. The original juristic treatises on jihad reflect these early conflicts between Muslims and non-Muslims, often in an "us versus them" or Abode of Islam versus Abode of War mentality.

Today much discussion centers on what are sometimes called the Quran's "sword verses" that call for killing unbelievers, such as, "When the sacred months have passed, slay the idolaters wherever you find them, and take them, and confine them, and lie in wait for them at every place of ambush" (Quran 9:5). During the period of expansion and conquest, many of the *ulama* (religious scholars and jurists), who enjoyed royal patronage, interpreted the Quran and *hadith* (traditions of Muhammad) in order to create Islamic rationales and laws legitimating the offensive warfare of powerful caliphs determined to expand their empires. These scholars claimed that the "sword verses" abrogated or overrode earlier Quran verses that limited jihad to defensive war. In fact the full meaning and intent of Quran 9:5 (cited above) is missed or distorted when quoted only in part. The rest of the verse qualifies this command: "But if they repent and perform the prayer and give alms, then let them go their way, for God is forgiving and kind" (Quran 9:5). The context in which the verse was revealed was ongoing tribal warfare with the Meccans, many of whom were kinsmen to the Muslims, making resolution of the conflict urgent. The fighting in this case was designed to bring an end to that conflict and restore a state of peace. The same is true of another often quoted verse: "Fight those who believe not in God nor the Last Day, nor hold that forbidden which hath been forbidden by God and His Messenger, nor hold the religion of truth [even if they are] of the People of the Book," which is often cited without the line that follows, "Until they pay the tax and agree to submit" (Quran 9:29).

Over the centuries, debate continued over such Quran verses, influencing the competing meanings of "struggling" to enjoin what is right and forbid what is wrong. Gradually the many positive injunctions emphasizing truces and peaceful coexistence, forgiveness, and patience during suffering, were weakened and the military aspect of jihad became strongly privileged, particularly in times of threats to the Muslim community, such as the Mongol invasions or the Crusades. Influential religious and legal scholars reinforced a system of politics and principles based on their pragmatic self-interest and gain (rulers were often patrons of religious scholars) rather than the more challenging original Quranic moral and ideological admonitions and noble pursuits. By the ninth century, political leaders and many jurists viewed jihad primarily as armed combat. This understanding is often revived during periods of threat, such as the European colonial era, when Sufi leaders used the framework of jihad in their resistance movements, and again during the independence movements of the twentieth century. In the modern period, jihad's meaning and power have been reflected in a multiplicity of ways. The mainstream majority see it as a cornerstone of their spiritual life, the "struggle" to be religiously observant Muslims in their personal lives and societies. For religious extremists it has become a clarion call, a source of recruitment and justification to others to join their militant jihads.

Does Islamic Law Mandate that All
Muslims Join in Military Jihad?

Jihad is rooted in the Quran's command to struggle (the literal meaning of the word jihad) in the path of God and in the example of Muhammad and his early Companions. In its most general meaning, jihad obliges all Muslims to follow and realize God's will: leading a virtuous life and extending the call to Islam through preaching, education, example, and writing. Throughout history, the call to jihad as military activity has rallied Muslims in both defensive and offensive wars. Jihad includes the right, and obligation, of the faithful to defend Islam and the community from aggression. Muslim rulers, with support from jurists, appealed to jihad to legitimate their wars and extend their empires and states through conquest.

The legal literature distinguishes between two types of jihad as military activity—those that are considered an individual duty and those that are considered a collective duty. Collective duty is the more historically prevalent variety and allows for recognition that different people fulfill different functions within the community. Because the jihad is a collective duty, only some of those eligible to fight in it actually do so. Others may be exempted for a variety of reasons, including their community and family duties. In cases of jihad as collective duty, young men need the permission of their parents to join the cause.

A situation must be truly dire in order to require every person to engage in jihad as an individual duty. Examples include direct military invasions of one's town and the fighting coming directly to your home. Because there is no time to plan for departure or make alternative arrangements, in this case jihad as an individual duty is a response to an immediate emergency, a life or death situation.

For Sunnis, jihad as a collective military obligation can only be declared by a legitimate ruler in consultation with religious scholars. Shia believe that only the Imam (who they believe will return from occultation to bring absolute justice to the world) can legitimately declare a jihad. However, in the interim, struggles to defend Islam are permissible before his return.

The ruler is responsible for leading the call for a jihad as well as providing equipment and determining war tactics and peace treaty provisions. Once issued, the call to participate in the jihad is incumbent on all who qualify. Legally qualified participants must be Muslim, free, adult, male, and physically and mentally sound. This meant that non-Muslims, women, minors, slaves, and those who suffered from a physical impairment or weakness were excluded. Family circumstances could also be taken into consideration, such as the number of dependents and whether arrangements could be made for their care. Provisions and support were to be provided to the family members of those engaged in jihad during the entire period of warfare.

Has the Concept of Jihad Changed in Modern Times?

In the twentieth and twenty-first centuries, the power of jihad as an ideological tool has expanded in many directions. Militant jihad in the form of fighting and warfare played a role in many struggles for independence from European colonial rule. Since then, focus has shifted to nation-building and public welfare (*maslahah*), particularly since the signing of the United Nations Charter, which establishes peace as the norm and war as the exception.

Since the late twentieth century, political Islam has been a significant factor in many Muslim countries, raising questions about the appropriate role for Islam in public life. Rulers have appealed to Islam and Islamic law to enhance their legitimacy, rule, and policies. Mainstream movements and political parties have appealed to Islam to claim authenticity and mobilize popular support. Mainstream Islamists who have been elected as presidents and prime ministers and served in cabinets and parliaments in Muslim countries have called for laws and governments reflecting Islamic values rather than Western, secular values. Religious leaders and scholars researching Quranic texts and hadiths are reemphasizing the wide variety of nonmilitant jihad goals, both individual and collective. At the individual level, these include the quiet struggles of patience and forbearance, striving in charitable works, seeking knowledge, and working hard to support one's family. At the collective level of society, working for nonviolent change, social justice, the elimination of corruption, and more moral and ethical government constitute a form of civilian jihad that can also be carried out by elected officials.

At the same time, extremist organizations, both national and transnational, have waged military jihads of violence and terrorism in the name of Islam. Al Qaeda and later ISIS have waged transnational global jihads against Muslim rulers (whom they see as abandoning their Islamic beliefs) and against the West. These terrorist movements have gone beyond the Quran and classical Islamic law's criteria for a just military jihad or war. Such groups recognize no limits but their own, employing any weapons or means, however brutal, to achieve their end. They reject Islamic law's regulations and limitations regarding the goals and legitimate means for a valid jihad, including declaration by a legitimate ruler or head of state; proportionality of violence; use of only the necessary amount of force to repel the enemy; and, finally, not targeting innocent civilians (noncombatants, women, and children). They have further claimed that their jihads qualify as individual duties that require every person to take up arms, rather than a collective duty to be spread across the community. They do not respect prohibitions against torture, mutilation, destruction of life and property, and bans on certain types of killing, such as burning people alive. Their vision of the world is completely bipolar and uncompromising with no apparent space for treaties or peace.

Across the world, Muslim jurists have used Islamic law to voice their consensus in condemning the criminal acts of Al Qaeda whom they characterized as *muharibun*, a term akin to "terrorist." They have collectively denounced these acts as *hiraba* (terrorism) for which severe penalties, often capital punishment, are prescribed. A compilation of these statements was tracked online from 2001 to 2010 as "Islamic Statements against Terrorism." A powerful Open Letter to Abu Bakr al-Baghdadi was issued in 2014 to delegitimate al-Baghdadi and ISIS, challenging the ISIS leader on many points of Islamic law that he is violating.

How Does Islamic Law View Martyrdom?

As in other faith traditions, martyrdom carries the connotation of offering the ultimate witness by giving one's life for the faith. The Arabic word for martyr, *shahid* (to bear witness), is used in the Quran to refer to a legal or eyewitness. Shahid comes from the same root as the word for the Muslim profession of faith (*shahadah*) in which a Muslim bears witness that "There is no God but God, and Muhammad is the messenger of God." The term shahid is never used in the Quran to refer to people killed in military battle.

Quran 3:169 has been taken to describe rewards for those who are killed "in the path of God," although the term shahid does not appear: "Never think that those who are slain in the path of God are dead. They are alive with their Lord, well provided for." The early hadith (traditions of Muhammad) literature explains that being "slain in the path of God" could refer to a variety of circumstances, including dying a painful death, dying in one's sleep, dying in childbirth, drowning, falling off a horse, or dying from fire, in a plague, or another serious illness. Thus, like jihad, martyrdom has had many meanings both in the past and today. Anyone (a preacher, teacher, scholar, or warrior) who dies bearing witness to his or her faith in God may be called a martyr. Muslims who die fulfilling a religious obligation or commandment (such as while reciting the confession of faith [shahadah] or making the pilgrimage to Mecca); in their efforts as missionaries, preachers, or teachers; while bringing medical assistance to others; or waging war to defend Islam and Muslims are today called "martyrs." The term has been used by Arab Christians as well as Muslims. Today, the concept of martyrdom is often claimed by militant jihadists and suicide bombers.

What Is Islamic Law's View of Suicide Attacks?

Suicide attacks, especially those that target innocent civilians or noncombatants and thus violate Islamic law, precipitated a sharp debate in the Muslim world, garnering broad condemnation on religious grounds—as well as some support. Prominent religious leaders have differed sharply in their legal opinions (fatwas).

Traditionally, Islam forbids suicide because only God has the right to give and take life. There is only one phrase in the Quran that appears relevant to suicide: "O you who believe! Do not consume your wealth in the wrong way—rather only through trade mutually agreed to, and do not kill yourselves. Surely God is Merciful toward you" (Quran 4:29). However, there are many hadith (traditions of Muhammad) that condemn suicide, such as one asserting that the person who commits suicide will spend eternity repeating the act of suicide. There is little discussion of suicide in the legal literature, in large part because there was broad agreement that it was prohibited.

Historically, both Sunni and Shia Muslims have forbidden "sacrificial religious suicide" and acts of terrorism. In the eleventh and twelfth centuries, Nizari Ismailis, popularly called the Assassins, became notorious for sending suicidal assassins against their enemies. They were rejected by mainstream Muslims as fanatics. However, in the late twentieth century, the issue resurfaced as some, Shia and Sunni alike, came to equate suicide bombing with "self-designated martyrdom," or relinquishing one's life for the faith. The change in terminology shifted it from a concept of despair and depression to the impression of agency and empowerment. Yet such "self-designated martyrdom" is not just about giving up one's own life—it is about taking those of others in the process, given that suicide attackers target other people. Thus, some deny any possibility of martyrdom in these acts and label them murder instead.

Although suicide attacks, or "self-designated martyrdoms," have occurred in many places ranging from Indonesia to the United States, the majority of cases are associated with Muslims engaged in resistance and retaliation against Israeli occupation and oppression. Increased Israeli military power and targeted assassinations compared with the lack of comparable weapons (in their eyes) to fight and defend themselves reinforced the belief among many Palestinians that suicide bombers were not committing an act of suicide but one of self-sacrifice, their only option for resisting and retaliating against an enemy with overwhelming military power and foreign support. Al Qaeda and ISIS-inspired militants in Europe and the United States have made similar arguments.

The September 11, 2001, attacks against the World Trade Center and the Pentagon resulted in sharp denunciations by many Muslim leaders of both the attacks and other acts of terrorism as an extreme twisting of Islamic principles that violated "true" Islam. After those attacks, newspaper ads in the *New York Times* and elsewhere (taken out by embassies of countries such as Egypt, Saudi Arabia, and the United Arab Emirates) sought to make the voices of mainstream Muslims and religious authorities heard. They denounced the terrorist acts as against Islam and Islamic law. The Becket Fund for Religious Liberty took out a full-page ad in the *New York Times* on October 17, 2001, head-lined, "Osama bin Laden Hijacked Four Airplanes and a Religion" and containing statements condemning the attacks by some of the world's most prominent Muslim leaders and religious authorities. These leaders and authorities noted the grave departure of the terrorists from classical and medieval Islamic law and the rules of engage-ment for military jihad, particularly by targeting civilians. Many leaders of terrorist organizations lack formal reli-gious training and are not qualified to issue fatwas. They are not heads of state and, therefore, cannot legitimately declare jihad.

World events, the rise of ISIS, the ongoing Palestinian-Israeli conflict, and the Syrian civil war continue to spark debates involving sharp distinctions between acts of self-sacrifice and self-defense versus the killing of non-combatants, women, and children, which is consistently condemned.

The "war of fatwas" between prominent religious authorities and scholars in the Muslim world provides a spectrum of legal views about suicide attacks and martyr-dom. Sheikh Ahmad Yasin, the late religious leader and founder of Hamas in Palestine, and Akram Sabri, the Mufti of Jerusalem, along with many other Arab and Palestinian religious leaders, have argued that suicide bombing is necessary and justified to counter Israel's illegal occupation and overwhelming military power. Although Shaykh Yusuf al-Qaradawi had been one of the first religious scholars to issue a fatwa in 1995 justifying suicide attacks in Israel on the premise that Israelis were not civilians but combatants in a war of occupation waged against the Palestinians, he subsequently condemned the 9/11 attacks. Abdulaziz Al Al-Shaykh, Grand Mufti of Saudi Arabia, condemned all suicide attacks without exception as un-Islamic and forbidden by Islam. He called upon all Muslim religious scholars to clarify that Islam never accepts such actions. Sheikh Muhammad Sayyid Tantawi, former Grand Mufti of Egypt and former Grand Sheikh of al-Azhar University and thus among the highest religious authorities globally, similarly denounced such attacks on innocent people as punishable on Judgment Day. He further labeled extremism as an enemy of Islam and not a legitimate jihad, which he confined to defense of one's land and help for the oppressed.

9

CRIMINAL LAW AND JUSTICE

Criticisms of Islam and Islamic law often focus on reports and media coverage of harsh hudud punishments in Muslim countries. This chapter compares the rationales and goals of Islamic criminal laws in their original context with hudud punishments in the post-colonial period. The original rigorous requirements and limitations in Islamic law have been all but forgotten by today's government-appointed prosecutors and judges.

Politics, power, and patriarchy have sometimes led to narrow codes and draconian penalties justified in the name of "Islamic" legitimacy. In addition, militant extremists have used their interpretation of Islamic criminal law to legitimate and enhance their "Islamic" authenticity and power. Lost in this process have been the Shariah principles of the common good (*maslahah*), justice, and protection of life and property, as well as many historical protections for women in the areas of sexual crimes, honor killings, and domestic violence. Some progress toward reining in abuses is seen in the fact that penalties like amputations and stoning are not allowed in fifty-two of the fifty-seven countries that constitute the Organization of Islamic Cooperation.

What Does Islamic Law Say about Retaliation or "an Eye for an Eye"?

Retaliation, "an eye for an eye," was a pre-Islamic Near Eastern cultural practice rooted in the principle of vengeance as a tribal obligation designed to restore lost family honor. A symbol of masculinity, vengeance was the prerogative—and obligation—of the male family members of the victim's tribe. The practice of retaliation was a reflection of the context in which it existed—a tribal, largely nomadic society in which there was no centralized state, law enforcement, or punishment mechanism. Pre-Islamic Arabs did not believe in an Afterlife, so they thought that justice had to be obtained in the present life. Vengeance was the localized mechanism for administering justice. The Quran modified this pre-Islamic practice by abolishing distinctions based on tribe, making the lives of all free people equal, and encouraging the substitution of either financial compensation or forgiveness in lieu of retaliation.

It was up to the victim or the victim's family to decide which of the three options—retaliation, financial compensation, or forgiveness—to pursue. In order for retaliation to be an option, the case would have to be proven in court according to strict rules of evidence and witnessing. If the evidence was insufficient or incomplete, the victim or victim's family could be assigned financial compensation instead. Perpetrators could also be imprisoned at the discretion of the court. In addition, retaliation could only be enacted against the individual responsible for the specific injury or who administered the death blow; it could not be assigned collectively to a group of attackers, although they could be held collectively accountable for financial compensation to the victim or victim's family.

Both financial compensation and retaliation are mentioned in the Quran. "Proportional retribution" is described as a right of the deceased's family in the case of murder. By limiting the right of retaliation to the deceased's immediate family, and making the object of retaliation only the individual killer, the Quranic rule is intended to save lives and deter violence (Quran 2:178–179). Financial compensation serves as "alleviation" and provides justice to the victim. In many cases, there was strong social pressure to accept financial compensation rather than retaliation because it provides justice without causing further harm. Forgiveness is believed to bring religious blessing and serves as a role model to the community of respect for human life and physical well-being. Forgiveness can be easier in a case where the perpetrator shows remorse for the crime, but forgiveness does not depend upon such remorse.

Outside of death penalty cases, retaliation was not intended to kill the perpetrator. If the convicted party had a temporary condition, such as illness or a condition (such as pregnancy) that would have created the risk that the process of physical punishment would result in death, that punishment was to be put off until the condition had ended. If the condition was permanent (such as an incurable disease or a weak heart), financial compensation was to be assigned instead. In addition, retaliation could not be assigned to certain parties, such as minors, the insane, or an unconscious person. Because retaliation was intended to be proportional, if the injury could not be precisely replicated in the attacker, the victim's only choice was compensation. The point of retaliation was to provide justice to the victim, and this might be carried out as effectively by financial compensation.

Today, some countries, such as Tunisia and Morocco, have done away with retaliation as part of national processes of modernization and development that shied away from corporal punishment other than the death penalty. Others, such as Sudan and the northern Nigerian states, have readopted retaliation as part of what they call "Islamization" programs designed to restore authenticity and legitimacy by bringing some version of Islamic law back into the public sphere. These attempts have often been piecemeal and have tended to focus on punishments, ignoring the original rules for evidence and witnessing. Despite classical prohibitions, some countries permit punishment of minors, defined as persons under the age of eighteen, by retaliation.

Overall, implementation of retaliation is rare today, although there are some instances where governments have chosen to use retaliation to try to promote public awareness of strong government prosecution of serious crimes, particularly where the victims are women.

Does Islamic Law Demand Harsh Punishments like Amputation and Stoning?

As in many premodern legal systems, the imposition of severe punishments (hudud) for certain crimes was intended to deter potential criminals, even if the likelihood of being caught and punished was minimal. The historical record contains few examples of these punishments. Discussion of such punishments accounts for only about 2 percent of the content of a typical jurisprudential work, suggesting that they were not a defining characteristic of Islamic legal theory or practice historically. Far more attention was given to matters related to worship, the Five Pillars, and family law. Despite this, some Muslim countries seeking to assert their Islamic credentials have made implementation of hudud punishments central to their Islamization programs.

Western law categorizes crimes as either civil (wrongs committed by personal parties against each other) or criminal (wrongs committed against the state). Islamic law divides crimes according to the rights of God versus the rights of human beings. Hudud crimes were considered violations of the rights of God. All other matters, including the right to physical safety, dignity, property, religion, and family, were encapsulated in the rights of human beings. Violation of rights entitled the offended party to compensation for damage caused.

Hudud means "boundaries" or "limits." Hudud crimes are therefore crimes that violate the "limits of God" or boundaries of socially acceptable behavior in a way that is detrimental to the safety and well-being of the community, private property, public order, sexual order, or personal honor. Many interpreters also add the public goods of protection of the state, morality, and social cohesion. Knowledge that certain behaviors that transgressed those boundaries were punishable was intended to strengthen the community. Muslims are warned in the Quran not to transgress or even approach these limits (Quran 2:187).

Because of their detrimental effect on community life and because they are considered to be crimes against God, hudud crimes are assigned fixed, mandatory, corporal punishments in the Quran and Sunna (Muhammad's example). Punishment for these crimes cannot be overridden or forgiven by a judge or head of state. There can be no substitution of financial compensation because the infraction is understood to have been committed against God, not human victims. However, the Quran verses describing the crimes and punishments indicate that God always offers the option of mercy and forgiveness to those who repent, giving the individual offender ultimate agency in redressing this crime against God. Many options are offered to the perpetrator of the hudud crime to repent and thereby avoid the prescribed punishment, although the act may still be punishable to a lesser degree according to the judge's discretion. In the event that the hudud punishment is assigned, it is to be carried out in public as a deterrent to others.

Hudud crimes include theft; banditry or highway robbery, which over time came to include other crimes of violence, such as piracy and, today, terrorism; unlawful sexual intercourse; slander, meaning unproven accusations of unlawful sexual intercourse; drinking alcohol; rebellion; and, according to some law schools, apostasy. Fixed punishments are typically lashes but include amputation for certain types of theft and capital punishment for crimes falling under the broad category of "banditry," certain sexual crimes, and apostasy. Banditry was considered the paradigmatic case of "causing corruption on earth," which was particularly egregious. Possible punishments depended on the severity of the defendant's conduct and could range from banishment (which includes imprisonment), if only threats of violence or minimal violence were used; to amputation of one or more of the defendant's limbs, if the defendant amputated the limbs of any of the victims during the crimes; or death, if the defendant committed murder in connection with the crime (Quran 5:33), in addition to punishment in the Afterlife. Lashing, when applied as a punishment, was not intended to kill the guilty party or cause harm to an innocent party, such as an unborn child. In the event of mitigating temporary circumstances, the punishment was to be put off until such circumstances no longer existed.

While many would concur that terrorism, piracy, and rebellion are very serious crimes, it is difficult for many today to accept as crimes those actions that are personal choices, such as alcohol consumption and choice of sexual partners. In Islamic law, the crimes included among the hudud were perceived to have a serious negative social impact that went beyond individual decision making.

Sexual crimes carried the potential for illegitimate off-spring that would have an impact on the family as well as inheritance rights. Alcohol consumption carried the potential for disruption or damage to private property, aggressive behavior, and sexual misconduct. Thus, although these were inherently personal choices, they were seen as having a broad adverse social impact.

Historically, hudud crimes required very strict preconditions for proof, including procedure, multiple eyewitness testimony, confession, strict rules of evidence, absence of doubt, and use of the specific terminology of the crime. Circumstantial evidence and hearsay were not admissible to prove hudud crimes. Only an adult Muslim of sound mind who was aware that an act was prohibited by God and still intentionally engaged in it could be tried for the crimes of drinking alcohol or sexual misconduct. Minors, the insane, and unconscious persons; persons acting under duress, such as the threat of death, serious injury, or harm to a loved one; or persons acting in defense of self, property, kin, or honor, such as a woman defending herself from sexual assault, could not be convicted of hudud crimes. Confessions had to be freely given by the perpetrator in court and could be retracted at any time up until the execution of the punishment. Coerced confessions were not considered permissible evidence.

Only free Muslim men were permitted to serve as witnesses in hudud cases. Women, slaves, who might be coerced to give false testimony, and non-Muslims were not permitted as witnesses in hudud cases, although they could testify in non-hudud cases. Scholars have argued that this restriction was designed to make conviction for a hudud crime difficult. Witnesses could further withdraw their testimony at any time and were neither legally nor morally obligated to testify. In fact, they often were discouraged from testifying based on the Quranic prohibition of seeking out offenses committed in private and encouragement to turn a blind eye to private misconduct (Quran 49:12), although a person would be obligated to hold another accountable for an act openly committed in that person's presence. A story from the second caliph, Umar, illustrates this point. While walking in Medina one day, Umar heard loud voices from a house. He decided to climb over the wall around the house to investigate and found a man with a woman who was not his wife and also the presence of wine. Umar confronted the man with his sin, but the man replied that Umar had committed three in confronting him—seeking out faults in others (Quran 49:12), climbing over the wall of a house (Quran 2:189), and entering a home without permission (Quran 24:27). Umar admitted fault and left.

Additional challenges to convicting a person of a hudud crime included the presence of doubt—whether about the facts of the case or whether the person knowingly and willingly committed a crime. If doubt was present, the crime could not be punished with a hudud punishment. It reverted to the judge's discretion. Finally, judges were actively discouraged from assigning hudud punishments. A hadith (saying of Muhammad) commanded, "Ward off [hudud] punishments from Muslims on the strength of doubt as much as you can. For it is better to err in forgiveness than to make an error in punishment." The historical record reflects significant maneuvering by both defendants and judges to avoid assignment of hudud punishments so that these severe punishments were reserved for serious cases fulfilling all of the required parameters. Religious scholars often wrote that wine drinking, prostitution, homosexuality, and fornication were rampant, but they were powerless to do anything but complain about it. Ultimately, despite their presence on the books, amputations and death by stoning were very rare in the historical record. Flogging, on the other hand, was frequently assigned, particularly where imprisonment as punishment for a crime was not the norm.

Finally, the state had the option of suspending hudud in mitigating circumstances. The second caliph Umar, for example, made implementation of hudud punishments contingent upon the state's fulfillment of its obligations to the people. In situations such as famine or drought, Umar suspended prosecution for hudud crimes such as theft because the state could not guarantee that people had enough to eat. Thus, the state's exercise of power was contingent upon its ability to fulfill its obligations to protect the lives and personal security of its subjects.

Many of these parameters and limitations on hudud punishments appear to be all but forgotten in the contemporary era, as hudud punishments have often been subverted into claims for "Islamic" authenticity, legitimacy, or resistance to the West for states trying to shore up their records in the post-colonial era. Only a very few states, such as Saudi Arabia and Yemen, held on to Islamic criminal law throughout the colonial period. Since 1972, seven countries—Libya, Pakistan, Iran, Sudan, Northern Nigeria, the Kelantan state of Malaysia, and the United Arab Emirates—as well as some nonstate actors, such as militant extremists like Al Qaeda, the Taliban, Boko Haram, al-Shabab, and ISIS—have reinstated Islamic criminal law, although actual practice has varied.

Recent years have seen widespread imposition of draconian punishments, often at record rates and in flagrant disregard for the classical parameters of evidence and testimony. This is in part because the state-appointed judges and prosecutors are political appointees seeking convictions rather than Islamic legal experts trying to ensure justice. In addition, in some countries hudud punishments have been extended beyond the classically defined crimes. New crimes today include offenses against public morals or the breach of any religious taboo in Iran, both of which are punishable by flogging. Some countries have tried to bridge their legal systems with universal human rights standards by requiring that amputations be performed under anesthesia, by a physician. In the process, the Shariah principles of the common good (maslahah), justice, and protection of life and property are often overlooked in favor of the state's prerogative to exercise power and violence.

What Does Islamic Law Say about Illicit Sex (Fornication, Adultery)?

Typically mistranslated as adultery, *zina*, or illicit voluntary genital sexual intercourse between a man and a woman who are not married to each other, is considered a crime under Islamic law. Under Islamic law, licit sexual intercourse can only occur within marriage or, in the past, between a master and a slave. Thus, both fornication and adultery are punishable crimes.

Historically, the Islamic social order was based on marriage, with children of known parentage. Control over sexual intercourse and reproduction was a public duty. A man found to have engaged in sexual intercourse with an unmarried woman became liable for the average bridal gift and might be subject to prosecution.

Because zina represented a serious crime against the social order and carried the potential for the death penalty, rules of evidence and witnessing were extremely strict under classical Islamic law. In order to be convicted of zina as a hudud crime, there either had to be four adult male witnesses to the actual act of genital penetration (per Quran 24:4) or the non-coerced confession of the accused had to be repeated four times in the court to parallel the four witnesses. The judge had to be convinced that the accused acted freely and knowingly, without coercion and with full knowledge that the action constituted a crime.

Like other hudud crimes, zina was notoriously difficult to prove. Scholars have speculated that the serious punishment associated with zina was intended to serve as a deterrent, not as a moral crackdown on society. Witnesses were neither obligated nor encouraged to testify in such cases and it was considered commendable not to notify the authorities or testify in court because the punishment was so severe. Testimony and confession could be withdrawn at any time up until execution of the punishment. Furthermore, the testimonies of eyewitnesses had to be identical in order to obtain a conviction. Even minor discrepancies could invalidate the testimony. Circumstantial evidence was not admissible, so a woman's pregnancy could not be used as evidence against her, except in the Maliki law school, which softened this by asserting that a woman could theoretically be pregnant for up to five years, thereby creating "plausible ambiguity" in the case of a woman who had previously been married. Penetration of anything other than the vagina by anything other than the penis was generally believed to fall outside of the parameters of hudud, although possibly still punishable at the judge's discretion.

Accusing someone of zina was a serious act that opened the accuser to punishment if the crime could not be proven in accordance with the law's strict standards. Quran 24:4–5 specifies that anyone accusing an honorable woman without the requisite four adult male eye witnesses to genital penetration is to be punished with eighty lashes. In addition, the accuser is deemed to be a perjurer whose testimony is never to be accepted in court again. Witnesses whose testimonies did not satisfy the legal requirements also became subject to punishment with eighty lashes.

Finally, once an investigation into zina began, the accuser and witnesses could not withdraw the charges, so that the possibility of being charged themselves with false accusation of zina was opened at the same time. Interestingly, the Quran only specifies unfounded accusations against a woman, suggesting that God was gravely concerned about protecting women from false accusations of misconduct by issuing such harsh penalties against their accusers. Muslim jurists, however, applied the same rule to accusations of unlawful sex made against men.

Muhammad's example also allowed for latitude in the wording and questioning about the surrounding circumstances in order to circumvent the hudud punishment. He asked, for example, if the couple had only been kissing rather than engaging in sexual intercourse or if perhaps someone who saw them had made a mistaken assumption about what they were actually doing. The point was to create opportunities for alternative explanations that would avoid the hudud punishment, although the activity still might be punishable at the judge's discretion. Only in situations where a person came to Muhammad and repeatedly confessed to zina and insisted upon punishment was it approved. Historical court records show that women accused of zina often claimed to have been drugged with sweets or some kind of food resulting in unconsciousness or that they were raped. Men claimed to have engaged in alternative acts that did not involve vaginal penetration by the penis.

Although punishment for zina in the form of stoning to death has become notorious in the contemporary era, the Quran does not call for the death penalty. Quran 4:15 states that a woman found guilty of illicit sex is to be confined to her home until she repents. Quran 24:2 calls for 100 lashes apiece for both parties. Jurists, other than those of the Hanafi law school, often added banishment for a year, although the Maliki law school limited this to the man.

The death penalty for zina comes from the hadith and was generally limited to adult, free Muslims who had previously enjoyed licit sexual relations in marriage—in other words, people who knew what the social requirements were. Shia also limited the death penalty to those who had a legal sexual partner available to them, such that seeking out illicit sex was clearly unnecessary. In general, if proven, jurists agreed that zina was punishable by 100 lashes for unmarried free persons, fifty lashes for slaves, and death by stoning for married or previously married persons.

Today, many of the historical protections for women's reputations have been set aside in countries claiming to "implement Shariah" in the form of hudud punishments. Women are disproportionately singled out for punishment in zina cases, while men often walk free or receive lighter sentences of lashes. The standards of evidence are rarely, if ever, met, particularly for the four adult male witnesses, and sentences are sometimes assigned in situations where illicit activity is suspected simply on the basis of finding an unmarried man and woman together, regardless of the surrounding context.

Although stonings have actually occurred only in Iran, Pakistan, and Somalia, stoning as punishment for zina is in the legal codes of Mauritania, the twelve Muslim states of northern Nigeria, Qatar, Saudi Arabia, Somalia, Sudan, the United Arab Emirates, and Yemen. Stoning occurs most frequently in Somalia, particularly in areas controlled by groups like al-Shabab and Hizbul Islam; in Iran; and in areas controlled by ISIS. In Afghanistan, Iraq, and Mali, stoning is not condoned by national legislation, but sentences and executions are carried out by nonstate actors, such as tribal leaders, local councils, or extremist groups. In Afghanistan, this tends to be in areas controlled by the Taliban and tribal leaders and is on the rise.

Reformers and women's rights activists continue to work for reforms to provide justice to women, particularly given that the charge of zina has become a catch-all for any degree of disobedience on the part of a woman toward her male family members and often has nothing to do with sex. All instances in Pakistan have occurred outside of the legal system. Circumstances are further complicated in Pakistan by the reality that charges of sexual misconduct can be made with impunity against a woman to pressure or punish her for rebelling against male authority, force her to divorce or remarry for the financial benefit of a male family member, or even coerce her into giving money to a male family member to cover debts or a habit such as alcohol, gambling, or drugs. A woman accused of zina is imprisoned until her case comes to trial, regardless of how flimsy the evidence against her is. In addition, the Zina Ordinance of 1979 allows a man to make a false accusation without punishment if he claims that he did so for the public good or if he has lawful authority over the woman. Even if the woman is found not guilty and is freed, she may remain subject to family discipline to the point of being killed in order to "restore" the family's "honor."

At the same time, there are also cases in which the hudud punishment for zina is on the law books but is not implemented in practice. For example, in Northern Nigeria, although the stoning punishment remains on the books, no one has been stoned for the past fourteen years. In the Sudan in recent years, the courts have overturned stoning sentences on appeal. Some reformers, such as Tariq Ramadan, have called for an end to punishment by stoning altogether because it is disproportionately applied to women and the poor and is used to mask deeper economic and political conflicts.

What Is the Islamic Legal View of Homosexuality?

Historically, Islamic law has held a negative view of homosexuality. Defined as an act rather than an inherent tendency, desire, orientation, or identity, homosexuality was generally classified as illicit sexual activity because it occurred outside the parameters of marriage or ownership and did not produce children. Classical Islamic law held a particularly negative view of anal intercourse between males.

The main challenge with respect to homosexuality in Islamic law is that, from a legal perspective, licit sex can only occur between a man and a woman. Homosexual activity is, therefore, necessarily illicit from a legal perspective because there is no legal way for it to take place. On the one hand, some scholars have argued that homosexual acts are no more offensive than other types of sexual transgression and are not inherently more sinful. On the other, the lack of a licit mechanism means that there is no means of remedying this purportedly sinful act other than by not committing it. This creates a serious challenge for same-sex couples today to find ways to both be committed to their lasting relationship and be faithful to Islam.

The Quran itself says very little about homosexuality and never addresses it directly. Instead, it condemns lewdness on the part of women (Quran 4:15), which some interpreters believe refers to lesbianism, and on the part of two men (Quran 4:16). While the woman is to be punished by being confined to her home until repentance, there is no specific punishment mentioned for men, although they are to be left alone if they repent and mend their ways. Like the Bible, the Quran includes the story of Lot in which the townsmen are accused of lusting after other men (Quran 7:80, 27:54, and 29:28), which is described as corruption and evidence of the immorality of the town, although no specific sexual acts are identified. Some contemporary exegetes in both the Christian and Islamic traditions have reinterpreted the story of Lot as one condemning the violence and nonconsensual aspects of the sexual motivations of the townspeople, as well as violation of the principle of hospitality and failure to respect God's status, word, and will, rather than a story condemning homosexuality; however, this is the interpretation of a decided minority.

A report in the hadith (records of Muhammad's sayings and deeds) specifically assigns capital punishment for two men caught having anal sex. The majority of jurists drew a parallel between vaginal sex and anal sex, arguing that both qualified as zina, which was punishable by either lashing or death, depending on the status of the defendant. The Hanafi school of law, which claims the largest number of adherents among Sunnis, held a more literal interpretation of zina, limiting it exclusively to illicit sexual acts involving vaginal penetration by the penis, with the result that anal penetration was a separate—and non-hudud—act, although it could, nevertheless, be punished at the judge's discretion. Under this definition, only repeat offenders might be put to death. The Shafii and Shia law schools held particularly negative views of male-male anal sex and allowed for a wall to be collapsed over the perpetrators or for them to be burned alive.

Sodomy remains punishable by death in a number of Muslim states, including Yemen and Saudi Arabia, the Muslim states of northern Nigeria, Mauritania, and areas of Somalia controlled by al-Shabab and al-Hizbul Islam. It is also punishable as a criminal act in countries such as Egypt and Malaysia, where accusations are often used as a political tool against opposition leaders, most infamously against the former deputy prime minister of Malaysia, Anwar Ibrahim. Iran also punishes homosexual acts with corporal punishment, typically lashes.

Female-female sex is not discussed much in legal literature and is not specifically mentioned in the Quran. There
are very few mentions of it in the hadith literature and those
hadith that do mention the act are considered to be unreli-
able. Although it did not qualify as a hudud crime because
of the absence of penetration by the penis, it was nonethe-
less viewed as an illicit sexual act. Accordingly, most jurists
considered it punishable at the judge's discretion.

Large majorities of Muslims as of 2013 remained strongly
opposed to homosexual behavior as morally wrong—more
than 75 percent of those surveyed in thirty-three of thirty-
six countries in a 2013 Pew Research Center Poll, with
highest rates of disapproval in Thailand and Cameroon
(99%), Ethiopia (98%), Lebanon and Ghana (97%), Kenya
and Jordan (96%), Indonesia (95%), and Egypt, Malaysia,
and Nigeria (94%). In only three countries did 10 percent
or more of the population find homosexual behavior morally acceptable—Uganda (12%), Mozambique (11%), and
Bangladesh (10%).

Today, there is growing recognition of homosexuality as
an identity and orientation in some circles, particularly in
the United States and Europe, and a recognition that it has
always existed in Muslim societies, as evidenced by literature and poetry celebrating same-sex love, particularly in
Turkey and Iran. A small minority of Muslims have called
for embracing same-sex love as a matter of justice, liberation, and opposition to oppression.

Polls in America show a trend of accepting homosexuality among American Muslims, like the US public as a
whole. A first Pew Research Center survey of Muslims in
2007 reported that 61 percent of Muslims said homosexuality should be discouraged and only 27 percent believed it
should be accepted. By 2011, Muslims were roughly evenly
split on this question. Today a Pew 2017 survey of American
Muslims reports that those who say homosexuality should

be accepted by society largely outnumber those who say it should be discouraged (52% versus 33%).

Are Honor Killings Permissible under Islamic Law?

Although honor killings, also known as honor crimes and honor-related violence (HRV), are often associated in the media and popular culture with "Islam," honor killings are a global phenomenon that transcends religion, countries, and social classes. Honor killings have their origins in pre-Islamic and Near Eastern cultures, India, Mediterranean Europe, and Latin America and were thought necessary to maintain the family's honor, which rested in the sexual conduct of its female members. Honor killings occur among Muslims, Christians, Hindus, Sikhs, and Yazidis and are currently found around the world in countries as diverse as Bangladesh, Pakistan, India, Morocco, Egypt, Israel and the Palestinian territories, Turkey, Jordan, Yemen, Uganda, Brazil, Ecuador, Italy, Sweden, and Great Britain.

The biggest legal problem with respect to many honor killings is that the entire process—recognition of a case, investigation, judgment, and punishment—occurs outside the court system. There is no guarantee that the woman has a chance to defend herself—or is even aware that she is suspected of dishonorable behavior. There is no opportunity for appeal. In the majority of cases, the victim of an honor killing is a woman accused of some kind of sexual misconduct, such as having an "illegitimate affair" with a man; losing her virginity; being the victim of rape, incest, a rumor, or suspicion; going missing from home for a time; marrying a man of a different faith; being pregnant out of wedlock; or dressing or engaging in a lifestyle in opposition to family beliefs or traditions. In some cases, although the family claims that the killing is in response to loss of virginity or suspected unchastity, in reality the woman may be killed so that someone can collect on her financial or inheritance interests while avoiding legal punishment for murder.

An honor killing is a murder conducted by a family member of an individual who is considered to have transgressed the boundaries of acceptable social or moral behavior, thereby dishonoring the family's reputation and/or image. The family's honor is believed to be restorable only by killing the guilty party. Because the killing takes place within the family in order to benefit the broader family unit, it is not considered by the family to be an act of murder. Some states, including Algeria, Jordan, Kuwait, Morocco, and Syria, show agreement through lighter sentences specified in the penal code than would be the case for murder. In other countries, such as Turkey and Pakistan, although lighter sentences are not part of the penal code, in practice, sentencing tends to be lenient. Women's and human rights activists and reformers have called for tougher sentences. Although some progress has been made, such as in Jordan, sentences for honor killings do not yet match those imposed for murder.

The Quran and hadith (records of Muhammad) do not mention honor killings, whether as an act or in terms of crime and punishment. The hadith and classical legal literature gave permission for an honor killing if a man's wife is a consenting party and only if this is the sole way to prevent the crime from continuing, provided that the defendant can prove these elements. Otherwise, the defendant would be subject to the ordinary rules applicable to a case of murder. In the event of rape, the attacker may be killed if this is the sole means of stopping the crime. The legal literature specifically refers to the man's preservation of his honor in the process. Classical legal literature sets very strict limitations on an honor killing, which occurs within discussions of zina (illicit sexual intercourse). This was carried down into the modern period through reliance upon the 1858 Ottoman Penal Code, influenced by the 1810 French Penal Code, which legitimated a "crime of passion," namely a husband killing a wife and her lover found in a compromising position.

Islamic law consistently upholds the principle that trial and punishment of crimes must be handled within the court and by a judge, not by individuals. The tradition asserts that extrajudicial killing is itself punishable as a crime. Given the difficulty of a conviction for zina, leaving the case to the courts to punish can appear risky to a family that believes its honor is at stake, particularly where extramarital pregnancy is present, as most law schools consider this circumstantial evidence and, thus, inadmissible for a hudud crime.

Contemporary efforts to address honor killings include work by reformists and women's rights activists as well as a United Nations General Assembly resolution passed in 2000 entitled "Working towards the Elimination of Crimes against Women Committed in the Name of Honor"; however, some countries abstained from voting on the resolution, including Egypt, Iran, Pakistan, and Saudi Arabia. Some senior religious scholars, including Muhammad Husayn Fadlallah (Shia) and Yusuf al-Qaradawi (Sunni), have categorically denounced honor killings. Significant media attention has also sought to create public awareness and a culture of opposition to honor killings. A 2013 Pew Research Center Poll, "The World's Muslims: Religion, Politics and Society," found that at least half of those polled in fourteen of twenty-three countries said honor killings were never justified against women. In Southern-Eastern Europe and Central and Southeast Asia, at least eight in ten said honor killings were never justified. Only in Iraq and Afghanistan (60%) did a majority say honor killings were often or sometimes justified. Honor killings remain a significant challenge in Pakistan, where around 1,000 women are killed annually, according to the Pakistani rights group the Aurat Foundation.

How Does Islamic Law Treat Domestic Violence?

Domestic violence is a global phenomenon that is not limited to any religious or ethnic group, culture, socioeconomic class, or age. Defined as emotional, verbal, financial, physical, or sexual abuse of one family member by another in a domestic setting, it encompasses spousal, parental, child, and elderly abuse. Women are disproportionately the victims of domestic violence. The United Nations has estimated that about one-third of women globally are victims of physical or sexual violence. It remains largely underreported despite rising global attention since the 1980s.

The Quran describes the ideal relationship between men and women as being protectors of one another (Quran 9:71). Men are particularly reminded to be fair to their wives and not intend to harm them or commit aggression toward them (Quran 2:231). The Quran warns against wrongdoing, harsh treatment, and causing harm or injury, calling instead for justice, mercy, and forgiveness. The Quran further guarantees women the right to life through the prohibition of female infanticide and murder. Muhammad is known to have criticized those of his followers who struck their wives or children.

Yet, throughout history, legal and religious scholars have been reluctant to try to override Quran 4:34. This verse specifies that if a wife is disobedient, the husband is first to advise her of her misconduct. If that doesn't resolve the issue, then he is to refrain from sleeping with her. If that still doesn't work, then he is given permission to strike her lightly. Although it opens with an admonition to men to take good care of their wives and provide for them financially, this verse has been used by legal and religious scholars as a justification for a man to discipline his wife physically if she is disobedient. It is important to remember that these scholars worked and wrote in a patriarchal, pre-colonial context in which husbands were understood to be the head of the family with both the right and the obligation to discipline subordinates within the family as a matter of preserving the social order.

Therefore, instead of arguing that men should not hit their wives, scholars tried instead to limit the ways in which a man could strike his wife to assure that it did not cause physical injury, such as by specifying that such a strike is only to be done lightly, such as with a handkerchief or toothbrush. They also warned that there should be no heavy hitting that causes harm or bruising or leaves marks. Many also specified that it should not cause pain. The Maliki school recognized physical abuse as grounds for divorce and gave the aggrieved wife a right to compensation from her husband for injuries he may have caused her.

Legal scholars throughout history have debated what, exactly, constitutes disobedience on the wife's part, other than marital infidelity, and whether the specific term used in the Quran is better understood as obedience or being devout. The difference is important as obedience can be related to either the husband or God, but being devout is something only God, not a husband, is capable of judging.

This raises the question of what purpose striking a wife was supposed to fulfill. When Quran 4:34 is read in context, the following verse—4:35—places dealing with a disobedient wife within the context of marital disputes that could potentially lead to divorce. Quran 4:35 calls for bringing in an arbiter from each family to work toward reconciliation. If those efforts fail, then divorce becomes an option. Ultimately, therefore, the purpose of the verse is to outline steps for dealing with a disobedient wife with the goal of saving the marriage through a change in behavior.

Historically, domestic violence typically gave rise to court cases only if the wife was killed. If the husband beat his wife and she died as a result, he was liable for homicide if there were eyewitnesses to the beating. If not, but there were witnesses to the marks left on the wife's body and the husband still swore fifty oaths that he didn't kill her and didn't know who had, he was still liable for paying financial compensation to the wife's family. Only if he found his wife in a compromising situation with a man did the husband have the right to kill them—but only if this was necessary to stop the crime of adultery from continuing. Legally, such a situation was found to coincide with grounds for impunity because of the necessities of defending one's honor and halting a crime in progress. However, if the man came upon another man raping his wife, he was only permitted to kill the rapist.

Some contemporary scholars have tried to reinterpret Quran 4:34 in a restrictive, rather than permissive, manner. They note that Quran 4:34 already represented a limitation on a man's right to engage in violence against his wife by restricting the circumstances in which he had this right and by making it the last resort rather than the starting point in the case of a marital dispute. Others have looked at the intended purpose of the broader passage—saving the marriage—to argue that if the intended purpose of saving the marriage is no longer being fulfilled, then there needs to be a revision in interpretation. If domestic violence today ultimately ends the marriage, then it is no longer fulfilling its original purpose of saving the marriage and therefore is no longer useful. Similarly, some have questioned whether the husband's failure to provide for the family negates his right to strike his wife and whether a wife's financial contribution to the family's support similarly negates such a right. In addition, some scholars have noted that use of the term *nushuz*, typically translated as "disobedient," is not restricted to women in the Quran. Men are also declared to be capable of nushuz in Quran 4:128, specifically by engaging in ill-treatment or cruelty toward their wives. The verse further states that any woman fearing such behavior on the part of the husband is not to be blamed for seeking divorce. This raises serious questions as to why so little attention is given to this command to men not to abuse their wives compared to the purported right of the man to strike his wife in a specific context.

Malaysia was the first country in the Asia-Pacific region to pass anti–domestic violence legislation in 1994. Today, domestic violence is considered a criminal act in some thirty-two Muslim-majority countries, including Egypt and Saudi Arabia most recently. There also remain some Muslim-majority countries in which domestic violence is not criminalized, including Lebanon and the United Arab Emirates. Conservative lawmakers in Lebanon have opposed bills against domestic violence, despite vocal and widespread demands for these laws.

How Does Islamic Law Handle Cases of Rape?

The Quran does not directly address rape, although there are several passages that prohibit men from forcing women into prostitution (Quran 24:32) or receiving widows as an inheritance against their will (Quran 4:19). (Inheritance of women following the death of their husbands was an ancient Near Eastern practice that is also mentioned in the Old Testament.) Because Shariah is designed to protect life, personal security, and public safety, rape as nonconsensual sexual intercourse is considered a criminal act and is subject to punishment under Islamic law, regardless of the religious affiliation, class status, or sex of the victim. There are historical examples of court cases involving both male-female and male-male rape.

Classical Islamic law recognized two broad categories of sexual intercourse—licit and illicit (zina). Licit sexual intercourse can only occur within marriage or an ownership right (with a concubine or slave). Any sexual intercourse taking place outside of marriage or an ownership right is considered illicit and is subject to the accompanying rules for evidence and punishment. Historically, rape was placed in the category of illicit sex because it occurred outside of marriage. (There is no concept of marital rape in classical Islamic law.) Consent, or lack thereof, was then addressed within that category. Jurists recognized a variety of methods of coercion—physical force, duress, fear of harm to oneself or one's family, and inability to consent, such as in the case of minor, insane, or unconscious persons.

Under classical Islamic law, punishment for rape was restricted to the perpetrator who could receive either a hudud punishment, if the case was proven according to the standards for zina (four adult male witnesses to genital penetration or confession by the perpetrator), or by the judge's discretion if a hudud case could not be proven but there was nevertheless sufficient circumstantial evidence that a crime had occurred. Although only the Maliki law school admitted pregnancy as circumstantial evidence in zina cases in general, all the major Sunni law schools accepted pregnancy as circumstantial evidence in rape cases, although the Hanbali school required additional corroborating evidence, such as witnesses who heard the victim screaming, but did not require direct eyewitnesses to the rape itself. The Hanafi and Shafii law schools simply accepted a woman's word that she had been raped in the event that she was found to be pregnant and unmarried, unless four adult male witnesses to genital penetration testified against her. If rape was proven, they then held the perpetrator liable for financial compensation for the rape and financial provision for the child and punished him with flogging. Victims were not subject to punishment because they were coerced into the action and were, therefore, not morally accountable. This approach is consistent with the hadith (records of Muhammad) and records of the Rightly Guided caliphs (the first four caliphs ruling after the death of Muhammad).

In the event of injury beyond the actual act of rape, the perpetrator could also be subject to paying financial compensation, including payment of the equivalent marriage gift. Both Sunni and Shia jurists recognized the potential for physical injury beyond the rape itself and required compensation to the victim commensurate with the extent of damage. Sunni legal literature specifically mentions the potential for serious harm leading to incontinence or even death for the victim and required compensation accordingly. Shia jurists sometimes added the marriage gift to assigned compensation. Because of the presence of intent on the part of the rapist, Shia jurists further assigned the death penalty, rather than flogging, as punishment to the perpetrator. The later Maliki tradition came to consider rape to be a form of banditry—a hudud crime—rather than merely illicit sex combined with force.

In the contemporary era, some states working to Islamize their legal codes have reimplemented hudud punishments as evidence of the state's religious commitment. In some places, such as Pakistan and Nigeria, the classical parameters have been distorted with respect to rape. While including rape in the category of zina is consistent with classical historic practice, placing the burden of evidence on the victim is not. Under these contemporary regulations, the victim is required to prove that she has been raped by producing four adult male eyewitnesses or she becomes subject to conviction for unlawful intercourse based on her unproven accusation. Her accusation of rape is taken as a "confession" to having committed unlawful intercourse, despite the fact that classical Islamic law required an unco-erced confession four times in court in order for it to be admissible.

These rape regulations also overlook the classical par-ameter of doubt—as to whether a crime had been know-ingly committed or whether the accused was a willing participant—which negated a hudud claim. Under the contemporary parameters, the victim might face add-itional punishment for false accusation of zina against a male attacker—the opposite of the original purpose of this protection, namely, preservation of a woman's reputation. In practice, these contemporary regulations have resulted in the prosecution of rape victims, rather than prosecution of the perpetrators, who tend to go unpunished due to lack of eyewitness evidence against them. This has seriously deterred women living in these countries from reporting rape, rendering them victims of both the rapist and the state that fails to provide justice.

Pakistan became particularly notorious for prosecut-ing rape victims following the 1979 Hudood Ordinances, which made illicit sex a crime against the state, punish-able by death. The ordinances became a tool for pressuring women to conform to family expectations and demands out of fear of being charged with zina. Modern forensic evi-dence was considered circumstantial evidence and, there-fore, was not admissible in Shariah courts. Subsequent trials focused on whether a woman could prove or dis-prove her consent, rather than whether forceful coercion or violation had occurred. In a final bizarre twist, a group of men who gang-raped a woman could testify against her as eyewitnesses, resulting in her punishment for zina while they walked free, despite the fact that they participated in the thus proven act of zina themselves. The Women's Protection Bill of 2006 finally resolved this issue by dissociating rape from zina and placing it under a separate category in the penal code. Rape is now tried in civil law courts where forensic evidence is admissible.

There are occasional reports in the news of tribal councils in places such as Pakistan and India prescribing rape as retribution for some perceived dishonor to a tribe; this has no basis in Islamic law. Islamic law recognizes rape as a crime. It is never regarded as a punishment. In some instances, a woman might be pressured to marry her rapist in order to spare him punishment as well as to preserve the family honor on both sides. This is more correctly understood as a carryover of ancient cultural traditions (see the comparable prescription in Deuteronomy 22:28–29) than a matter of Islamic law. In some places, such as Kazakhstan, Kyrgyzstan, and Yemen, this has been carried forward in a cultural practice of "bride kidnapping," in which men choose their brides by kidnapping them and taking them into the family home where they must cook, do housework, and provide sex until the women accept the marriage. This practice has no basis in Islamic law.

What Does Islamic Law Say about Female Genital Mutilation/Cutting?

Female genital mutilation/female genital cutting (FGM/FGC), also called female circumcision, is a cultural practice found in Africa and parts of the Middle East and Asia that involves altering or cutting off all or part of the external female genitalia. It is not connected to any specific religion. In some countries, including Egypt, Sudan, Mali, Kenya, Nigeria, Ethiopia, and Eritrea, it is practiced among both Christian and Muslim populations. More Christian than Muslim women are affected in Kenya and Ethiopia.

The practice of FGM/FGC predates Islam and is neither religiously mandated by Islam nor mentioned in the Quran. The Quran generally prohibits mutilation or permanent altering of the body. There is no consensus in the hadith (sayings of Muhammad) about female circumcision, and many of the hadith believed to refer to it are considered weak in chains of transmission. Those hadith that specifically mention female circumcision warn against harming women. Law schools are divided on whether FGM/FGC is permitted, obligatory, forbidden, or to be left to parental discretion. Some legal scholars describe female circumcision as a commendable or meritorious act, although this does not necessarily extend to all forms of FGM/FGC.

Contemporary legal scholars vary in opinion as to whether FGM/FGC should be eradicated, reduced in impact, or encouraged. Those calling for an end to the practice cite medical evidence of a negative impact on a woman's physical and mental health and potential damage to the reproductive system. Some countries, such as Oman, have declared their intent to raise awareness about medical concerns, although there is as yet no concrete evidence of this happening. In other countries, such as Iran and Egypt, there has been a significant decrease in the practice. Yet efforts to eradicate the practice have been met with strong resistance in other countries, particularly Malaysia and Indonesia. In Malaysia, FGC has become a widespread practice among the middle class, which considers it a religious obligation. Although the government has outlawed the practice, the National Fatwa Council declared it obligatory in 2009. Organizations such as Sisters-in-Islam in Malaysia and internationally, a global Muslim movement for equality and justice in the Muslim family, have pressed for greater government action to end it. Similarly, in Indonesia, where 85 percent to 100 percent of girls are believed to have undergone FGC or are at high risk of it, it is believed to be an Islamic requirement. In 2013, the Indonesian Ulama Council issued a statement that female circumcision is recommended, but not mandatory.

Major contemporary fatwas on FGM/FGC include one issued by leading Sunni Shaykh Yusuf al-Qaradawi who leaves the choice to parents, although he personally supports it to protect girls' morality. However, after many years of permitting it, al-Azhar's Dean of the Faculty of Sharia, Ahmed Talib, stated in 2005 that FGM/FGC was a crime that had no relationship to Islam and declared it nonobligatory. Al-Azhar's Grand Mufti Ali Gomaa also denounced the practice in 2006. Among Shia, Ayatollah Khamenei of Iran declared FGM permissible but not obligatory in 2011, although he asserted the husband's right to demand that his wife be circumcised. Ayatollah Ali al-Sistani of Iraq issued a fatwa in 2014 declaring that FGM is not a religious tradition and denied parents' permission or justification for having the procedure performed on their daughters.

How Does Islamic Law Define and Punish Theft?

Theft is generally defined as the unlawful taking of property belonging to another party. The threat of severe punishments for theft, which is included among the hudud crimes, was intended to serve as a deterrent. Scholars also believe that it had fulfilled the practical purpose of marking a thief at a time when there was no centralized government or prison system to investigate and punish thieves. Amputation was a clear and immediately visible sign of a person's conviction of theft. Quran 5:38 orders that the hand of the thief be amputated. Classical Islamic law permitted the amputation of the right hand for a first offense and a left foot for a second offense (cross-amputation).

Some reformers today are calling for attention to the underlying purpose of the punishment rather than literal readings of the Quran. They argue that the purpose of making someone's status as a thief evident today could just as easily be made clear through a prison sentence, which protects the security of the community and private property without causing bodily injury. This interpretation would permit setting aside the punishment of amputation.

In classical law, not all thefts qualified as hudud crimes. Only the specific crime of theft of a piece of movable property above a certain minimum value from a guarded or locked location in a stealthy manner was punishable by amputation. There could be no prior relationship between the thief and the property, such as partial ownership or having been entrusted with overseeing or keeping the property. Similarly, if the thief stole from a relative, such as a spouse or son, or a debtor, then the theft was not considered a hudud crime. Embezzlement did not qualify as a hudud crime because of the preexisting relationship between the thief and the property. Theft of items left unguarded or in public or open areas, such as in the street or in front of a mosque, did not qualify as hudud because these public places are neither guarded nor locked. The Hanafi law school further did not include perishable food in the definition of movable property because the value diminishes over time and ownership of something necessary to life is questionable, particularly in times of duress.

Strict rules of evidence and witnessing also had to be met for a hudud punishment to be assigned. These included prompts to the accused thief in court to deny the theft. Even if the thief was caught red-handed, there had to be at least two eyewitnesses to the act of theft. If a thief claimed that the item was his or denied that he had stolen it, this was understood to create enough doubt to prevent the hudud punishment. Although the victim could not pardon the accused once the accusation was registered, the victim could choose to donate the stolen property to the thief in order to allow him to avoid the hudud punishment. Similarly, the thief could circumvent the punishment by choosing to return the stolen property to the victim. The thief could also pay damages to the victim as an alternative.

These legal loopholes to the hudud punishment for theft meant that in most cases, punishment for theft fell to the judge's discretion for punishment rather than the fixed punishment for a hudud crime. The required parameters for theft combined with the strict requirements for evidence, witnessing, and testimony from the accused made it nearly impossible, practically, to sentence anyone to the hudud punishment for theft. The historical record shows that judges were generally conservative with respect to assigning hudud punishments and that instances where the hands of thieves were actually amputated were shocking to local populations. In some Islamic empires, special prisons were established for thieves, providing a practical alternative for punishment.

Today, amputations are rare, but they occur occasionally in Iran, Yemen, Sudan, Somalia, Saudi Arabia, northern Nigeria, and Afghanistan in areas controlled by the Taliban or tribes. Medical doctors are supposed to oversee these procedures to limit bleeding and infection, but most refuse.

What Does Islamic Law Say about Murder?

Islamic law recognized the gravity of murder as a violation of the Shariah values of personal security, public safety, and the right to life. Under Islamic criminal law, murder was generally considered a private claim because of the direct, personal harm caused to the victim and the victim's heirs, not just the state or surrounding community. It was up to the victim's heirs to bring the case to court and to participate in determining the punishment for the convicted killer. For this reason, ordinary cases of murder were not classified as a hudud crime because the punishment for it was not set, but was open to input from the family. In the event that the victim had no known family or heirs, the state could step in to demand prosecution and punishment. Premeditated murder, or murder committed in connection with banditry, however, was deemed to be a crime against the public and, accordingly, the state always took the lead in prosecuting such crimes.

Punishment for ordinary murder could take one of three forms: retaliation, financial compensation to the victim's heirs, or forgiveness by the victim's heirs. Retaliation took the form of capital punishment in response to murder by an individual. It could not be demanded in a case where a person was put to death by the state. The heirs were not entitled to financial compensation in this case, either, because the state was acting in the capacity of serving justice, not engaging in murder. In the event that a person was assaulted by a group of people and killed, only the person who administered the deathblow was subject to the death penalty. The other parties were subject to discretionary punishment rather than retaliation. In the cases of premeditated murder or murder committed in the course of banditry, however, capital punishment of the offender was mandatory, without regard to the consent of the victim's family.

Retaliation could be demanded only if the victim's status was greater than or equal to the status of the murderer. Under classical Islamic law, a person's status was determined by the religion of the victim/perpetrator and whether the victim/perpetrator was free or enslaved. Use of status to mitigate criminal liability was not uncommon across cultures and societies. The Hanafi school of law, however, rejected distinctions based on religion and status in application of criminal law. For those schools, such as the Malikis, that distinguished premeditated murder and murder committed in the course of banditry from ordinary murder, penalties for such crimes were applied to all perpetrators, regardless of the religion or status of either the perpetrator or the victim. Customary law, particularly in tribal areas, might also introduce distinctions based on social status, even if such distinctions were not legitimate under classical Islamic doctrine. Today, some of these categories have largely ceased to exist in mainstream societies. Slavery, in particular, has been abolished in most Muslim countries, although it is being reintroduced by the fringe extremist organization ISIS and some African countries to great criticism by Muslims around the world.

There are some areas of certain countries that still take tribal status into consideration, but this tends to be limited to specific locations and is not necessarily part of the national legal code. The only instances in which different valuations continue to be assigned in some, although not all, countries are based on sex, the compensation due for torts committed against a woman being less than that given to a man suffering similar injuries, and on status as a Muslim versus a non-Muslim. Because the few hadith that support differentiation are classified as weak, reformers are actively calling for doing away with such distinctions as violations of the Quran's egalitarian vision of all believers and Shariah principles of justice and right to life and personal safety that are supposed to be applicable to all people.

With respect to financial compensation, under classical Islamic law, the victim's heirs could pursue compensation as a private matter without a formal ruling by the judge, similar to how arbitration cases function today, albeit for civil matters rather than for a crime like homicide. However, this did not preclude the state from pursuing prosecution and assigning the death penalty or imprisonment or intervening in a case to set a financial value for a given situation, including in a situation where there was not sufficient evidence to assign the death penalty, but there was sufficient evidence that a murder had occurred. The state was also liable for compensating a victim's family if the guilty party could not be found. If the family reached an agreement with the killer, a written record of the agreement for financial compensation was to be drawn up. This agreement often contained a clause that the compensation would be paid only if the murderer was not executed. The Ottoman and Egyptian archives contain many examples of parties coming to such agreements through the nineteenth century for a variety of reasons, including avoidance of capital punishment. Indian courts also assigned compensation through the late 1770s when the British-directed Anglo-Muhammadan Law replaced financial compensation with prison sentences.

Following struggles for independence in the twentieth century, almost all Muslim-majority countries adopted European-inspired legal codes that did not contain provisions on retaliation or financial compensation. Such provisions have come back into play in only a limited number of countries, including Pakistan in 1990 and the Islamic Republic of Iran in 1991.

Finally, forgiveness is outlined as a possible outcome in Quran 2:178, which permits pardon of the murderer at the discretion of the victim's heirs. Quran 2:179 goes on to specify that such "fair retribution" saves life, which is understood to be a good thing. The passage ultimately highlights the Shariah principle that while justice is to be served, the impetus toward mercy in favor of the preservation of life is preferable. Forgiveness can be offered at any time up until the moment of execution of the punishment. There are many documented cases of forgiveness of a murderer, including in contemporary Saudi Arabia.

In general, in murder cases in which retaliation was being considered as a punishment, circumstantial evidence was not admitted, even if the killer was in possession of the murder weapon. Circumstantial evidence and incomplete evidence could only be presented in a case where financial compensation was under consideration. An example of incomplete evidence would be an accusation by a dying victim (because the victim could not personally appear in court) or testimony that someone saw a person beating another person who was later found dead, but the one who saw the beating did not personally witness the killing.

A central question in punishment for murder cases was intent. Intentional killing could result in the death penalty as retaliation, while unintentional killing could be punished at most by financial compensation. In the case of unintentional killing, if financial compensation was awarded, it was the responsibility of the killer's male family members to pay the compensation over a maximum of three years. In the case of intentional killing, liability fell upon the killer. Accidental or unintentional death was to be punished with financial compensation even if the death was caused by the direct action of the killer, such as taking a kidnapping victim to a city that came to be afflicted with a plague that killed the victim. Although the intent of the killer was kidnapping, rather than murder, the death of the victim occurred due to the direct action of the killer, thus making the unintended killer liable for financial compensation.

An interesting twist to murder in classical Shia Islamic law is the awarding of financial compensation to a woman whose husband practices coitus interruptus without her agreement. The jurists believed that the woman was robbed of a potential child in such a case and that she was owed restitution. A person who interrupted a couple during sex was similarly liable for compensation for the disruption of a potential life. Finally, according to both the Sunni and Shia schools of law, anyone who caused a pregnant woman to miscarry owed her compensation. The more developed the fetus, the more compensation was owed, particularly if the sex was discernible. The loss of a male fetus received twice as much compensation as that of a female fetus.

How Does Islamic Law Define and Respond to Cases of Personal Injury?

Shariah assures the principles of the right to life and personal security and the right of victims to receive justice. In the event of personal injury, Islamic law provided three options for justice: retaliation, financial compensation, or forgiveness, which could be offered at any point up until the execution of the sentence (Quran 2:178). Because the punishment was not fixed, personal injury did not fall within the parameters of a hudud crime. This meant that the victim had a direct voice in determining the punishment as part of the process of achieving justice.

Retaliation in the event of personal injury had roots in pre-Islamic Near Eastern cultural practices that operated in the absence of a centralized state and judicial system. If a member of a tribe suffered an injury at the hands of another party, it was the collective responsibility of the tribe to inflict retaliation on the offending party's tribe, not necessarily the direct offending party. Because retaliation was intended to vindicate the group's honor rather than achieve justice for the aggrieved individual, this approach tended to result in cycles of retaliation between tribes that continued for generations.

Classical Islamic law reformed the practice of retaliation by focusing on the immediate perpetrator and restricting the practice of retaliation to cases of intentional killing and injury that had been tried before a judge and resulted in a conviction. Strict rules of evidence and witnessing had to be observed, including the testimony of eyewitnesses and confession by the perpetrator, rather than circumstantial evidence. Finally, retaliation could not endanger the life of the person or cause harm to another innocent party, such as an unborn child. If retaliation was assigned to someone in a temporary state of disability, such as illness or pregnancy, retaliation could be delayed until that circumstance no longer existed. In the event of a permanent condition, only financial compensation could be assigned. Any case that did not satisfy the requirements for retaliation was similarly assigned financial compensation.

Those involved in personal injury cases did not have to appear before the court. It was always possible for the direct parties to negotiate and reach a settlement outside of court, thereby sparing the accused the possible assignment of retaliation, as well as the potential public embarrassment of litigation.

As with murder cases, the question of intent was central to determining the appropriate punishment. Intentional bodily injury carried the potential for retaliation as a punishment and would be indicated particularly by the use of a weapon, while unintentional bodily injury, such as that resulting from an accident or negligence, did not. In determining the liability of the perpetrator, the judge also had to consider the foreseeability of injury based on the activity being undertaken, causality, whether the accused could have known of the potential risk of injury, and intervening circumstances that interrupted the chain of causality. The status of the accused and the victim also had to be taken into consideration, as retaliation could only be assigned in the case of parity between the accused and the victim. A Muslim was considered equal to another Muslim, regardless of sex, but a slave was not considered equal to a free person and a non-Muslim was not considered equal to a Muslim under classical Islamic law, with the exception of the Hanafis, for whom all persons lawfully present in Islamic territory were equals for purposes of the law of retaliation. Even if retaliation could not be assigned, the victim was still eligible to receive financial compensation as a matter of justice. The amount of compensation was determined according to a variety of parameters that included sex, age, religion, and legal status (free person or a slave).

Today, personal injury is generally compensated financially, although some countries retain retaliation on the books for personal injury. In particularly egregious cases of injury, some courts have assigned retaliation as a deterrent to bring attention to the severity of the issue in question and to make it clear that behavior like that of the perpetrator is unacceptable. In these cases, the driving purpose is not so much a literal interpretation of the law as it is to send a broader social message about limitations on the rights of men with respect to women, in particular. It sometimes remains unclear whether these sentences have actually been carried out or are simply on the books as deterrents.

What Is Apostasy and How Is It Treated in Islamic Law?

Apostasy, as the public rejection of Islam by a Muslim, whether by words or by conduct, was considered a punishable offense under classical Islamic law. Apostasy could be implicit, such as by denying Muhammad's status as a prophet or claiming that the Five Pillars need not be followed, or explicit, such as by converting to another faith.

Classical Islamic legal literature contains many lists of actions deemed to represent apostasy, particularly focusing on disrespectful treatment of the Quran and Muhammad. However, not all Islamic schools of law considered it a hudud crime. Although apostasy clearly seems to fall within the parameters of the rights of God, it also has a social impact.

The Quran itself does not specify apostasy as a hudud crime with a set punishment. There are more than 100 Quran verses that affirm freedom of religion and freedom of conscience, as well as the truth of other divine revelations that specifically include the Torah, the Psalms, and the Gospels. Most important, Quran 2:256 assures that "There is to be no compulsion in religion," making it clear that religious affiliation is intended to be a personal choice rather than something enforced by a state. Thus, while unbelief is warned against and threatened with punishment by God in the Afterlife, there is no clear agreement as to whether it is to be punished during this life.

There is no record of Muhammad ever having put to death a person convicted of apostasy, despite encountering numerous instances of this. While a hadith attributed to him states, "Whoever changes his religion, put him to death," scholars have noted that this hadith was revealed in Medina during a period of ongoing and intensified conflict with Mecca in which some Muslims rejected Islam and joined forces with the Meccan enemy to fight against the Muslims. Therefore, they have argued that this hadith is not intended to be a blanket prescription against apostasy but was applicable only when accompanied by treason or sedition, which threatened communal safety, security, and unity.

This interpretation is bolstered by the historical example of the so-called Wars of Apostasy after Muhammad's death, when some Arab tribes tried to break away from the community, believing, according to tribal custom, that their political alliance had ended with the death of the leader. They had not rejected the religion of Islam. The wars were, therefore, fought over political acts of desertion and treason rather than religious faith.

A person charged with apostasy was not immediately executed. In order to receive the death penalty, the person had to be proven to be a sane adult who had previously been Muslim and had publicly and deliberately rejected belief in Islam. Anecdotal evidence was not sufficient for conviction. The accused usually had to make a direct and overt statement rejecting Islam to be convicted. Only in the case of deliberately insulting Muhammad was the death sentence to be carried out immediately after being assigned. Given the seriousness of the crime and its accompanying recommended death punishment, some schools of Islamic law recommended delaying the execution to give the accused time to reflect and repent and in order to remove any possibility of doubt, such as a situation of duress in which the person feared for his or her life and publicly renounced the faith but secretly remained Muslim within. The Hanafi school of law made this recommendation for a delay, although it did not consider it to be obligatory. The Shia allowed a delay only in the case of someone who converted to Islam, not someone born into the faith. Both schools permitted the death penalty only for male apostates. Female apostates were to be imprisoned until they repented.

With all of these exceptions and doubts, it is not surprising that, historically, punishment for apostasy varied across time and space, becoming increasingly rare by the nineteenth century. As with other types of crimes, alternative punishments, such as shunning, being disowned by one's family, public censure, intimidation, and even assault, were used as broad social threats against conversion to another religion.

Apostasy represented not only a breach in the person's relationship with God but also in the trust of the faith community. Assignment of the death penalty to apostates was, therefore, based in part on the potential negative impact it could have on the community of believers (*ummah*) and in part on the possibility that apostates could become potential enemy combatants. From the eleventh century on, some states used charges of apostasy against those who were viewed as hostile or a threat to rulers, despite warnings in the hadith that declaring another Muslim to be an unbeliever is a grave sin.

Today, apostasy is a highly sensitive and contested issue. It is listed as a capital offense in Sudan, Saudi Arabia, Qatar, the United Arab Emirates, Yemen, Afghanistan, Brunei, and Mauritania. Iran also punishes apostasy with the death penalty, even though this punishment is not listed in the Iranian Code of Criminal Procedure. Despite the laws on the books, there have been only two cases since 1994 resulting in conviction and execution (Sudan and Iran). Some laws specify that the death penalty is to be lifted in cases where the accused repents and returns to Islam.

Even in some countries where apostasy has been decriminalized, charges of apostasy can be used to prosecute scholars and other individuals for writings or comments on social media. Examples include the late Egyptian professor Nasr Abu Zayd, whose controversial writings led to accusations against him of apostasy. This then led to a claim before an Egyptian court by a third party seeking immediate dissolution of his marriage, insofar as apostasy of the husband results in immediate dissolution of the marriage under classical Islamic family law. The Egyptian courts that heard this divorce suit agreed with the complainant that Abu Zayd's writings amounted to apostasy and therefore dissolved his marriage against his own will and that of his wife in 1995, despite the fact that Abu Zayd claimed to be

Muslim and that he had never renounced his faith. Although many people called for his death, the state did not assign the death penalty. Instead, the state assigned him police protection out of concerns about vigilantism. In another example, Saudi Arabia threatened execution in the high-profile case of Hamza Kashgari, who was accused of insulting Muhammad in a series of social media Tweets in 2012, but he repented and was freed in 2013. Finally, in Pakistan in 1990, the Federal Shariat Court conflated apostasy and blasphemy in order to extend Pakistan's blasphemy laws to non-Muslims as well as Muslims. The current blasphemy law assigns the death penalty or imprisonment for life and a fine for any contempt expressed against Muhammad, whether spoken or written, direct or indirect, by insinuation, innuendo, or imputation.

Members of the minority Ahmadiyya and Christian communities have consequently found themselves charged under these vague laws because they do not believe in Muhammad as God's final prophet. Critics have charged that the laws are being implemented by political appointees rather than by scholars of Islamic law, rendering the laws a political tool in the hands of the government rather than a protection of faith per se. Pakistani politicians and judges speaking out against the laws have been harassed and even assassinated. In some countries, accusing someone of apostasy can block that person's ability to claim inheritance or custody of children. Even where apostasy is not punishable by law, there remains strong social pressure against leaving Islam in Muslim countries and among immigrant populations.

What Does Islamic Law Say about Drinking Alcohol?

The Quran prohibits drinking wine (Quran 5:90), although the punishment for doing so is specified only in the hadith (records of Muhammad). Muhammad and the first caliph, Abu Bakr, assigned forty lashes for consumption of wine. The punishment was raised to eighty lashes under subsequent caliphs. The law schools therefore vary in the number of lashes that were assigned for a proven case.

Proof of this crime varied considerably. Some law schools allowed conviction only if the alcohol could still be smelled on the offending party's breath when the person appeared before the judge or if the person confessed. Many jurists did not permit punishment if a person simply smelled of alcohol or was drunk because it was possible that the person was unaware of consuming it (the principle of doubt). This is based on the principle outlined by the founder of the Shafii school of law that people are only to be punished based on certainty. At the same time, being under the influence of alcohol did not excuse a person from committing a crime on the basis of lacking capacity because it was assumed that the person had already committed a crime by willfully drinking alcohol. This made it more likely for a person to be convicted of alcohol consumption in the presence of another crime than for a person to be convicted only of drinking alcohol.

Drinking alcohol is prohibited because of the intoxication that results. Intoxicated persons are regarded as presenting a potential threat to public safety, private property, and personal security because social and sexual inhibitions become diminished under the influence of alcohol and some persons may become violent or aggressive. Because Shariah is intended to protect personal security, property, and life, Islamic law expanded the prohibition on wine to include other intoxicating beverages producing similar effects as well as recreational drugs. A minority of jurists in the Hanafi law school, in the case of consumption of intoxicants other than wine, only allow for conviction if the person becomes intoxicated, leaving the door open to consumption of small quantities that do not result in intoxication. The majority, however, prohibit consumption of any quantity of alcohol unless there is a medically valid reason for doing so, such as use of a cold medication that contains alcohol if there is no nonalcoholic version available. This is based on the principle that the obligation to preserve life can make permissible what is normally forbidden on a temporary and urgent basis. Legal scholars are very careful to specify that this is an exception, rather than the rule, and doctors are encouraged to prescribe nonalcohol based medicines and treatments whenever possible.

Alcohol consumption is considered unlawful only for Muslims. Thus, some Muslim-majority countries, such as the United Arab Emirates and Bahrain, permit limited, and often private, sales of alcohol only to non-Muslims in locations largely visited or populated by them, such as hotels. Public drunkenness remains prohibited because of the concerns it raises for personal and public safety. The majority of Muslims globally find alcohol consumption to be morally wrong, with highest rates of disapproval in Southeast Asia, South Asia, the Middle East, and North Africa, according to a 2013 Pew Research Center Poll. Greatest acceptance is found in Southern-Eastern Europe and Central Asia, although more than half the population finds it morally wrong. It is important to note that believing something is morally wrong does not necessarily translate into believing that it should be punishable by law.

10

ISLAMIC FINANCE IN
A GLOBAL WORLD

The Shariah principle of moderation occupies a middle
position between liberal capitalism and socialism. Islam is
a practical religion. Its links to trade and commerce originated with Muhammad's experience with caravan trade
and his marriage to Khadijah, a wealthy merchant. The
prophetic messages in the Quran emphasize justice and
honesty in the marketplace as well as enjoyment of material possessions as long as this does not become excessive
and ignore the needs of others. For example, interest/
usury (*riba*) is viewed as unjustly profiting from another's
labor and property, focusing on profit alone rather than
the common good (*maslahah*). Shariah principles provide
a foundation for public interest that guides charitable giving, creating charitable endowments, and even establishing contemporary microfinance projects. These principles
also inform modern economic theories that support interest-free financial transactions enabling sharing of risk and
profits as well as providing a safer investment environment. They influence the way many Muslims handle their
private property, personal banking and loans, public commercial trade, and contracts of sale.

Some Muslim economists promote the use of Shariah
principles that emphasize long-term planning, moderation

in spending and investing, and preserving the resources and security of future generations. Criticism is aimed at the West's capitalist-driven progress and development, linked to the global environmental crisis and vast economic inequality, as well as the Muslim world's vast income disparities, widespread underdevelopment, and failure to encourage genuine economic growth and social welfare. Critics argue that more balanced and strategic planning for development in the global financial markets affecting East and West remains a critical mandate for the future.

How Are Muslims' Economic Transactions Guided by Shariah Principles and Values?

Economic transactions for Muslims are guided by the Shariah principles of social equity, fairness, justice, moderation, and not oppressing the poor. The Quran frequently mentions the importance of charity, care for widows and orphans, honesty and fairness in business, avoidance of exploitation and excess, support and respect for private property regardless of whether it is owned by a woman or a man, and the prohibition of usury. For example, Quran 26:181–183 commands believers not to cheat other people of what belongs to them, to be honest in market dealings so that people get what they pay for, and to weigh using correct scales. Quran 2:27–280 further calls upon Muslims to cease collecting debts based on usury and to be lenient with debtors who have difficulty paying what they owe, noting that it would be better to write such debts off as charity.

Charity is an important activity for Muslims, as enshrined in the Third Pillar—*zakat*—and encouraged in additional charitable giving. However, being charitable is not intended as a substitute for just business dealings nor is it to encourage the establishment of a welfare state.

Rather, Shariah principles are designed to assure that those engaged in business deal fairly with their customers and remember their social responsibility to the community at large at the same time that they earn their own living and a reasonable profit.

Like Jesus, Moses, and other prophets, Muhammad was an advocate of socioeconomic justice and the rights of the marginalized and oppressed, placing him at odds with the power holders and wealthy traders in his hometown. He advised his followers to earn an honest living, acquire what they needed, and not be excessive in their wants and desires. He warned that poverty is just as much of a material injustice as wealth and luxury and that both can be equally damaging to a person's moral integrity and faith.

Shariah principles call for moderation as a middle ground between the extremes of excessive consumption and materialism, on the one hand, and abject poverty and deprivation, on the other; moderation becomes an expression of virtue and balance. Islamic law outlines general expected behaviors but also includes exceptions to the rules. It is not a system of extremism, but rather one that is intended to be flexible enough to account for variations in human experiences. Thus, for example, although fasting during the month of Ramadan is generally required, exceptions are made for those for whom fasting would represent an undue hardship, such as a pregnant or lactating woman, children, the elderly, or those with medical conditions that would render fasting dangerous to their overall health and well-being. This principle of avoiding extremism is also applied to material possessions.

Charitable giving is encouraged in Islam. Charity taken to the extreme of depriving one's own family of their needs is not. There must be a balance between one's own needs and caring for those of others. Enjoying the material benefits of life is not sinful per se; it is only when such enjoyment is excessive or comes at the cost of depriving others of their needs that it becomes a problem. In a case where a person has lent money to a debtor who becomes insolvent, postponing repayment without charging anything additional would assure that neither party suffers unduly. If the person lending the money is able to forgive the debt, doing so brings additional blessing.

How Does Islamic Law View Interest/Usury (Riba)?

One of the greatest challenges facing Islamic finance today is the clear and unequivocal prohibition of riba in the Quran and Sunna (example of Muhammad). Riba is typically translated as "usury" or "interest," although scholars continue to debate what riba is and to what degree it is prohibited. Historically, many Muslim jurists have asserted that interest should never be charged on a loan because it exploits a person already in demonstrable financial need. Others have argued that riba refers only to exorbitant interest or usury, which was common practice during Muhammad's lifetime. Lower rate interest-bearing loans, such as those offered for credit today, were neither known nor understood at that time. The challenge today is that the global economy is based on credit and interest is integrated into contemporary financial mechanisms. Muslim economists have therefore worked to define what, exactly, constitutes riba and to develop alternative financial mechanisms that work around it, at least in name.

There are four Quran verses that prohibit riba. Quran 30:39 places riba in contrast with charity, commenting that those who charge riba to increase their own wealth at the expense of someone else's do not earn favor with God, while that which is given in charity does. This verse was revealed in the early years of Muhammad's ministry in Mecca, which was a major site of trade and pilgrimage.

The practices of riba and speculation at that time served to protect idle capital and exploit traveling pilgrims and traders. In other words, they were used to increase the wealth of those who already possessed it without requiring any effort or contribution on their part other than lending capital. Muslim scholars believe that this verse was designed to call attention to the two extremes of behavior toward those less fortunate—exploitation versus charitable giving—and thus to the bases of social justice and public welfare (maslahah) or the absence thereof.

Quran 4:160–161 defines riba as gaining wealth under false pretenses, something that had also been prohibited in the Old Testament. The passage asserts that God will punish all who participate in this condemned practice, regardless of their religious affiliation. Quran 3:130–132 connects the prohibition of riba to the very foundational identity of being a member of the Muslim community. In this passage, riba is tied to exorbitant interest that doubles or otherwise multiplies the amount originally loaned. The passage was revealed in the context of the Muslim loss at the Battle of Uhud, which may have been financed through riba. Some Muslim scholars therefore believe that this verse highlights the very real consequences that disobedience to this prohibition can have—to the point of causing God to abandon the guilty in the midst of battle.

The most extensive discussion of riba in the Quran is in Quran 2:275-281, distinguishing between trade, which is legitimate and permissible, and riba, which is forbidden. God's opposition to riba is made clear in the threat of war upon those who continue to demand it, while assuring blessing for those who give charitably. The core issue at stake is justice—those who deal unjustly with other people will be dealt with unjustly themselves, while those who practice mercy—for example, by giving someone in difficulty additional time to repay an outstanding debt—will also receive mercy, particularly if the creditor offers for-giveness of the debt as a matter of charity. God asserts the importance of changing one's ways once awareness of wrongdoing is raised. While riba will not be punished retroactively, believers are commanded not to repeat the offense into the future.

Muhammad's example also strongly condemns riba by voiding all claims to it after the conquest of Mecca and declaring it a crime against both God and his Prophet that would merit war if reinstated. At the same time, trade was encouraged. The issue was not earning a profit per se, but demanding an exorbitant profit that would produce injust-ice or oppression by taking advantage of those in a weak bargaining position. Part of the difference between trade and riba is that trade requires risk sharing and tangible input whereas riba simply lends money for a guaranteed return, regardless of the relative success or failure of the venture or its impact on society. In other words, trade is a joint venture in which each party makes a contribution and both take on risk, while riba represents an unbalanced power equation in which one party is guaranteed a return within a specific timeframe, regardless of the surrounding context.

In order to help stamp out the practice, Muhammad asserted that both the giver and the receiver of riba would be equally condemned. The purpose was to make pro-hibition of riba a community obligation and responsibil-ity rather than simply a matter of private arrangements between individuals or something that only affected certain segments of society. Even arrangements such as trading a commodity with a time delay and justifying an increase in profit based on that delay were condemned as riba.

These clear prohibitions and examples, designed to pro-mote economic justice, represent a serious challenge to par-ticipation in the contemporary global capitalist economy, which is based on credit and interest-bearing loans. Since the nineteenth century, Muslim reformers have worked to develop modern economic theories designed to work within the Western-dominated economy while respecting both the Quranic prohibition of riba and the entrepreneurial spirit the Quran encourages. Early economic theories tended to be reactionary, as they were formulated in the context of a Western-dominated colonial economic and social system that had devastated local economies and rendered them dependent on the West. These theories generally targeted interest as the cornerstone of the "immoral" Western capitalist system, highlighting the Quran's prohibition on riba as morally superior. Some self-defined Islamic states, such as Iran and Pakistan, have at times declared the goal of eradicating interest altogether and supporting "interest-free" financial alternatives, including "interest-free" government bonds to support their respective regimes. Yet doing away with interest altogether has proven to be impractical, leading some to conclude that a certain level of interest may be acceptable, provided that it is not excessive, given that any interest-bearing loan will multiply the original amount borrowed if extended for a long enough time.

Some countries, such as the members of the Gulf Cooperation Council and Malaysia, use Shariah as their official source of law, and they claim Shariah compliance in their national financial institutions. Virtually all Islamic banks have Shariah boards to verify that transactions are Shariah-compliant, including the three with the largest assets—Al-Rajhi in Saudi Arabia, Kuwait Finance House, and MayBank Islamic in Malaysia. Conventional banks offering Shariah-compliant products through Islamic windows also have Shariah boards. There are also international councils for assuring adherence to Shariah standards, the most important of which is the International

Islamic Fiqh Academy, in Jeddah, Saudi Arabia. These councils typically use *ijtihad*, or independent reasoning, as the mechanism for bringing classical scholarship and modern financial regulations into cooperation. Yet more attention is often given to adhering to the prohibition on riba than to examining how it plays out in practice in terms of exploitation of the poor or the promotion of social equity and welfare.

Contemporary Islamic financial instruments typically assert the illegality of all interest, focusing on literal prohibitions while essentially fulfilling the same function under alternative terminology. For example, Islamic banks advertise their compliance with Shariah through "interest-free financing." Rather than lending money at a fixed interest rate, Islamic banks engage in "silent partnership" by purchasing, for example, a car or home at a given price and then reselling it to the consumer at a profit. At the end of the day, the consumer pays a price similar to a conventional mortgage or car loan, but through a mechanism that allows the bank to mark up the commodity to earn a profit rather than charging interest per se. Some Muslim scholars have also sought to distinguish between riba as a usurious transaction that is intended to create perpetual debt versus risk-based profit that allows Muslims to make investments that ultimately allow societies to prosper. The focus is on the social justice outcome of this kind of investment rather than the terminology of interest.

Do Islamic Banking Practices Differ from Those of Western Banks?

In the quest for Shariah-compliant economic development and a Shariah-compliant parallel to the Western capitalist global system, Islamic banks have become a prominent fixture on the financial landscape throughout the Muslim world and, increasingly, in the West. There are currently more than 400 Islamic banks in more than fifty countries, offering a variety of services and banking practices intended to keep pace with the modern financial system while assuring adherence to Shariah principles. Although still relatively small, accounting for only 1 percent of the global financial system and about $2 trillion in assets, Islamic finance is growing rapidly—expanding 40.3 percent annually between 2004 and 2012 and projected to grow at a rate of 20 percent annually through 2018. About 12 percent of the world's Muslims hold investments in Islamic banks. The value and potential for growth have attracted the interest of major global financial institutions, including Goldman Sachs and Lloyd's, which offer Islamic financing options in Europe and elsewhere. HSBC offers Islamic finance in the UAE and Malaysia and through the Saudi British Bank of which it is a partial owner.

The Shariah principles guiding Islamic banks are upholding public interest (maslahah), sharing of both risk and profit, equity participation, fulfillment of contracts, and avoiding excessive risk-taking, giving or taking of interest (riba), exploitation of a person in need (i.e., the borrower), and commodification of food, money, or other life essentials. Certain practices, such as hoarding, profiteering, and investing in debt, are prohibited by Shariah principles because of their negative impact on public interest and inherent oppression of the less fortunate. Investment in prohibited substances, such as alcohol, narcotics, and firearms, is also forbidden.

The mechanism of Islamic banking is the distinction between risk and profit, on the one hand, and riba as usury or interest, on the other. Risk entertains the possibility that the investor may not get back the money originally put into a venture. Sharing both risk and profit is intended to ensure that neither party is being exploited by the other

and that both parties have a vested interest in seeing the
venture succeed. Riba, on the other hand, is seen as exploitation of a needy party by someone in a greater position of
financial power.

Focus on profit-sharing is not unique to Islamic law; it
is also found in the Jewish tradition of *heter iska* and the
Christian-European *commenda*. In principle, profit-sharing
asserts that money deposited in a bank is an investment
in the bank's portfolio, making the depositor a silent partner. The bank is expected to invest in Shariah-compliant
ventures, services, and instruments. Because it is an investment, although a return is expected, it is not supposed to
be guaranteed or securitized in theory. In practice, the realities of the contemporary financial industry have led to
regulations that pressure Islamic banks to guarantee transactions (demand deposits), although not investment profit
and loss-sharing deposits.

Specific services offered by Islamic banks include loans
governed by predetermined profit-sharing, making the
relationship one of investor and entrepreneur rather than
lender and borrower; advance purchase by the bank with
a higher resale price to the purchasing party rather than a
"loan" to a "borrower"; equity sharing; sovereign interest-
free bonds guaranteed by the government at a set annual
"profit rate"; corporate bonds not guaranteed by the government (which constitute the majority of bonds); and oper-
ational leasing contracts in which the lessee pays rent to the
owner of the asset and the owner retains most of the risk.

Redesigning "loans" into partnerships in which both risks
(potential for loss of money or goods) and profits are shared
creates a relationship in which both parties have rights and
responsibilities rather than one party simply being indebted
to the other. In theory, these arrangements respect Shariah
principles, although it has been noted that in practice, outcomes tend to be very similar to those seen with Western

banks. With respect to advance purchase, for example, the markup on the advance purchase on a car or house typically ends up at the same price as a conventional mortgage or car loan, although it uses a mechanism that avoids the terminology of interest. At the same time, although many Muslims prefer to finance significant purchases through Islamic banks, in cases where such services are not available, such as in non-Muslim-majority countries, conventional banking systems are still used as a matter of necessity or choice.

Although there are many complex financial products that claim to be Shariah-compliant, it can be difficult to distinguish Shariah-compliant from non-Shariah-compliant products. Because the end result is the same, a limited number of interest-paying investments have been approved by some major legal scholars. For example, al-Azhar's Grand Mufti Shaykh Tantawi approved government bonds, certificates of investment, and deposits. Nevertheless, broad juridical preference remains for the terminology of profits, rather than interest.

Many critics of Islamic banking charge that Shariah compliance extends only to services offered to investors rather than being applied consistently throughout the bank's practices. For example, some Islamic banks are known to hold investments in non-Shariah-compliant instruments, such as other companies or banks that charge interest or issue interest-based services. Although some institutions, such as the Islamic Fiqh Institute in Qatar, have tried to ensure that returns are a percentage of actual profits rather than a percentage of capital, it often proves difficult to maintain genuine adherence to risk-taking, as the only real risk in many cases is of default rather than a nonprofitable investment.

Another accusation is that Islamic banks have only changed the terminology of services rather than the substance of the arrangement, so that Shariah compliance is in name only. For example, although an increasing number of commercial banks claim to have Shariah-compliant departments, the products remain parallel pricewise to the offers of commercial banks and tend to be securitized, meaning that the investor does not actually take any risk.

A final criticism is that although a deposit is supposed to represent ownership of an entire undivided asset with all of its accompanying rights and obligations, it is unlikely that this is actually the case for each individual investor. For example, Islamic mutual funds are supposed to be investments in ownership of a share of the fund, not the underlying stocks, thereby meeting Shariah board requirements. However, Islamic Index tracker, exchange traded, and hedge funds are more complicated because some, or even all, of the investment finances the purchase of derivatives, which are not acceptable to Shariah boards.

Yet for all the criticisms, Islamic banks are perceived to be safer than Western banks, despite their susceptibility to the boom and bust cycles of the oil industry. Overall, Islamic banks fared better than their Western counterparts during the 2008 global financial crisis. In large part, this was because Shariah-compliant financing discourages risky behavior, thereby limiting the involvement of Islamic banks in the collapsing derivatives market, and encourages low investment in debt, which protects them from shocks to financial and capital markets. In addition, Islamic banks are mostly retail institutions with strong and stable customer deposits, rendering them less exposed to the interbank markets on which investment banks depend.

How Can One Establish a Charitable Endowment (Waqf) in Islam?

The importance of charity as an Islamic principle is emphasized in its inclusion in the Five Pillars. Zakat, or annual almsgiving of 2.5 percent of one's entire wealth for Sunnis and on specific portions of wealth for Shia, is an integral expression of membership in the Muslim faith community. Additional charity is always encouraged. The Shariah principles behind charity are the protection of public interest (maslahah), care for the less fortunate, and prevention of hardship and exploitation of the most vulnerable by assuring that their needs are met. One method for engaging in charity in a perpetual way, rather than on a one-time donation basis, is by establishing a *waqf*, or charitable endowment.

A waqf is a charitable endowment of a nonperishable, durable asset given to a specific cause with living beneficiaries in perpetuity. Anyone, female or male, can dedicate a waqf, provided they are legally and financially sound. Although the Quran does not specify the legal parameters, charitable endowments have been common since Muhammad's lifetime and feature prominently in Islamic jurisprudence.

There are three main types of waqf: religious (mosques or property used to maintain mosques); philanthropic (for example, supporting public or health services, scientific research, or environmental preservation); and familial (given to specific descendants, frequently daughters, often in order to supplement or circumvent the prescribed allocations in Islamic inheritance laws). The most common forms of waqf are mosques and schools. In fact, the oldest existing, continually operating university in the world, al-Qarawiyyin University in Fez, Morocco, was founded as a waqf consisting of a mosque and a school in 859 CE by a woman, Fatima al-Fihri. Other common forms of waqf historically were hostels for pilgrims and travelers, hospitals, and orphanages. Waqf served as an important mechanism for Muslim women's participation in public life and welfare.

Almost any asset can be given as a waqf, including money, real estate, hospitals, houses, businesses, agricultural assets, and even trees. The only restriction on an asset is that it may not promote anything immoral, such as gambling or alcohol consumption.

Once established, the waqf is managed by a specified individual or group. Historically, this was often a family member. The manager is responsible for upkeep of the waqf so that it does not fall into disrepair or lose its capacity to produce revenue. Waqf revenues can legitimately be used for this upkeep. Contemporary debates about waqf have questioned whether a waqf must permanently remain in the form in which it was established or if changing the form might be acceptable if doing so would better fulfill public interest (maslahah).

Because of their important role in social welfare, waqf have been managed and overseen by Islamic courts, departments, and ministries throughout history, from the original Caliphate to the Ottoman Empire and contemporary nation-states. For example, in 1812, about one-quarter of all land in Egypt was within the purview of a waqf. Similarly, in mid-sixteenth century Palestine, there were nearly 1,000 waqf properties. Many of these properties were commandeered by the state when various countries won independence.

Today, establishment of waqf remains an important and common form of charitable giving, including in the West. In 1973, the North American Islamic Trust (NAIT) was formed to hold titles to waqf in North America, including property titles of many mosques, Islamic centers, and schools across the United States and Canada.

How Does Islamic Law View Property Rights?

All aspects of creation, including property and life, are ultimately considered to belong to God in Islam. Human beings serve as God's vicegerents and, therefore, as caretakers of God's property, serving as its trustees. Within those parameters, private property rights and the principle of ownership are guaranteed by the Quran and form the cornerstone of Islamic economic theory. Property ownership is a matter of responsibility that requires maintenance of that property. Destruction of property, whether by active means, such as through fire, or passive neglect of crops, animals, or built structures, would be a violation of the Shariah principles of protection of property for the benefit of oneself and the community at large and caretaking of property as a trust from God.

Islamic law considers property rights to be both given and regulated by God. Islamic law generally recognizes three types of property—public, private, and waqf (religious endowment). Public property is defined as property that is collectively owned by an entire society or community with the intent of benefiting all or most of its members. Examples of public property include roads, forests, rivers, parks, natural springs, lakes, land designated for community use, land that is not privately owned, and mineral resources. The government is expected to administer public property in a way that best suits public interest (maslahah) in keeping with Islamic law. As long as public property continues to fulfill a community need, it cannot be acquired or owned by private parties. If a public property no longer fulfills a community need, a different property that would serve a similar purpose can be substituted. Public property that is not economically productive may be converted into private property if the acquiring party makes the unproductive land productive, such as by revitalizing land for agricultural or industrial use. The critical legal issue is one of making the property productive, such as by planting fruit trees, not simply by claiming ownership, such as by putting up a fence or otherwise setting boundaries.

Private property is that which is owned or overseen by a private individual or group. The God-given basic right to own private property means that no government, society, or legal system has the right to bar private ownership, including ownership by women and/or orphans, or to preclude possession based on race, religion, or ethnicity. Additionally, no Muslim government can seize private property without just cause and due compensation. Direct theft or theft by fraud of another person's property, whether material or abstract, such as intellectual property, is punishable by both Islamic law and God. Property involving substances or activities prohibited in Islamic law, such as pigs and pig by-products, alcohol and other intoxicating substances, gambling, and prostitution, cannot be owned by Muslims.

Islamic law guarantees property owners the right to use, enjoy, benefit from, and dispose of property, provided that the exchange is fair and that no other party is harmed in the process. Property owners are expected to care for and enhance their property. Wastefulness is forbidden, as is extracting from or enjoying one's property in a way that abuses, exploits, or oppresses other individuals or society as a whole. Any use of private property that causes harm to another, such as by reducing the sunlight that reaches a neighbor's property, or monopolizes some aspect of benefit from a property, such as by trying to circumvent Islamic inheritance law shares or taxation for charitable purposes, is prohibited.

Finally, with respect to water rights, classical Islamic law considered water to be held in public trust as a gift from God necessary to every form of life (Q 21:30). The concept of Shariah itself means "a path to water," emphasizing the central role of water both for survival and in drawing closer to God. Thus, water was considered a public trust and a community right rather than private property. While private individuals could certainly make use of public water sources, such as for irrigation, this could only be done in a way that did not cause harm to others or the community at large. Similarly, causing damage to a water supply, such as by polluting it or causing destruction to a distribution mechanism, was considered a public harm and thus punishable under Islamic law.

How Does Islamic Law Govern Trade and Contracts of Sale?

In keeping with Islamic law's recognition of private property ownership and the right of an owner to sell, trade, or transfer property, trade and contracts of sale have been part of the picture of Islamic finance since the lifetime of Muhammad. The Shariah principles guiding trade and contracts of sale include preservation of public interest (maslahah), protection of private property, protection of the individual from exploitation or oppression through usury, and ensuring justice.

Although the Quran was revealed to a society in which oral testimony and agreements were the norm, the Quran nevertheless specified that contracts were to be recorded in writing (Q 2:282). The verse further states that the contract is to be written by a scribe—a neutral party to the transaction—and that, regardless of the size of the debt, the amount of the debt and the timeline for repayment should be accurately recorded. In the event the debtor was incapable of contracting a debt or too weak in intellect to do so, the debtor's guardian was to act in the debtor's stead. In addition, the contract was to be witnessed by either two men or a man and two women "so that, if one of the two women should forget, the other can remind her." This written and witnessed document is declared to be "more equitable in God's eyes, more reliable as testimony, and more likely to prevent doubts from arising between you." In other words, the purpose of the contract was to assure justice for both parties as well as to maintain the social order: Such a contract would be legally enforceable and did not leave room for either party to forget or claim that the debt either never existed or had not been repaid. The verse also specifies that in the case of trade, merchandise is to be handed over when payment is received. Although a written receipt is not required, witnesses to the transaction are prescribed so that no harm is experienced by either party.

These clear and detailed guidelines for contracts and trade were intended to ensure that contracts were entered into in good faith and that the rights and responsibilities of both parties were guaranteed as recorded in the legal document. Breach of any of the terms of the contract constituted grounds for ending the business relationship and pursuing damages in court. This model is a direct parallel to the marriage contract (*nikah*) in form, with requirements for offer and acceptance, witnesses, and a guardian standing in for a person considered unable to engage the contract in the eyes of the law.

Insistence upon a written contract was somewhat unusual in a society in which oral testimony was considered to be more reliable than writing because of fears of forgery. Classical jurists generally preferred oral testimony as court evidence. Classical legal literature also raised concerns about apparent versus hidden intentions in negotiations of terms of sale and gave attention to methods of determining the certainty of the terms of a contract.

Financial transactions were far less complicated before the European colonial era, although there were core models of contracts of sale, and full elaboration of jurisprudence on contract law did not develop until modern times. The Ottoman Majallah/Mecelle of 1869 and 1886 was developed in response to the French Napoleonic Code and became the model for codification of contract law throughout the Arab world. Consequently, the civil codes of contract law in many Arab countries are more reflective of Western civil codes than Islamic precedents. Early examples from the Arab world include the more secular Egyptian Civil Code of 1949 that became the basis for contract law in Syria, Kuwait, and Libya. However, the 1953 Iraqi Civil Code returned to a more classical Islamic legal model and became the model that was followed by later civil codes in the Arab world. One notable exception to these developments is Saudi Arabia, which continues to follow classical (typically Hanbali) jurisprudence and does not have a civil code on contracts, although efforts toward codification have been made since 2010. Saudi Arabia has been ranked by the World Bank as 140th out of 183 economies in terms of facility of enforcing contracts, but it is nevertheless also ranked as the world's eleventh easiest economy in which to do business.

How Do Shariah Principles Guide the Capitalist Market Economy?

Because Islam is a practical religion that emphasizes actions in this world with implications for the Afterlife, it is to be expected that Islamic law would address questions related to trade and profit. Islam's connection to trade and commerce began with Muhammad. Before he became a prophet, he worked in the caravan trade and married a wealthy merchant. Many passages in the Quran call for justice and honesty in the marketplace. Throughout history, bazaars have been located next to mosques. The great Muslim empires of the past engaged in a flourishing transcontinental trade with state protection and support.

Shariah principles intended to guide commerce and trade include accuracy in measurements and proportions,

safeguarding the well-being of the general public, attention to fulfillment of public needs, and avoiding hardship and exploitation of the vulnerable. Muhammad said,
"May the mercy of God be on the one who is lenient when
he sells, lenient when he buys, and lenient when he makes
a demand." The Quran condemns both the extravagant
and wasteful use of what is otherwise permissible, such
as water or food, and spending on or investment in something that is unlawful, such as gambling or alcohol, because
one person's extravagance means another person's deprivation, exploitation, or corruption. Quran 7:31 warns that
God does not love prodigals and Quran 26:152 ties wastefulness to corruption, both of which are denounced.

These principles therefore permit participation in capitalist ventures but require attention to ensure that profits are not being made at the expense of public well-being
(maslahah) or are producing unfair results. Economic
activity, enterprise, and employment are encouraged for
all people and there is recognition that different people
have different talents and abilities, so that types and levels
of work may vary. At the same time, there is also recognition that some people may not be able to work for a variety
of reasons, such as age or infirmity, so that welfare benefits are also to be made available and distributed appropriately. The ultimate point is to create a balanced society
in which productivity is encouraged, the needs of all are
cared for, and the extremes of wastefulness and extravagance, on the one hand, and laziness and negligence, on
the other, are avoided.

Shariah is neither socialist nor liberal capitalist; it takes a
middle position between the two that emphasizes the common good (maslahah). It does not prescribe either national
or common ownership of property. Rather, Shariah accepts
and respects the right of individuals and organizations to
own private property, which can only be expropriated if it

was obtained unlawfully or is to be used for public welfare or service (maslahah). In the latter case, the prior owner must be fairly compensated. At the same time, property ownership, whether by private or public entities, cannot be used to inflict harm on others.

The rise of modern interest-based capitalism in the Islamic world is associated with the European colonial era. While some reformers, such as Sayyid Ahmad Khan (India, d. 1898), called for reconciliation of Islamic rules with contemporary norms, including charging interest, others called for the development of a modern system of Islamic finance designed to prevent the exploitation, moral decay, and vast income disparities associated with interest-based capitalism. The main critique was that focusing on profit alone left the economy subject to boom and bust cycles rather than being driven by concern for the common good (maslahah).

It is important to note that Islamic economic theory was developed within the context of the struggle for independence from colonial rule and its legacy. It therefore reflects the quest for authenticity and legitimacy rooted in the Islamic tradition that was the hallmark of the reformists of the nineteenth and twentieth centuries. Critics have charged that this renders Islamic economics a reactionary and defensive theory that is weak in its scientific and theoretical bases. Proponents counter that Islamic economic theory, as it has developed since the 1970s, in particular, has centered on the moral, ethical individual rather than selfish utility, so that it respects capitalism's support for private property and free enterprise but within the parameters of protecting the public from excessive materialism and economic inequality.

In the contemporary period, some Muslim scholars have connected the global environmental crisis and the skewed distribution of economic wealth with capitalist-driven progress and development. They charge that focus on short-term profit comes at the expense of long-term damage to both human and nonhuman life and living environments. For example, Malaysian scholar and social activist Chandra Muzaffar has connected the quest for profit to rampant speculation in basic commodities, such as food and fuel that has a disproportionate negative impact on the global south. Statistics showing that the world's richest 10 percent own over 50 percent of the world's resources and the populations of wealthy countries consume as much as ten times more natural resources than poor countries support the contention that contemporary free-market capitalism fails to serve the common good (maslahah) at the global level. Some have even gone so far as to argue that the global financial market is a nonmilitant form of extremism that results in poverty, crime, radicalization, and even more deaths than militant extremism ever has, marking its clear failure to serve the common good (maslahah).

Muslim economists have also expressed concerns about the instability and excess of the capitalist market economy, seen most spectacularly in the 2007 US subprime crisis that rapidly became a global financial crisis, the reverberations from which are still being felt today. Following Shariah principles would require long-term planning, moderate spending and investment, and consideration of the impact that decisions today may have on the financial security, availability of resources, and environmental security of future generations

How Does Islamic Law View Poverty, Microfinance, and Economic Development?

Shariah principles call for attention to issues related to poverty, including the imperative to protect public welfare (maslahah), ensure that the needs of all people are fulfilled, and avoid hardship and exploitation of the vulnerable. In the past, the mechanisms for addressing poverty were charitable giving (both the annual obligatory almsgiving called zakat and supererogatory, or extra, charity called *sadaqah*), the foundation of waqf (charitable endowments), and curbing excess profits. While these were not mechanisms for promoting economic development per se, they were intended to constantly redistribute portions of the wealth of the Muslim community to assure that the needs of the most vulnerable were met.

Attention to economic development began with the rise of the European colonial era and, especially, the Industrial Revolution. The accompanying growth and dominance of Western capitalism had a negative impact on local economies and brought about the economic dependence of many Muslim-majority countries on the West. The domination of Western capitalism and industrialization is often asserted as a contributing factor to the ends of the great Mughal and Safavid empires and the decline of the Ottoman Empire.

In the nineteenth century, reforms like the Ottoman Tanzimat and the initiatives of Muhammad Ali in Egypt tried to break this dependence on the West. However, they met with limited success because revamping the economy required new large-scale infrastructure that could only be financed through Europe and the Western-owned banks (mostly British) in the region. At the same time, domestic regimes focused on achieving and maintaining political power rather than economic development, and they were filled with mismanagement and corruption, with individuals at the top claiming large portions of state budgets for themselves. State revenues were not being invested in the two most important components of the modern economy—industry and human capital, further delaying economic development.

The discovery of oil in many countries held the promise of promoting modernization and economic development and advancement. Instead, it led to the development of rentier states (states whose main revenues are derived from exports of indigenous resources). The hallmarks of these rentier states have become vast income disparities, bloated government bureaucracies, populations dependent upon government subsidies, and lack of government accountability. Concerns about the finite nature of nonrenewable natural resources, declining oil profits, and overdependency on a single commodity have led to renewed attention to economic development and diversification since the last quarter of the twentieth century.

Some countries, such as Malaysia, have chosen to follow a "middle path" of affirmative action in addressing poverty rather than nationalizing wealth or taking wealth from one community and giving it to another. Malaysia claims a success rate of reduction of absolute poverty from 50 percent to 60 percent of the total population in the 1970s to only 3 percent by 2011.

In other countries, such as Egypt, private collective savings club programs have proven helpful in promoting economic development as groups of individuals pool their resources by paying into a fund from which members can then borrow—and repay—loans, one at a time. Women have found this to be a particularly helpful way to purchase home appliances like refrigerators and washing machines, essentially borrowing directly from each other without involving banks and interest. The downside of this arrangement is that some members have to be more patient than others, as borrowing is staggered. It also remains a purely private arrangement rather than an institutionalized or national one, limiting its impact to the borrowers directly involved.

Institutionally, the development of microfinance in Bangladesh in the 1970s by economist Muhammad Yunus through the foundation of Grameen Bank brought credit and banking to the poorest of the poor. Because the poor had been shut out of standard banks and loans due to lack of capital, Yunus created a banking structure specifically designed to lend to the poor, with preferential lending to women, to finance entrepreneurial projects that would begin to earn immediate profits, albeit on a microscale. Grameen's model has been replicated in many other countries and has been recognized as a practical program for eliminating poverty, resulting in Yunus winning the Nobel Prize for Peace in 2006. Although Grameen Bank has been criticized for "un-Islamically" charging interest on these microloans, Yunus has argued that charging interest is necessary for the bank to function and that, essentially, borrowers are paying interest to themselves because every borrower not only must open a microsavings account at the time of the loan but also becomes a shareholder in the bank.

Yet for all of the theoretical support for poverty alleviation and economic development offered by Shariah, the reality remains that much of the Muslim world remains financially underdeveloped and even impoverished. Despite professed adherence to the values of caring for the least fortunate and the equality of all believers, vast income disparities and lack of integration of the poor into society are rampant throughout the Muslim world. Even investment projects funded by what are supposed to be "Shariah-compliant" financial mechanisms have often been criticized by Human Rights Watch for failure to analyze the social impact of the investments, including often dangerous working conditions, wage exploitation, and indebtedness to and dependency upon recruiters for work visas. Many of these projects finance opulent luxury developments in Muslim-majority countries that cater to the rich rather than encourage genuine economic development, poverty alleviation, or projects promoting social welfare.

How Does Islamic Finance Interact
with the Global Financial Market?

Islamic economic theory is based upon the Shariah principle of upholding public interest (maslahah). It reflects a famous hadith (saying of Muhammad) that says, "Harm may neither be inflicted nor reciprocated." This means that the law must act in such a way as to eliminate harm from society to whatever extent possible, provided that this does not result in an even greater harm. In the event that harm cannot be avoided altogether, public interest requires the choice involving the least harm. In theory, this consideration of potential harm establishes a framework that prohibits any harmful act or abusive exploitation, whether of resources or human beings. In practice, it also allows for negligible harm to be tolerated if redressing it would potentially overburden the general public. In the event of manifest or exorbitant harm, the state would be obligated to step in and take legal action.

These issues come into play with respect to the global financial market because national governments are responsible for looking out for their own interests in economic development while at the same time trying to prevent their countries from being controlled by multinational corporations and other powerful, external entities. Although international conventions and treaties can help to establish legal parameters with state actors, today's reality is that nonstate actors, ranging from businesses and research interests to pirates and guerrilla groups, are increasingly part of the global financial picture due to their impact on stability, security, and the environment. Elimination of harm without causing greater harm, whether to development plans or the human population, is increasingly challenging today.

At many levels, Shariah should in theory empower Islamic governments to block projects and enterprises that would cause damage to their people, their living conditions, and/or the environment—for example, multinational corporations entering a country to extract natural resources at the cost of destruction of the surrounding environment and the associated negative impact on the lives, health, and well-being of citizens. The legal principles of placing prevention of harm over acquiring benefit and of assuring that necessities are met as a matter of public interest should provide governments with guidelines to ensure the personal security and well-being of their citizens. Yet, in practice, governments often overlook such concerns in favor of their own financial benefit, thereby violating the Shariah principles they are supposed to uphold.

Financial globalization was touted as a means of increasing capital flows from wealthy to poor countries in order to move economic development forward. The reality has often been the opposite, as capital has flowed from poor to wealthy countries. Even influxes of capital into poorer countries have resulted in market bubbles, overinflated stocks, rising prices for basic commodities including food, and increased unemployment rather than real growth or investment. At the same time, consumerism has overtaken many aspects of society with the outsourcing of previously public jobs to private industries. All of these results challenge the Western conventional wisdom that the free market polices itself and acts in the public's interest (maslahah).

Given the widening gap between wealthy and poor both within and across countries, concerns about deleterious effects on local economies, and rising awareness of Western tendencies toward socializing risks and problems and privatizing profits, some Islamic scholars have called for a more balanced and strategic approach to participation in the global financial market. They acknowledge the benefits of trade and knowledge transfer in the fields of communications and technology while urging greater caution with respect to financial matters.

There are calls today for greater attention to poverty eradication, economic development, and social justice as the most effective means of ensuring security, stability, and job growth. While charity and charitable work remain important, development is often touted as a more effective means of fighting poverty in the long term and creating lasting investment and employment opportunities. There is widespread concern that poverty, unemployment, and unequal distribution of resources lead to social unrest and create fertile ground for extremism, violence, and other social ills, such as drug abuse and human trafficking. The public interest (maslahah) with respect to globalization clearly lies in thoughtful development that retains a degree of control over participation in the global financial market.

11

SCIENCE, BIOETHICS, AND HUMAN LIFE

In the twenty-first century, it is crucial to understand the relationship between Shariah and scientific questions about life, including medical, bioethical, and environmental decisions. Historically, Muslims viewed scientific exploration as a way to express and deepen one's faith. From 800 CE to the beginning of the modern era (fifteenth century), Islamic scientific achievements flourished in astronomy, mathematics, and medicine as well as alchemy, chemistry, botany, geography, cartography, physics, zoology, ophthalmology, and pharmacology,

Following the colonial period, as Muslim societies faced new realities and discoveries, Islamic revival and reform movements again focused on revitalizing not only interpretations of Islam and Islamic law but also the relationship between religion and science.

Bioethical and environmental issues are influenced by the Quranic view of human beings as God's vicegerents (representatives) responsible for all of God's creation, including plant and animal life, as well as by Shariah principles promoting the value of human life and Muslims' responsibility to preserve and protect the body, both matter and spirit.

This chapter details the influence of these responsibilities and values on Islamic legal perspectives. It describes Islamic legal parameters related to global environmental issues as well as Islamic moral and legal views on medical research. Questions focus on debates about cloning, stem cell research, and genetic engineering as well as multiple responses to bioethical questions regarding family planning and abortion, organ donation, and euthanasia. Beyond Islamic jurisprudence and texts, the role of individual conscience also plays a major role in Islamic bioethics, encouraging a case-oriented approach that focuses on individual circumstances guided by Shariah principles.

What Is the Relationship between Science and Shariah?

Given the sometimes troubled relationship between science and religion in Christianity and Islam today, it may be surprising to learn that historically Islam encouraged scientific and medical exploration. Muslim scientists believed that such exploration was a religious duty as it encouraged deeper understanding of and appreciation for God's creation, including human life and well-being. Many fields of mathematics, including algebra and trigonometry, and of science, ranging from astronomy and optics to surgery, owe their origins and development to Muslim scientists and physicians who built upon the heritage of ancient Greece and transmitted it to the West. In the classical era, there was no conflict between Islam and science; rather, scientific exploration was viewed as a means of expressing and deepening faith.

Since the onset of the European colonial era, in the Muslim world the relationship between religion and science has become more complex. The conquest of Muslim empires and countries by European Christian countries seemed to suggest an inherent weakness in Muslim societies, which was attributed by some to a stagnant, past-oriented religion that failed adequately to engage in a process of reform. Islamic reform movements in the late nineteenth and early twentieth centuries sought to revitalize not only interpretations of Islam and Islamic law capable of addressing new realities and discoveries, but also the historic constructive relationship between religion and science. Today, Muslim scientists, such as Nobel Prize winners Ahmed Zewail (unshared, Chemistry, Egypt-US), Mohammad Abdus Salam (joint, Physics, Pakistan), and Aziz Sancar (unshared, Chemistry, Turkey), are making important contributions in this regard.

A Pew Research Center Poll (2013) of Muslim opinions throughout Africa, Asia, and Europe found that overall, the majority of Muslims globally (54%) believe that there is no inherent conflict between religion and science. Regional variations were noticed, with strongest support for no inherent conflict found in the Middle East/North Africa region (MENA) at 75 percent, followed by 61 percent in Central Asia, 54 percent in Southeast Asia, and 50 percent in Southern-Eastern Europe. In South Asia, a strong minority (45%) supported the idea of no inherent conflict. Perhaps most surprisingly, Turkey, the only Muslim-majority country to have applied for membership in the European Union, had the most evenly split population, with 44 percent seeing no conflict and 40 percent perceiving conflict.

In comparison, 59 percent of American Muslims—higher than the global average—said they believe science and religion are fully compatible—a rate higher than that of American Christians (39%) or the American general public (37%).

The poll also found that, globally, 53 percent of Muslims believe in human evolution. In thirteen of the twenty-two countries surveyed, the majority indicated belief that human beings and other living things have evolved over time. In only four countries did majorities assert that human beings have existed in their present form since the beginning of time—Iraq (67%), Afghanistan (62%), Indonesia (55%), and Tajikistan (55%). Nevertheless, evolution has proven to be a thorny and contested issue. Like Christians, Muslims believe that God specifically and deliberately created human beings with a divine purpose. This belief is seen by many to be at odds with the premise that human beings evolved over time from other life forms. Some have also expressed concern that belief in evolution removes God and moral values from society and fails to affirm the special role of human beings as God's vicegerents on earth, as taught by the Quran. For many Muslims, as for many Christians, belief that human beings have a special purpose in the divine plan and are at the top of the hierarchy of creation is central to their faith.

American Muslims are evenly split in their belief in evolution (45%) versus denial (44%). In this, they are comparable to American Christians, 46 percent of whom say they believe in evolution, as compared to 52 percent of Americans overall.

What Parameters Does Islamic Law Establish for Dealing with Environmental Issues?

While God is the ultimate Creator and Sustainer of all that exists, the Quran nevertheless teaches that God created human beings to serve as God's vicegerents (*khalifah*) (Quran 2:30) and inheritors of the earth (Quran 6:165 and 10:14). Human beings are therefore responsible for taking care of all of God's creation, including plant and animal life. Historically, this status has often resulted in assumptions about human superiority that allow for domination of the earth and all of its life forms. Today, however, Islamic environmentalists look at the Quran and Sunna (Muhammad's example) in light of contemporary realities and call for a reinterpretation of the concept of khalifah as one of responsibility toward the earth and nature.

As God's creation, the earth and all forms of life it sustains are to be respected and protected. The Quran describes different weather patterns, including rain, wind, and sunlight, as well as natural phenomena, such as trees, plants, soil, mountains, and stars, as signs of God's power and blessing that should be responded to with gratitude (Quran 14:32, 31:20, 45:3–5). God promises that those who believe and are faithful to God's commands will be blessed with rain to bring forth fruits and grains, but that drought, poor harvests, and harsh weather will be the lot of those who do not (Quran 2:21–22, 11:52, 17:68–69). Thus, there is a clear connection between human behavior and the state of the environment.

The Sunna of the Prophet pays attention to environmental issues that include water conservation, cultivation and sustainability of the land, and maintaining a sanitary environment (not polluting walkways, shaded areas, or watering places). Water conservation was particularly important in a desert environment in which water was scarce and unfair distribution was literally a matter of life and death. Muhammad created two types of protected zones: private pasture (*hima*) and forbidden areas or zones (*haram*). Forbidden areas were often declared around wells in order to prohibit overuse of water. Private pasture areas were usually designated as wildlife reserves. Today, private pastures serve in many countries as conservation land. Muhammad also warned against overconsumption, not only because of the potential harm it caused to the land but also because it meant inattention to the less fortunate: "The person is not a proper Muslim who eats until he is full but leaves his neighbor hungry."

Muhammad encouraged people to plant trees and vege-
tation: "If a Muslim plants a tree or sows a seed, and then a
bird or a person or an animal eats from it, it is regarded as
a charitable gift (*sadaqah*) from him." Bringing unused land
under cultivation was highly praised. Similarly, cleaning
up harmful things from pathways was considered a charitable act. Even in times of war, Muhammad commanded
that the natural environment should not be destroyed.
Classical jurisprudence (Islamic law) prohibits poisoning
water supplies, destroying crops, cutting down trees, and
demolishing beehives because of the vital role food and
water play for all sources of life.

Muhammad also called for kindness to animals, such as
giving a thirsty dog or cat water to drink and respecting
and protecting bird's nests with eggs in them; he criticized
those who abused their animals, including animals used
for farming, warfare, and travel. He warned that anyone
who wrongfully killed even a sparrow would face God's
interrogation. With respect to slaughtering animals for
meat, he prescribed rules (*halal*) allowing for as quick and
painless a death as possible and avoiding needless suffering, particularly through the use of sharp knives. The
hadith (prophetic sayings) specify that animals are not to
be slaughtered in front of other animals and that animals
should not see the sharpening of the knives.

Some contemporary Muslims see tools in these Quran
verses and Muhammad's own example for addressing the
growing global environmental crisis and climate change.
The realities of climate change are seen quite starkly in
Muslim countries in the Middle East, Africa, and South
and Southeast Asia where droughts, overuse of farmland,
desertification, soil erosion, deforestation, water shortages,
disappearance of lakes and wetlands, increasing cata-
strophic natural disasters, and rising sea levels are everyday realities with a disproportionate impact on the poor,

many of whom are Muslims. Yet, as is often the case in less developed countries globally, significant conversations about environmental issues tend to take a back seat to concerns related to development. Muslim countries often point to Western patterns of overconsumption as leading to environmental degradation and economic exploitation of their countries at the same time that they seek to improve the consumption levels of their own people. Thus, for many Muslim countries, addressing environmental issues is not a national priority and Muslim environmental activists are a sometimes persecuted minority. An example is the mass arrests of those who protested the 90 percent shrinkage since the 1970s of Lake Oromiyeh in Iran.

Islamic environmental activism is a relatively new phenomenon dating to the 2000s. Most adherents are in Western countries and have had a relatively small impact so far. Nevertheless, groups like the Islamic Foundation for Ecology and Environmental Sciences (IFEES) and Wisdom in Nature provide educational workshops, programs, and training sessions to encourage grassroots activism and raise awareness of the environmental crisis among Muslim populations around the world. Their work includes organizing pro-environmental demonstrations, participating in interfaith environmental gatherings and activities, teaching organic farming practices, encouraging purchase of organic and sustainably raised foods, promoting Islamic conservation principles and practices, implementing recycling programs, and promoting "greening" of mosques by installing solar panels and water heaters, light-emitting diodes (LEDs), and low-flow toilets. In addition, IFEES convened Muslim scholars from around the world to respond to Pope Francis's encyclical, *Laudato Si'*. The result, the Islamic Declaration on Global Climate Change, rooted in the Quran and Sunna (Muhammad's example) and drawing on scientific evidence, calls upon Muslims everywhere in all positions in life to make changes in their lifestyles and government policies to address these contemporary realities that affect all people.

The guiding Shariah principles (*maqasid al-Shariah*) of preserving life, preventing exploitation, and promoting well-being all have critical environmental dimensions related to agriculture and animal husbandry. For example, some Muslim jurists permit the use of genetically modified organisms (GMOs) based on the principle of public interest (*maslahah*). Supporters argue that the greater good of providing a secure food supply to an ever-growing population by making crops more resistant to disease, insects, and a less than ideal growing environment is more important than concerns about the genetic composition of plants. Jurists who are opposed cite risks to both the environment and the human population, as the potential impacts of GMOs remain largely unknown and/or undocumented.

Similar questions are raised with respect to factory farming of animals. While supporters of factory farms argue that they permit mass production of a needed product to feed people at a reasonable price, Muslim animal rights activists counter that such mass production fails to respect animals as God's creations, in addition to failing to adhere to the guidelines established by God for halal meat slaughtered in the correct manner. They believe that greater attention should be given to the whole life of the animal, citing Muhammad's concern for animal welfare, such as forbidding beating or branding animals, cutting off their tails, or otherwise mutilating them. In addition, it is questionable whether factory farms practice proper methods of slaughter. Some Muslims, notably in the West, have begun exploring vegetarian options out of concern about factory farms and due to the difficulty of determining whether available meat sources are genuinely halal.

What Is the Islamic Legal View of Medical Research, such as Cloning, Stem Cell Research, and Genetic Engineering?

Shariah asserts the inherent value of human life and charges Muslims with the responsibility of protecting and preserving human life and preventing its forcible end, whether by murder or suicide. The Quran (Quran 3:145) assigns power over life and death to God alone and teaches that God gives each human being a soul (Quran 38:72 and 15:29). The value placed on human life as a gift from God raises moral and ethical questions for Muslims, as for Christians and Jews, with respect to medical research on human subjects or materials, such as stem cell research, human genetic engineering, and human cloning.

Stem cell research involves extraction and experimentation with undifferentiated cells that can develop into many different cell types. It is their capacity to renew themselves and become either organ- or tissue-specific cells with special functions that has made stem cells particularly interesting to medical and scientific researchers as a potential means of treating, and even curing, diseases such as diabetes. Stem cells could be used to grow new tissues or organs either to repair or to replace damaged ones.

Although there are both "adult" and embryonic stem cells, differences in their characteristics have led to preference for the greater potential found in embryonic stem cells, particularly those extracted from a blastocyst (3–5 day old embryo), for constructing all types of specialized cell types and organs. Beginning in 1998, such cells became available through embryos that were created for reproductive purposes through in vitro fertilization (IVF) and then donated for research when they were not needed. Ethicists from many religious traditions questioned the use of such embryos without first addressing questions related to when life begins, whether these potential lives had rights, and whether lives were being destroyed through such research, given that the extraction of stem cells ultimately destroys the embryo.

Classical Islamic law teaches that the fetus receives a soul either 40 or 120 days into pregnancy. Prior to ensoulment, the fetus was considered to have the potential for life but was not yet a human life. Although revisited by some contemporary jurists in light of scientific and medical advances, classical jurisprudence has proven central to contemporary discourse about stem cell research.

In fall of 1989, a committee of the Islamic Organization of Medical Sciences approved the use for research purposes of embryos left over from IVF treatments. Drawing upon classical jurisprudence, they observed that an aborted fetus is treated differently from a born baby. Fines for abortion were lower than those for murder and, although an ensouled fetus had the right to burial, the fetus was not given a name. Therefore, they concluded that an embryo is not yet technically a human being and, thus, could be used for scientific research.

However, a meeting of the Organization of the Islamic Conference (OIC) in spring 1990 ruled the exact opposite. Arguing that human dignity is not exclusively linked to human life, they pointed to the respectful treatment prescribed for the deceased. Even in death, the body was to be respected as God's creation. Although a fertilized egg could not yet be considered a human life, they nevertheless asserted its human dignity, thus prohibiting its destruction for research purposes. This is particularly true in the case of a frozen embryo, which is technically alive.

Legal systems in different countries reflect these varying perspectives. Iran, for example, has permitted stem cell research since 2002 when Ayatollah Ali Khamenei, Supreme Leader of Iran, issued a fatwa declaring embryonic stem cell research in keeping with the principle of saving life and therefore consistent with Shia practice. Among Sunnis, the strongest government and financial support for stem cell research comes from Qatar and Saudi Arabia. Malaysia hosted the first National Stem Cell Research Congress in 2012, declaring that Islam commands the use of science for human benefit as a public good (maslahah). Similarly, Jordan passed a law in 2014 to regulate stem cell research and therapy, permitting it as a public good that improves human health, but also assuring that legal parameters are in place to respect human life. At the same time, some countries prohibit stem cell research. Pakistan, for example, does not permit any lab to process or separate stem cells.

Similar debates have taken place with respect to genetic engineering. The majority of Muslim jurists oppose genetic engineering because it involves tampering with God's creation. Nevertheless, they make exceptions in the case of medical or scientific advancements that will benefit human life and welfare.

The majority of Muslim jurists also prohibit human cloning because the replication of an entire human being not only reproduces God's creation but also suggests that individual human beings are not unique and can be mechanically reproduced. Cloning further suggests, they believe, a human claim to share God's power in giving life. Some jurists have expressed concerns about the impact of cloning on issues related to lineage and inheritance. Does a clone have the same legal status as the original person? Some jurists accept cloning of body parts for the purpose of medical treatment but do not accept cloning of the entire person. A minority of jurists permit it, including the late Shia authority Ayatollah Mohammed Hussain Fadlallah, who consider cloning analogous to bringing a sperm and an egg together in the human act of reproduction.

Some Muslim jurists have accepted animal cloning, provided that certain conditions are met, namely, that there is benefit for human beings, such as through scientific or medical advancement. This potential benefit must be greater than the potential harm, and care must be taken that the animal experiences neither unnecessary harm nor suffering.

What Is the Relationship between Medicine and Shariah?

The central issue at the heart of bioethics is life—birth, death, and obligations and responsibilities during life and in facing the end of life—for oneself, for other people, and for other forms of life. Shariah asserts two main principles to guide human behavior—the injunction to save life and the prohibition against killing life—based on the belief that God is the one who holds the power, both to give life and to take life away. The practical implementation of these principles is the role of Islamic law.

Parallel to Western principles of medical ethics—doing good, autonomy, justice, and doing no harm—the Shariah principles behind medical discovery and practice are public welfare (maslahah), neither harm nor harassment, necessity, protection against distress, and averting a probable harm. The classical legal literature describes the practice of medicine as a communal obligation whose underlying purpose is to preserve life, offspring, property, religion, and reason. There may be times when necessity or extenuating circumstances require overriding the general rules or norms that would otherwise apply. For example, although consumption of pork products is generally prohibited, using a pig's heart valve for a transplant is considered permissible because the purpose is to preserve a human life.

Passages such as Quran 16:90—"Behold, God commands justice, and the doing of good, and generosity toward [one's] fellow people; and He forbids all that is shameful and all that runs counter to reason, as well as misdeeds"— point to the centrality of the public good (maslahah). In considering specific cases, Sunni jurists tend to emphasize divine command ethics—determining whether an act is good or bad based on what God has commanded about it in scripture, while Shia jurists use deontological ethics (looking at the good or evil present in the act itself based on whether it adheres to certain rules), and teleological ethics (determining the moral obligation of an action based on the good or desirable end it achieves).

Historically, the Islamic vision of the human body as consisting of both matter and spirit required both mental and physical health to be treated in the event of illness. Thus, even music had a role in curative treatments because of its ability to tap into human emotions. While the heart was known to be the center of the physical system, it was also viewed as the seat of love, anger, and perception. In order to treat the whole person, physicians were expected to study physics, ethics, and logic as well as medicine.

In classical Islamic medicine, personal conduct was important in treatment because it established the quality of the physician-patient relationship. The physician was expected to be not only knowledgeable but also well mannered and professionally dressed. The patient was expected to be honest and obedient. Being in physical contact with the patient through touch, observation, perception, and conversation in order to establish a trusting relationship was seen as critical to appropriate treatment. This approach lasted in the Near East and South Asia until the mid-nineteenth century, when the European colonial era brought modern medicine to the region. Vestiges of prior practice can be seen in many parts of the Muslim world today, particularly in an authoritarian and paternalistic approach to medicine that calls upon the patient and his or her family to do as they are told rather than participate in decision making. Patients may also deemphasize personal autonomy in favor of obedience to God or to their family, and they may accept suffering as a test or punishment from God.

Some of the differences between traditional and Western medicine have an impact on how the body is viewed. The rise of scientific medicine in the seventeenth-century West led to a split between philosophy and medicine and resulted in a more mechanical, physiological view of the body as a series of systems, separate from the psyche or self. Thus, in Western medicine, the heart is viewed as a pump within the cardiovascular system, fulfilling the function of circulating blood; it is no longer viewed as the center of love or emotion. Although patient autonomy and patient-centered care are major bioethical principles in Western medicine, the physician today, rather than a trusted participant, is more of an observer, taking a quantitative approach to examination and diagnosis—collecting and recording data, making measurements with instruments, using statistics, standardizing treatment, and maintaining objectivity. A relationship of trust and professional demeanor are not as critical to this more clinically detached approach.

Muslim critics have argued that this Western mechanistic approach results in a worldview in which the body is seen as a site for experimentation, through drugs, procedures, or machines such as life-support systems, all guided by rules and regulations, rather than a sense of personhood. Such a mechanical approach to the body, they maintain, does not consider a given treatment's impact on the person or family relations in cases such as keeping a loved one "alive" with machines or, conversely, deciding to terminate life support. In addition, emphasizing biotechnology often overlooks other pressing health issues, particularly preventable ones such as obesity, diabetes, or diseases caused by smoking, which need to be addressed with behavioral changes.

The challenge for Islamic bioethics today is to bridge the past and the present, holding on to respect for life and personhood while drawing upon knowledge gained from scientific study of the human body and human development. Space can also be left open for individual interpretation (*ijtihad*) where something is not definitively known—such as the exact moment when life begins in utero or whether absence of electrical activity in the brain truly constitutes death. Overall, the Islamic ethics of life places great value on every human life, so that issues like abortion, organ donation, and euthanasia involve decisions that have implications for the gift of life.

Islamic approaches to bioethical questions such as family planning and abortion first appeared in the 1960s, a time when population control programs were being introduced throughout the Middle East. Relevant Arabic legal texts were discovered that placed the issues within a historical perspective. In the late 1960s and early 1970s, organ transplants became the focus of controversy; many religious scholars (*ulama*) were reluctant to permit them. In the 1980s, bioethical debates led by the Muslim World League (MWL) and the Organization of the Islamic Conference (now the Organization of Islamic Cooperation) addressed issues such as the use of artificial respiration and the use of modern technology in reproductive assistance. Since the 1990s, Muslim participation in global conversations about bioethical concerns has increased significantly, as have Muslim contributions to debates about bioethics, particularly where stem cell research is concerned.

How Does Shariah Influence Muslims' Medical and Bioethical Decisions?

Many Muslims believe in the importance of "adhering to Shariah." How this is defined, however, what it means, and the extent to which "Shariah" is a determining factor in decision making is more individualized. Bioethical decisions reflect family and economic concerns. Additionally, popular preachers are often more influential in such situations than traditional Islamic authorities and official fatwas.

Because many medical decisions are considered private family matters, individual conscience often plays a greater role than formal legal opinions. Muslims are expected to bear in mind their individual accountability, knowing that they will answer to God on Judgment Day, and to discern the intention behind any given action. For example, killing is generally considered wrong. However, in the case of self-defense, where the intent is to preserve one's own life, killing might be considered acceptable.

It is also important to recognize that the Islamic approach to bioethics emphasizes communal security over the rights or needs of an individual person. For example, if carrying her pregnancy to term would endanger the mother, because she already has a relationship with many other members of the community—husband, other children, parents—her life takes precedence over that of the unborn child who has yet to form such relationships.

At the same time, Islamic bioethics also attempts to maintain a case-oriented approach where the specific circumstances of a case are taken into consideration and decisions are guided by principles rather than strict rules and regulations carried from one case to another. While some have argued that this leads to incoherence because continuity from one case outcome to another is lost, others have seen this approach as a strength because it allows each situation to remain individualized and personalized.

How Are Blood and Organ Donations Treated in Islamic Law?

At the heart of legal discussions about blood and organ donation are views of life, death, and the human body. Shariah asserts the principles of saving and protecting life, preventing harm, protecting from exploitation, and protecting dignity. The human body is to be respected as God's creation and property.

Historically, respect for the human body called for its preservation in both life and death. Muhammad forbade the pre-Islamic practice of corpse mutilation, which he considered disrespectful to God's creation. In the early years of organ transplants (late 1960s and early 1970s), Islamic legal scholars were largely opposed to such procedures because of the damage to the donor's body and because of the relatively low rates of long-term success. However, by the late 1980s, as transplants began to show long-term success, some jurists came to support organ donation, seeing preservation of human life as a higher priority than preservation of bodily integrity after death.

Western post-Enlightenment thinking considers the human body to be the property of the individual who is entrusted with decision-making power over its treatment. Technology is viewed as a tool to be used in maintaining life and avoiding death for as long as possible. Western medicine further holds a mechanical view of the body as a series of systems. If one piece breaks down, it can be replaced with another viable part in order to restore functionality to the system. For example, the heart, as a pump, can simply be replaced with another pump. It is a mechanical, rather than a moral, issue.

However, the Islamic view recognizes an intimate connection between the body and the soul. In this vision, transplanting an organ from one body to another is not a mechanical procedure but an act of receiving part of another person into oneself. Some jurists believe that the heart, in particular, retains some of the preferences of the person from whom it was transplanted, and some scholars are uncomfortable with transplants for that reason.

The ultimate legal issue is whether organ donation and transplantation constitute safe and helpful technology that seeks to preserve human life or represents desecration of the body and interference with God's will. Citing the religious duty to preserve human life, Shia jurists generally split donations into two types—minor organs (tissues that can regenerate, including blood) and major organs (those which cannot regenerate and without which life is not possible). Donation of minor organs during life is permitted without restriction. Donation of major organs is generally limited to those that do not desecrate the appearance of the body. In the case of major organs, preference remains for transplants from nonhuman animals, even those otherwise considered ritually impure, such as pigs and dogs.

The majority of Sunni jurists permit blood and organ donation based on two central principles—necessity and overall benefit. There must be clear benefit to the recipient, voluntary donation, no harm to the donor, and no financial compensation to the donor. Organ donations are restricted to necessary transplants—those in which the person's life depends on receiving the organ. Non-necessary transplants, such as plastic surgery procedures, are theoretically forbidden, although they do occur in practice. Donating an organ as an act of love or charity or out of concern for the recipient is permitted and even encouraged as a noble act that God will generously reward, particularly if the recipient is in dire need. Making use of technology to preserve and enhance human life is deemed to be in keeping with Islam's long history of encouraging scientific and medical discovery. At the same time, these jurists prohibit the sale or commodification of any part of the body as lacking respect for the body and God's ownership of it.

A minority of Sunni jurists who are opposed to organ donations cite concerns about the inevitable rise of an organ black market and the lack of respect for the body as God's creation that is inherent in thinking of it in purely mechanical terms. Some are uncomfortable with the idea of organ donation as a personal decision by one human being to save the life of another because the power of life and death is supposed to reside with God. Supporters of organ donation have counterargued that God still retains power, as not all organ transplants are successful. It is thus wrong to consider organ donation "playing God" because it does not guarantee the continuation of life. It simply provides the mechanism by which this may occur.

Even among those who approve organ donation, there is great concern about the potential for exploitation of the poor via organ trafficking, particularly for kidneys, in areas where there are large disparities in wealth. Children are the most disproportionately affected as nonvoluntary "donors." Gulf countries rely heavily on poor living donors recruited from India, Pakistan, the Philippines, Eastern Europe, and, increasingly, China. "Transplant tourism" is becoming popular, with donors in Pakistan, India, and Indonesia supplying organs to tourists coming from the Indian subcontinent and the Middle East. Kuwait and Saudi Arabia receive many living donors from East and Southeast Asia. Some jurists, rather than issuing a blanket statement permitting organ donations, insist that the economic circumstances of the donor be taken into individual consideration because of the realities surrounding people in poor countries and war zones. There are also concerns among jurists that marginalized family members are sometimes pressured to donate organs to more prestigious members. Statistics show that a rising number of young women, aged twenty to thirty, are donating kidneys due to social pressure. Prevention of this exploitation requires concern for the preservation and protection of human life in both directions. Many countries have passed laws and there are fatwas prohibiting paid donations and the sale of human organs. In addition, Egypt has a law requiring that the donor and the recipient share the same nationality.

Some hesitation has also been expressed with respect to nonliving donors. Concern about the potential for misdiagnosis of brain death because of the desire to harvest the person's organs and about exploitation of the poor and vulnerable led the Islamic Fiqh Academy of the Organization of the Islamic Conference in 1986 to issue a statement on what constitutes legal death, citing either complete and irreversible stoppage of the heart and breathing or complete and irreversible stoppage of all vital brain functions. This guideline provided a foundation for approving transplants from brain-dead donors and those without a beating heart. Additional statements on organ donation since then include fatwas from Egypt's Dar al-Ifta (House of Fatwas) and the Islamic Charter of Medical Ethics issued to the World Health Organization, and statements by regional societies such as the Islamic Medical Association of North America. Although these fatwas and statements do not constitute national legislation, they nevertheless have an impact on debates and reflect consensus among Islamic and other biomedical statements that oppose the exploitation of individuals for organ donation through financial incentives.

In practice, of all Middle Eastern countries, only Saudi Arabia, Qatar, Kuwait, and Iran permit nonliving donation. Saudi Arabia, Iran, and Kuwait permit commercial trade in organs from deceased donors. Iran even offers government compensation for kidney donors, whereas Egypt and Pakistan permit transplants only from living donors. The

UAE does not permit any transplant procedures, although it sponsors nationals to go abroad for transplants and assists in paying the costs of the surgery.

In comparison, despite the widespread practice and encouragement of organ donation in the United States, American Muslims remain largely reluctant to donate organs. African American Muslims are the most resistant because of concerns about their potentially being exploited due to their race in the market for organs.

How Are Contraception and Family Planning Treated in Islamic Law?

Historically, Islam, like Christianity and Judaism, celebrated human fertility as a gift from God and ongoing evidence of God's creative power. Large families assured a strong and flourishing faith community and met the needs of society. Procreation and the formation of the Muslim family were considered among the primary purposes of marriage, although not the only ones. At the same time, practical concerns about the cost of supporting a large family and about the health and well-being of the mother resulted in a long history of discussion and debate about the legality of contraception and family planning. Unlike Christianity and Judaism, which, historically, have had more restrictive views on contraception, the Islamic tradition also emphasized the intent of human responsibility in controlling fertility out of concern for the welfare and well-being not only of the potential child but also for the family unit as a whole.

Although the Quran does not make any explicit mention of contraception, hadith (prophetic traditions) record Muhammad's approval of the use of coitus interruptus. Use of this method was not simply the husband's prerogative, however; the wife's consent was required because she would be giving up the possibilities of children and sexual satisfaction, to which she was legally entitled. The vast majority of legal scholars and all of the major schools of Islamic law have accepted coitus interruptus as permissible between husband and wife.

Using a combination of sacred texts, biological knowledge, and reason, Muslim jurists expanded the permissible methods of family planning and contraception from earliest times, using the legal tool of analogy (*qiyas*) to permit other forms of birth control. Legal justifications for the practice of contraception by married couples include avoiding pregnancy due to health risks for the wife or for a breast-feeding child, concerns about the negative impact of repeated pregnancies on the wife and other children, the need to space out pregnancies, preventing transmission of infectious or hereditary diseases, avoiding genetic risks due to consanguinity, economic hardship, and the need to provide for the education of existing children.

Modern jurists, both Sunni and Shia, have used analogy to permit modern chemical and mechanical forms of birth control, ranging from contraceptive pills and intrauterine devices (IUDs) that prevent implantation to barrier methods such as condoms and diaphragms. The critical criterion for permissibility is that the method must be temporary, rather than permanent, so as not to limit or counter God's creative power. Temporary methods leave open future potential fertility and are not foolproof, so that God's intervention remains possible. Although there is no clear text in the Quran or example of Muhammad forbidding more permanent measures, such as sterilization, jurists have consistently opposed the practice because it gives the impression of seeking to limit God's creative power by permanently altering what God has created; human beings should not seek to control divine power.

In keeping with the spirit of Shariah, general rules and guidelines can always be overridden in the case of necessity. For example, Muslim jurists may be opposed in general to permanent, irreversible measures such as vasectomy or tubal ligation, but they permit it in cases where the wife's life would be endangered by a future pregnancy. In such cases, the imperative to preserve her life would permit what would otherwise be forbidden. There are some contemporary debates about whether sterilization simply to avoid having more children should be considered religiously acceptable in a time of concerns about global overpopulation, but the vast majority of jurists remain opposed to this method except when there is a medical reason for it.

A conservative minority of jurists and local religious leaders today claim that contraception overall is prohibited by Islam because Muhammad commanded an increase in the number of Muslims. They say that contraception is infanticide, which is expressly forbidden in the Quran, that it is contrary to belief in God's power and control over destiny, that it ignores the Quranic mandate to trust and rely on God, that it ignores the understanding that procreation is at the heart of marriage, and that birth control campaigns and programs are part of a Western conspiracy to limit the number of Muslims and thus subdue Islam. However, the majority of jurists today uphold the permissibility of family planning, provided that this is a mutual decision made by the husband and wife.

As with other bioethical issues, the reality of practice throughout the Muslim world varies with the opinions of jurists. In northern Tanzania, for example, despite broad juridical disapproval, sterilization has become an attractive option for Muslim women with at least six children. These women justify sterilization in the belief that a smaller number of children means greater ability for quality parenting, as well as providing the economic means necessary for their education. They also argue that sterilization is more efficient than temporary methods—easier and with no side effects, requiring one hospital visit rather than the ongoing use of other methods.

Despite widespread juridical approval for family planning, a 2013 Pew Research Center poll surveying twenty-one countries in Africa, Asia, and Europe found that in only three of those countries did majorities of the population find it acceptable for married couples to choose to limit the number of children they have—Indonesia (61%), Tajikistan (58%), and Tunisia (51%). Otherwise, although the majority generally did not object to family planning as morally wrong, they nevertheless remained reluctant to practice it. At the same time, concerns about population explosions in areas with limited and shrinking resources, the impact of urbanization and the associated increased cost of living, and the ongoing struggle against poverty and illiteracy have led to government-sponsored family planning programs and policies in many Muslim countries, including Indonesia, Egypt, Iran, and Bangladesh. Success has been mixed. The methods most likely to be successful are those that enjoy the support of religious leaders who promote the legitimacy of birth control within the Islamic tradition.

How Does Islamic Law View Assisted Reproductive Technology (ART) and Other Fertility Treatments?

Islam places high importance on the family, procreation, and preservation of children. The Quran celebrates human fertility as a gift from God. The main goal of marriage in Islam is the formation of a stable and pious family. This centrality of the family in Islam has always rendered infertility a source of frustration and worry for married couples, as infertility constitutes grounds for divorce by either spouse.

In the past, infertile couples had few options. Fostering an orphan or family member was encouraged as an act of charity, based on the example of Muhammad, who was raised by his grandfather and then his uncle following the deaths of his parents. However, adoption in the sense of claiming an adoptee as your own progeny was generally forbidden because of the associated claims for lineage and inheritance.

The guiding Shariah principle with respect to infertility treatments is integrity of the marriage. Any procedure that uses the egg and sperm of the married couple, such as artificial insemination or in vitro fertilization with the husband's sperm, use of drugs or hormonal therapies to promote ovulation, or methods to increase the husband's sperm count is considered licit. Even though no sexual act takes place, procedures using the egg or sperm of a third party are considered illicit because of the legal implication of adultery. The resulting child is not the product of the husband and wife and is considered illegitimate and thus not permitted to share in lineage or inheritance. This line of reasoning parallels that of the historical prohibition on adoption.

An important exception on third-party donation is found in Iran, where Supreme Leader Ayatollah Ali Khamenei legalized third-party sperm and egg donation in 1999. Although sperm donation was subsequently banned by legislators in 2003, egg donation remains permissible because of the legal precedents established in Shia jurisprudence, which accepts polygyny and temporary marriages (*mutah*). Embryo donation was legalized in 2003.

The importance placed on procreation helps to explain the popularity of and national investment in infertility treatment, particularly through assisted reproductive technology (ART), in the Muslim world. For example, all Gulf Cooperation Council (GCC) states have legalized ART exclusively for married heterosexual couples. There are fifty licensed in vitro fertilization (IVF) centers in the Gulf serving a regional population of about 55 million people.

Because the science and technology used in ART are very new, multiple legal and ethical dilemmas are still being debated because there are no crystal clear precedents in the Quran or Sunnah.

Questions considered by jurists include what to do if the husband dies before the embryo is implanted or if the couple divorces, in which case the child would no longer be born to a married couple. Most jurists oppose implantation in such cases. Yet laws in the GCC countries do not require the husband's presence for the embryo transfer.

Some questions focus on the health of the future child. Should the embryo be tested for genetic diseases and chromosomal anomalies and, if these are found, can the couple choose not to implant the embryo? If not implanted, what should happen to the embryo? Is it a human life, a potential human life, or no life at all? Does it have any associated rights? Jurists are divided over these questions. Some believe that the embryos represent life or potential life and should not be destroyed, while others say potential life occurs only after implantation.

Some jurists fear abuse of God's gift of fertility. They divide over questions such as whether it is right to use ART for sex selection or eugenics to produce "designer" babies. Some jurists accept sex selection so that families can balance the ratio of boys and girls, while others reject this as "playing God."

Other jurists are concerned about potential human error, such as transferring the wrong embryo, or the possible misuse of "extra" embryos for research or sale without the couple's knowledge or consent. Do these possibilities justify forbidding the practice altogether?

A commonly discussed moral and ethical dilemma involves the "potential life" status of "extra" embryos that are fertilized but not transferred due to concerns about multiple pregnancy or to save them for a later time. Or, if multiple embryos are implanted, which embryo can be removed to ensure the survival of the remaining embryo(s)? Which potential life has greater value over another?

In Theory and Practice, How Is Abortion Handled in Islamic Law?

Neither the Quran nor the Sunnah (Muhammad's example) makes a clear statement about abortion, but the Quran places high value on human life and its preservation. Killing one's offspring is prohibited, even in the case of extreme poverty or hunger (Quran 17:31). Quran 4:93 further promises punishment in both this life and in the Afterlife for the unlawful killing of a human being. The fundamental objectives of the Shariah—preserving life, offspring, property, and religion, and use of reason—further underscore the value of life and human responsibility for it. Given Islam's emphasis on life and support for the importance of procreation in marriage, it is not surprising that Muslims, like Christians, give great attention to the question of what, exactly, constitutes life and when life begins when dealing with the thorny question of abortion.

The Quran declares God to be the deliberate and purposeful Creator of human life. Verses such as Quran 23:12–13 describe the seven stages of a human embryo's development, which jurists interpret to mean that the fetus gradually progresses toward becoming human. Quran 38:72 describes God giving each fetus a soul: "When I have shaped him and breathed from My Spirit into him, bow down to him."

Receiving the soul distinguishes human beings from the rest of creation (Quran 15:29), but the Quran does not specify exactly when ensoulment—the joining of the soul to the body that marks the beginning of life—takes place. This is a critical issue for jurists dealing with abortion because after ensoulment the fetus is considered a person with rights, including the right not to be aborted, the right to a funeral/burial in the event of miscarriage, and rights of lineage, inheritance, and bequests.

Many classical jurists determined that the fetus received its soul one hundred twenty days into pregnancy, based on a hadith (prophetic saying) in which Muhammad outlined three distinct forty-day phases of development prior to ensoulment: "The germ of every one of you is concentrated in his mother's womb in the form of a drop for forty days; then he becomes a clot of blood for the same period; then he becomes a piece of flesh for the same period; then the angel is sent to ensoul him." One hundred twenty days into pregnancy further corresponds to the "quickening," or time when the mother is first able to perceive movement. Other jurists ruled that ensoulment occurs forty days into pregnancy.

Regardless of the timeline, jurists consistently ruled against abortion of an ensouled fetus, considering it the killing of an innocent life. While some conservative jurists consider abortion to be prohibited at any stage of pregnancy because the fetus is "on its way" to receiving a soul, others did not object to ending pregnancy in its first trimester because the fetus was not yet seen as a person with legal rights. Although it was permissible, abortion was nevertheless considered reprehensible. Limited grounds for licit abortions were set, with the most important requirement being the consent of both husband and wife.

In addition to consulting these classical sources, Muslim jurists when considering abortion today must also address

contemporary medical, scientific, and technological discoveries. Sophisticated images of fetal development have
led some jurists to question whether it is still possible to
assign a date at which ensoulment occurs, as this cannot
be quantified scientifically. At the same time, it is possible to recognize human features in a fetus at much earlier stages. Therefore, like the Vatican, some jurists, hold
that life begins at conception. Nevertheless, the majority
prefers a less absolutist approach that permits consideration of extenuating circumstances, rather than fetal
development alone.

Because Islamic law is intended to be flexible and not
absolute, exceptions to the general rules against abortion
have always existed. Islamic law calls for addressing each
case individually and considering all specific circumstances. Unlike Christians who tend to focus on the sanc-
tity of each individual life, Muslims emphasize community
life with each individual living in relationship with others.
An individual's life is seen as one good among many others and, so, new life occurs within a complex and growing
web of existing relationships.

Thus, the most important and consistent exception to
prohibitions against abortion occurs when the mother's
life is in danger. Because she already lives in relationships
with others and has family responsibilities and duties, her
life takes priority over that of the fetus. Historically, many
jurists also considered a nursing child to have priority over
a fetus because the nutritional needs of the child could be
disrupted by a pregnancy.

In the case of a pregnancy resulting from rape, legal
scholars are divided about the issue of "harm." While the
rape itself is clearly a harm, the resulting fetus might not
necessarily be considered a harm unless it poses a risk to the
mother's life. Some jurists have further expressed concern
about abortion constituting a harm to the innocent fetus.

On the other hand, contemporary realities, like systematic rape used as a war tool in the Bosnia and Kosovo wars, the 1990 Iraqi invasion of Kuwait, and ISIS atrocities, have led some muftis to permit abortions or abortifacient medicines. They recognize the potential gross harm to mother and child—stigma, discrimination, isolation, social and emotional injury, and impact on a woman's marital status, either susceptibility to divorce or restriction of marital opportunities.

Other abortion controversies involve quality of life, as in the case of a deformed fetus, and economic circumstances, such as financial ability to support a child or provide a good standard of living for existing children. The most sensitive cases involve abortions for the sake of sex selection or resulting from an illicit relationship, both broadly prohibited.

The complex issues surrounding abortion reflect the sharp contrast between theoretical permission in legal literature and actual practice. Regardless of legal justification in certain circumstances, the surrounding ethical climate remains opposed to abortion, given the emphasis on the values of life and community morality. In practice, a 2013 Pew Research Center Poll found that the majority of Muslims globally believe that abortion is morally wrong, with the highest rates of disapproval in Thailand (99%), Cameroon (95%), Tanzania (94%), and Indonesia (93%). Of the twenty-three countries polled, in only five did 10 percent or more of the population believe that abortion is morally permissible. At the same time, thirteen countries, mostly in the Middle East/North Africa region, said that abortion was not a moral issue, and in eleven countries, at least 10 percent of those polled said that the morality depends on the situation. The issues are, therefore, not as clear-cut as legal literature might suggest.

National laws of Muslim-majority countries do not necessarily reflect Shariah, either, and Islamic legal scholars do not always agree with the national laws. Only three Muslim-majority countries permit abortions for reasons other than the mother's health. Tunisia has the most liberal abortion laws, permitting abortion on demand during the first trimester. Turkey also permits abortion on demand during the first ten weeks. Iran permits consideration of a list of certain serious conditions for either the mother or the fetus, but only within the first sixteen weeks of pregnancy and then only if two doctors affirm the seriousness of the physical or psychological condition. Although abortion is illegal in Indonesia outside of issues related to the mother's health, there are nevertheless scholars such as Achmad Ghazali who have ruled that abortion should be an option in cases of rape and incest. Other jurists have used the legal concept of public welfare (maslahah) to argue against abortion, expressing concerns about social disintegration and the negative impact on family cohesion that abortion can produce. Abortion, they argue, stands in direct contradiction to the main goal of marriage in Islam—the formation of a stable and pious family.

Abortion is typically condemned by religious leaders and absent from public sector programs, often due to concern that availability of abortion could result in an increase in sexual promiscuity. In most Muslim countries, public health abortion services are not available, so services are limited to those who can afford to pay for them privately. As in many other countries in the world, the unavailability of legal abortions does not necessarily reduce the demand for abortion. Where licensed physicians are unable or unwilling to provide such services, women often turn to other practitioners, often with fatal consequences. In Egypt today, the most frequent cause of maternal mortality is illegal abortion.

How Is Euthanasia Seen in Islamic Law?

Shariah calls for the preservation of human life and prohibits taking it away, whether by murder or suicide. As Quran 3:145 explains, God holds power over both life and death. Historically, death was understood to be the moment when the soul was separated from the body and was defined as the moment when the heart stopped beating. Death was a family matter and typically occurred in the privacy of the family home. Strokes, brain injuries, aneurysms, kidney disease, and severe infections often ended in death.

Modern medicine's ability to prolong the life of the body past its otherwise appointed time raises new questions about how life and death are defined, whether all life is worth preserving, and in what circumstances euthanasia might be considered. Many conditions that once inevitably led to death are treatable today. The patient may be left dependent on ventilators and other technologies that keep the body alive, despite brain death. Death is now more likely to occur in hospitals or nursing homes rather than in the privacy of the family home.

In Islamic law, death carries important legal implications for inheritance, marital status, and business contracts. In addition, a person who is dying is considered to be in an altered mental state and cannot make certain types of legal and financial decisions. Circumstances such as brain death, in which a person's status is ambiguous, have led to significant debates among Muslim jurists.

Brain death became broadly accepted as the criterion for declaring a patient dead in the landmark 1968 report "A Definition of Irreversible Coma." Debates among Muslim legal scholars about brain death and euthanasia date to the 1970s. In 1986, the Islamic Fiqh Academy issued a statement redefining legal death in terms of certain irreversible conditions, either when the heart and breathing have completely stopped or when all of the vital functions of the brain have stopped and the brain begins to degenerate. The physician is responsible for determining when death has occurred. The critical issue is body functionality rather than quality of life, which tends not to receive much attention in Islamic legal literature, given the Shariah's emphasis on the value of all life as a gift from God. Accordingly, there is no life that is not worth living.

Since the 1980s, Sunni jurists have largely accepted the concept of brain death, although, theoretically, God always retains the option of intervention and recovery. Some Sunni jurists prefer to think of brain death as an intermediate state between life and death during which some functions, such as heartbeat, may continue. A minority of Sunni jurists, citing the potential for overdiagnosis in order to harvest organs, do not recognize brain death. Shia jurists generally prefer the more classical definition of death as the cessation of heart function.

The 1981 Islamic Code of Medical Ethics rejects euthanasia, or "mercy killing," outright, arguing that modern medication and neurosurgery provide effective means of controlling pain, thus eliminating "quality of life" arguments based on unbearable suffering. Pain control is always permitted since it does not impact the ultimate outcome of the illness.

Western ethical debates about euthanasia tend to focus on the "right to die" and patients' dignity and control over their bodies. Muslim jurists, by contrast, see human dignity residing in patients' relationship with God and their responsibility to care for the body God has entrusted to them. Decisions regarding the body, such as forcing a premature end to life for oneself or for someone else, carry implications for the Afterlife. Importantly, Muslims believe that they have both the right and the duty to seek medical treatment for illness or injury because healing comes from God.

Like Western ethicists, Muslim jurists distinguish between "active" and "passive" euthanasia. The central legal issue is the decision maker's intent. Muslim jurists overwhelmingly reject active euthanasia because it involves a physician's direct intervention in terminating a life by lethal means. This action, whether voluntary (when a patient agrees to terminate his or her life) or involuntary (when someone else makes the decision), is viewed as killing. Although voluntary euthanasia carries a connotation of suicide, jurists do recognize a qualitative difference since, unlike suicide, euthanasia either speeds up an inevitable process of death or removes hindrances to a naturally occurring death. Similarly, although involuntary euthanasia carries connotations of murder since a deliberate choice is made by someone other than the patient to end that patient's life, jurists nevertheless consider the context to be comparable to killing a mortally wounded person rather than an act of murder. The act of killing is still rejected but is considered a lesser harm than murder because the patient was going to die anyway.

Passive euthanasia, withdrawing care to allow a terminally ill patient to die naturally, is more broadly accepted, but only when the patient's condition is permanent, irreversible, and expected to lead to death within days or weeks, such as when a terminally ill cancer patient elects to end chemotherapy treatments. However, palliative care is recommended and hydration and nutrition are always required.

The greatest challenges involve terminally ill or lethally injured patients, who have already been placed on life support, with no prospects for recovery. Most jurists would consider it acceptable to have allowed such patients to die of natural causes prior to life support. Removing life support is more problematic because it involves a deliberate

444

4444

human action causing death. Some opposed to ending life support argue that as long as the heart is still beating, the patient is still alive, and so life support must continue and any secondary illness or infection be treated. Disconnecting life support would constitute killing. However, others permit removing machines if a physician determines the heartbeat is due exclusively to the machine, which already marks human interference with natural death. Still others argue that indefinitely leaving a person on life support constitutes disrespect of the body, exposing it to useless treatment and preventing the person from entering the Afterlife.

In practice, Muslims overwhelmingly condemn suicide as immoral and generally consider euthanasia to be morally wrong. A 2013 Pew Research Center poll found that 75 percent of Muslims globally condemn suicide as immoral, with highest rates of disapproval found in Southeast Asia (92% or higher). Rates of disapproval for euthanasia were more than 75 percent in seventeen of thirty-seven countries surveyed, although minorities in six countries said that the moral status of euthanasia depends on the context in which it occurs.

BIBLIOGRAPHY

Abdel Haleem, Muhammad. *The Qur'an: A New Translation*.
New York: Oxford University Press, 2008.

Abdel Haleem, Muhammad. *Understanding the Qur'an: Themes and Style*.
London: I.B. Tauris, 2011.

Abdul Majeed, Abu Bakar. "Islam in Malaysia's Planning and
Development Doctrine." In *Islam and Ecology: A Bestowed Trust*, edited
by Richard C. Foltz, Frederick M. Denny, and Azizan Baharuddin,
463–76. Cambridge, MA: Harvard University Press, 2003.

Abdul-Matin, Ibrahim. *Green Deen: What Islam Teaches about Protecting
the Planet*. San Francisco: Berrett-Koehler Publishers, Inc., 2010.

Abou El Fadl, Khaled. *The Authoritative and the Authoritarian in Islamic
Discourses: A Contemporary Case Study*. 2nd ed. Austin, TX: Dar
Taiba, 1997.

Abou El Fadl, Khaled. *Speaking in God's Name: Islamic Law, Authority,
and Women*. Oxford: OneWorld, 2001.

Abou Ramadan, Moussa. "The Transition from Tradition to
Reform: The Shari'a Appeals Court Rulings on Child Custody
(1992–2001)." *Fordham International Law Journal* 26, no. 3 (2002).

AbuBakr, Aaishah. "Rape: Fallacies of the Four Witness requirement."
The Express Tribune, December 23, 2011.

Afsaruddin, Asma. *Contemporary Issues in Islam*. Edinburgh: Edinburgh
University Press, 2015.

Afsaruddin, Asma. *The First Muslims: History and Memory*.
Oxford: OneWorld, 2008.

Afsaruddin, Asma. *Striving in the Path of God: Jihad and Martyrdom in
Islamic Thought*. New York: Oxford University Press, 2013.

Ahdar, Rex, and Nicholas Aroney, eds. *Shari'a in the West*. New York: Oxford University Press, 2010.

Ahmad, Ahmad Atif. "Al-Ghazali's Contribution to the Sunni Juristic Discourses on Apostasy." *Journal of Arabic and Islamic Studies* 7 (2007): 50–73.

Ahmed, Habib, Mehmet Asutay, and Rodney Wilson, eds. *Islamic Banking and Financial Crisis: Reputation, Stability, and Risks*. Edinburgh: Edinburgh University Press, 2014.

Ahmed, Leila. *Women and Gender in Islam*. New Haven, CT: Yale University Press, 1992.

Ali, Kecia. *Sexual Ethics and Islam: Feminist Relfections on Qur'an, Hadith, and Jurisprudence*. Expanded & revised ed. Oxford: OneWorld, 2016.

Ali, Wajahat, et al. "Fear, Inc.: The Roots of the Islamophobia Network in American." The Center for American Progress, August 2011.

Alkhatib, Ihsan Ali. "Shariah Law and American Family Courts: Judicial Inconsistency on the Talaq and Mahr Issues in Wayne County, Michigan." *The Journal of Law in Society* 14 (2013): 83–105.

Alwani, Zainab. "Domestic Violence." In *The Oxford Encyclopedia of Islam and Women*, edited by Natana J. DeLong-Bas, Vol. 1. New York: Oxford University Press, 2013.

Amanat, Abbas, and Frank Griffel, eds. *Shari'a: Islamic Law in the Contemporary Context*. Stanford, CA: Stanford University Press, 2007.

Amir-Moezzi, Mohammad Ali. "Dissimulation." [Supplement 2017]. In *Encyclopaedia of the Qur'ān*, edited by Jane Dammen McAuliffe, Georgetown University, Washington DC. <http://dx.doi.org/10.1163/1875-3922_q3_EQCOM_050513>

Ammar, Nawal. "Ecological Justice and Human Rights for Women in Islam." In *Islam and Ecology: A Bestowed Trust*, edited by Richard C. Foltz, Frederick M. Denny, and Azizan Baharuddin, 377–89. Cambridge, MA: Harvard University Press, 2003.

An-Na'im, Abdullahi Ahmed. *African Constitutionalism and the Role of Islam*. Philadelphia: University of Pennsylvania Press, 2006.

An-Na'im, Abdullahi Ahmed. *Islam and the Secular State: Negotiating the Future of Shari'a*. Cambridge, MA: Harvard University Press, 2009.

An-Na'im, Abdullahi Ahmed. *Toward an Islamic Reformation: Civil Liberties, Human Rights, and International Law*. Syracuse: Syracuse University Press, 1990.

An-Na'im, Abdullahi. *What Is an American Muslim?: Embracing Faith and Citizenship*. New York: Oxford University Press, 2014.

An-Na'im, Abdullahi, and edited by Mashood E. Baderin. *Islam and Human Rights: Selected Essays of Abdullahi An-Na'im*. New York: Routledge, 2010.

An-Na'im, Abdullahi A., ed. *Cultural Transformation and Human Rights in Africa*. London: Zed Books, 2002.

An-Na'im, Abdullahi A., ed. *Islamic Family Law in a Changing World: A Global Resource Book*. London: Zed Books, 2002.

Anwar, Etin. "Female Genital Mutilation." In *The Oxford Encyclopedia of the Islamic World*, edited by John L. Esposito. New York: Oxford University Press, 2009.

Anwar, Ghazala. "Irtidad." In *The Oxford Encyclopedia of the Islamic World*, edited by John L. Esposito. New York: Oxford University Press, 2009.

Arenfeldt, Pernille, and Nawar Al-Hassan Golley, eds. *Mapping Arab Women's Movements: A Century of Transformations from Within*. Cairo: The American University in Cairo Press, 2012.

Asem, Sondos. "US International Religious Freedom Policy from an Egyptian Perspective." *The Review of Faith & International Affairs* 11, no. 1 (2013).

Auda, Jasser. *Maqasid al-Shariah as Philosophy of Islamic Law: A Systems Approach*. Herndon, VA: The International Institute of Islamic Thought, 2008.

Awad, Abed. "The True Story of Sharia in American Courts," *The Nation*, June 13, 2012.

Azam, Hina. "Rape." In *The Oxford Encyclopedia of Islam and Law*, Oxford Islamic Studies Online, edited by Jonathan A.C. Brown. New York: Oxford University Press, 2013.

Azam, Hina. *Sexual Violation in Islamic Law: Substance, Evidence, and Procedure*. New York: Cambridge University Press, 2017.

Barlas, Asma. "Believing Women." In *Islam: Unreading Patriarchal Interpretations of the Qur'an*. Austin: University of Texas Press, 2002.

Basarudin, Azza. *Humanizing the Sacred: Sisters in Islam and the Struggle for Gender Justice in Malaysia*. Seattle, WA: University of Washington Press, 2016.

Berkey, Jonathan P. *The Formation of Islam: Religion and Society in the Near East, 600–1800*. New York: Cambridge University Press, 2003.

"Best Practices: Progressive Family Laws in Muslim Countries." Woodrow Wilson Center for Scholars: Middle East Program and Rand Corporation, August 2005.

Black, Ann. "In the Shadow of Our Legal System: Shari'a in Australia." In *Shari'a in the West*, edited by Rex Ahdar and Nicholas Aroney. New York: Oxford University Press, 2010.

Bonney, Richard. *Jihad: From Qur'an to bin Laden*. New York: Palgrave Macmillan, 2004.

Brinner, William M., and Devin J. Stewart. "Conversion." In *The Oxford Encyclopedia of the Islamic World*, edited by John L. Esposito. New York: Oxford University Press, 2009.

Brockopp, Jonathan E. *Early Maliki Law: Ibn 'Abd al-Hakam and His Major Compendium of Jurisprudence*. Leiden: Brill, 2000.

Brockopp, Jonathan E. *Islamic Ethics of Life: Abortion, War, and Euthanasia*. Columbia, SC: University of South Carolina Press, 2002.

Brockopp, Jonathan E., and Thomas Eich, eds. *Muslim Medical Ethics: From Theory to Practice*. Columbia, SC: University of South Carolina Press, 2008.

Brown, Jonathan A.C. *Hadith: Muhammad's Legacy in the Medieval and Modern World*. Oxford: OneWorld, 2009.

Brown, Jonathan A.C. *Misquoting Muhammad: The Challenge and Choices of Interpreting the Prophet's Legacy*. Oxford: OneWorld, 2014.

Brown, Nathan J. *The Rule of Law in the Arab World: Courts in Egypt and the Gulf*. New York: Cambridge University Press, 1997.

"Can Non-Muslim Children Inherit from Their Muslim Father?" Sunnah.org, As-Sunnah Foundation of America, July 26, 2013. http://sunnah.org/msaec/articles/inherit.htm.

"Capital Punishment." In *The Islamic World: Past and Present*, edited by John L. Esposito. New York: Oxford University Press, 2004.

Charrad, Mounira M. *States and Women's Rights: The Making of Postcolonial Tunisia, Algeria, and Morocco*. Berkeley, CA: University of California Press, 2001.

Cochran, Cybele. "Women and the Law in Islamic Societies: Legal Responses to Domestic Violence in Saudi Arabia and Morocco," *al-Nakhlah*, Spring 2009.

Cook, Michael. *Commanding Right and Forbidding Wrong in Islamic Thought*. New York: Cambridge University Press, 2000.

Coulson, Noel James. *A History of Islamic Law*. Edinburgh: Edinburgh University Press, 1964.

Coulson, Noel James. "Shari'ah." In Encyclopedia Britannica Online. Encyclopedia Britannica Inc, 2016. <http://www.britannica.com/topic/Shariah>.

"Country Reports on Human Rights Practices – 2004: Tunisia." Bureau of Democracy, Human Rights, and Labor, US Department of State, February 28, 2005.

Debs, Richard. *Islamic Law and Civil Code: The Law of Property in Egypt.* New York: Columbia University Press, 2010.

DeLong-Bas, Natana J. *Islam: A Living Faith.* Winona, MN: Anselm Academic, 2018.

DeLong-Bas, Natana J. *Wahhabi Islam: From Revival and Reform to Global Jihad*, rev. ed. New York: Oxford University Press, 2008.

DeLong-Bas, Natana J., Editor-in-Chief. *The Oxford Encyclopedia of Islam and Women.* 2 vols. New York: Oxford University Press, 2013.

"Depriving Women of Inheritance Violates Islam: Egyptian Cleric," *Al Arabiyya News*, April 22, 2012.

"Domestic Violence against Women in Turkey," Turkish Republic Prime Ministry Directorate General on the Status of Women, 2008.

Doumani, Beshara B. *Family Life in the Ottoman Mediterranean: A Social History.* New York: Cambridge University Press, 2017.

Dugger, Celia W. "Report Finds Gradual Fall in Female Genital Cutting in Africa." *The New York Times*, July 22, 2013.

"Egypt: Are Attitudes to Rape Beginning to Change?" IRIN. http://www.irinnews.org/report/76827/egypt-are-attitudes-to-rape-beginning-to-change.

El Alami, Dawoud Sudqi, and Doreen Hinchcliffe. *Islamic Marriage and Divorce Laws of the Arab World.* London: Kluwer Law International, 1996.

El-Ashker, Ahmed, and Rodney Wilson. *Islamic Economics: A Short History.* Leiden: Brill, 2006.

El Feki, Shereen. *Sex and the Citadel: Intimate Life in a Changing Arab World.* New York: Pantheon Books, 2013.

Elliott, Andrew. "The Man behind the Anti-Shariah Movement." *The New York Times*, July 30, 2011.

Elver, Hilal. *The Headscarf Controversy: Secularism and Freedom of Religion.* New York: Oxford University Press, 2012.

Esposito, John L. *The Future of Islam.* New York: Oxford University Press, 2010.

Esposito, John L. "Pluralism," in *The Oxford Encyclopedia of the Islamic World*, edited by John L. Esposito. New York: Oxford University Press, 2009.

Esposito, John L. "Pluralism in Muslim-Christian Relations." ACMCU Occasional Paper, Washington, DC, April 2008.

Esposito, John L. *What Everyone Needs to Know about Islam: Answers to Frequently Asked Questions, from One of America's Leading Experts*. 2nd ed. New York: Oxford University Press, 2011.

Esposito, John L., ed. *The Oxford Dictionary of Islam*. New York: Oxford University Press, 2003.

Esposito, John L., ed. *The Oxford Encyclopedia of the Islamic World*. New York: Oxford University Press, 2009.

Esposito, John L., and Ibrahim Kalin, eds. *Islamophobia: The Challenge of Pluralism in the 21st Century*. New York: Oxford University Press, 2011.

Esposito, John L., and Dalia Mogahed. *Who Speaks for Islam? What a Billion Muslims Really Think*. New York: Gallup Press, 2007.

Esposito, John L., and Emad Shahin, *The Oxford Handbook of Islam and Politics*. New York: Oxford University Press, 2013.

Esposito, John L., Tamara Sonn, and John O. Voll. *Islam and Democracy after the Arab Spring*. New York: Oxford University Press, 2016.

Esposito, John L., with Natana J. DeLong-Bas. *Women in Muslim Family Law*. 2nd ed. Syracuse: Syracuse University Press, 2001.

Fadel, Mohammad. "Muslim Reformists, Female Citizenship, and the Public Accommodation of Islam in Liberal Democracy." *Politics and Religion* 5 (2012): 2–35.

Fadel, Mohammad. "Political Liberalism, Islamic Family Law, and Family Law Pluralism: Lessons from New York on Family Law Arbitration." In *Marriage and Divorce in a Multi-Cultural Context: Reconsidering the Boundaries of Civil Law and Religion*, edited by Joel Nichols. New York: Cambridge University Press, 2011.

Fadel, Mohammad. "Review: A Tragedy of Politics or an Apolitical Tragedy?" *Journal of the American Oriental Society* 131, no. 1 (January–March 2011): 109–27.

Fadel, Mohammad. "The True, the Good, and the Reasonable: The Theological and Ethical Roots of Public Reason in Islamic Law." *Canadian Journal of Law and Jurisprudence* 21, no. 1 (2008).

Failinger, Marie, Elizabeth Schiltz, and Susan J. Stabile, eds. *Feminism, Law, and Religion*. New York: Routledge, 2013.

"Female Genital Mutilation Still Widespread in Africa," *Channel News Asia*, August 4, 2013.

Firestone, Reuven. *Jihad: The Origin of Holy War in Islam*. New York: Oxford University Press, 1999.

Foltz, Richard C. *Animals in Islamic Traditions and Muslim Cultures*. Oxford: OneWorld, 2005.

Foltz, Richard C. *Worldviews, Religion, and the Environment: A Global Anthology*. Belmont, CA: Wadsworth Publishing, 2002.

Foltz, Richard C., Frederick M. Denny, and Azizan Baharuddin, eds. *Islam and Ecology: A Bestowed Trust*. Cambridge, MA: Harvard University Press, 2003.

Franck, Matthew. "A Solution in Search of a Problem." *National Review Online*, June 15, 2012, http://www.nationalreview.com/content/solution-search-problem.

Friedmann, Yohanan. *Tolerance and Coercion in Islam: Interfaith Relations in the Muslim Tradition*. New York: Cambridge University Press, 2003.

Gaudreault-DesBiens, Jean-Francois. "Religious Courts, Personal Federalism, and Legal Transplants." In *Shari'a in the West*, edited by Rex Ahdar and Nicholas Aroney. New York: Oxford University Press, 2010.

Al-Ghannushi, Rashid. *Al-Hurriyat al-'Ammah fi al-Dawlah al-Islamiyyah*. Bayrut: Markaz Dirasat al-Wahdah al-Arabiyyah, 1993.

Al-Ghannushi, Rashid. "Interview Transcript," *The Financial Times*, January 18, 2011.

Goldziher, Ignaz. *Introduction to Islamic Theology and Law*, translated by Andras and Ruth Hamori. Princeton, NJ: Princeton University Press, 1981.

Gottlieb, Roger S., ed. *The Oxford Handbook of Religion and Ecology*. New York: Oxford University Press, 2006.

Haddad, Yvonne Yazbeck, and John L. Esposito, eds. *Islam, Gender, and Social Change*. New York: Oxford University Press, 1998.

Haddad, Yvonne Yazbeck, and Barbara Freyer Stowasser, eds. *Islamic Law and the Challenges of Modernity*. Walnut Creek, CA: Altamira Press, 2004.

Hajjar, Lisa. "Religion, State Power, and Domestic Violence in Muslim Societies: A Framework for Comparative Analysis." *Law & Social Inquiry* 29, no. 1 (Winter 2004).

Hallaq, Wael B. *A History of Islamic Legal Theories: An Introduction to Sunni usul al-fiqh*. New York: Cambridge University Press, 1997.

Hallaq, Wael B. *An Introduction to Islamic Law*. New York: Cambridge University Press, 2009.

Hallaq, Wael B. *The Impossible State: Islam, Politics, and Modernity's Moral Predicament*. New York: Columbia University Press, 2013.

Hallaq, Wael B. *The Origins and Evolution of Islamic Law*. New York: Columbia University Press, 2005.

Hallaq, Wael B. *Sharia: Theory, Practice, Transformations*. New York: Cambridge University Press, 2009.

Haq, S. Nomanul. "Islam and Ecology: Toward Retrieval and Reconstruction." In *Islam and Ecology: A Bestowed Trust*, edited by Richard C. Foltz, Frederick M. Denny, and Azizan Baharuddin, 121–54. Cambridge, MA: Harvard University Press, 2003.

Haque, Jahanzaib. "Pakistan's 'Shame': Rape Cases in 2012." *The Express Tribune*, December 31, 2012.

Hashmi, Sohail H., ed. *Just Wars, Holy Wars, & Jihads: Christian, Jewish, and Muslim Encounters and Exchanges*. New York: Oxford University Press, 2012.

Haworth, Abigail. "The Day I Saw 248 Girls Suffering Genital Mutilation." *The Guardian: The Observer*, November 17, 2012.

Heffening, W. "Sarika." In *Encyclopedia of Islam*, 2nd ed, edited by P. Bearman, Th. Bianquis, C.E. Bosworth, E. van Donzel, W.P. Heinrichs. Leiden: Brill, 1954–2005.

Hefner, Robert W., ed. *Shari'a Politics: Islamic Law and Society in the Modern World*. Bloomington, IN: Indiana University Press, 2011.

Heper, Metin. "A Democratic-Conservative Government by Pious People." In *The Blackwell Companion to Contemporary Islamic Thought*. Malden, MA: Blackwell, 2006.

Henry, Clement, and Rodney Wilson, eds. *The Politics of Islamic Finance*. Edinburgh: Edinburgh University Press, 2004.

Al-Hibri, Azizah Y., and Hadia Mubarak. "Marriage and Divorce." In *The Oxford Encyclopedia of the Islamic World*, edited by John L. Esposito. New York: Oxford University Press, 2009.

Hidayatullah, Aysha A. *Feminist Edges of the Qur'an*. New York: Oxford University Press, 2014. http://www.nytimes.com/2011/12/22/us/politics/in-shariah-gingrich-sees-mortal-threat-to-us.html?_r=2&.

Hussain, Jamila. *Islam: Its Law and Society*, 3rd ed. Sydney: The Federation Press, 2011.

Huus Kari. "Federal Court Deals Blow to Anti-Shariah efforts." *NBC News*, January 10, 2012.

"In-depth Study of All Forms of Violence against Women." United Nations, General Assembly, July 6, 2006.

Iqdal, Munawar, and Rodney Wilson, eds. *Islamic Perspectives on Wealth Creation*. Edinburgh: Edinburgh University Press, 2005.

"Islamic Inheritance." Muslim Women's League, September 1995. http://www.mwlusa.org/topics/rights/inheritance.html.

Izzi Dien, Mawil. "Islam and the Enviroment: Theory and Practice." In *Islam and Ecology: A Bestowed Trust*, edited by Richard C. Foltz, Frederick M. Denny, and Azizan Baharuddin, 107–20. Cambridge, MA: Harvard University Press, 2003.

Jafri, S.H.M. *The Origins and Early Development of Shi'a Islam.*
New York: Oxford University Press, 2000.

Juergensmeyer, Mark, Margo Kitts, and Michael Jerryson, eds. *The
Oxford Handbook of Religion and Violence.* New York: Oxford
University Press, 2013.

Kabeer, Naila. "Resources, Agency, Achievements: Reflections on the
Measurement of Women's Empowerment." *Development and Change*
30, no. 3 (July 1999).

Kaltner, John. *Introducing the Qur'an for Today's Reader.* Minneapolis:
Fortress Press, 2011.

Kamali, Mohammad Hashim. "Are the Hudud Open to Fresh
Interpretation?" *Islam and Civilizational Renewal* 1, no. 3 (2010).

Karic, Enis. "Gambling." In *Encyclopaedia of the Qur'ān,* Vol. II, edited by
Jane Dammen McAuliffe. Leiden: Brill, 2002.

Kassam, Tazim R. "The Aga Khan Development Network: An
Ethic of Sustainable Development and Social Conscience." In
Islam and Ecology: A Bestowed Trust, edited by Richard C. Foltz,
Frederick M. Denny, and Azizan Baharuddin, 477–96. Cambridge,
MA: Harvard University Press, 2003.

Kechichian, Joseph A. *Legal and Political Reforms in Saudi Arabia.*
London: Routledge, 2013.

Khadduri, Majid. *The Islamic Conception of Justice.* Baltimore and
London: Johns Hopkins University Press, 1984.

Khalidi, Tarif. *Arabic Historical Thought in the Classical Period.*
New York: Cambridge University Press, 1994.

Kim, Eun-Jung Katherine. "Islamic Law in American Courts: Good,
Bad, and Unsustainable Uses." *Notre Dame Journal of Law, Ethics &
Public Policy* 28 (2014): 287–307.

Klausen, Jyette. *The Islamic Challenge: Politics and Religion in Western
Europe.* New York: Oxford University Press, 2005.

Kohlberg, Etan. "Some Imami-Shi'i Views on Taqiyya." *Journal of the
American Oriental Society* 95, no. 3 (July–September 1975).

Kramer, Gudrun, updated by Joseph A. Kechichian.
"Minorities: Minorities in Muslim Societies." In *The Oxford
Encyclopedia of the Islamic World,* edited by John L. Esposito. New
York: Oxford University Press, 2009.

Kugle, Scott Siraj al-Haqq. *Homosexuality in Islam: Critical Reflection on
Gay, Lesbian, and Transgender Muslims.* Oxford: OneWorld, 2010.

Kuran, Timur. "Economic Theory," subentry under "Economics." In *The
Oxford Encyclopedia of the Islamic World,* edited by John L. Esposito.
New York: Oxford University Press, 2009.

Kurzman, Charles. *The Missing Martyrs: Why There Are So Few Muslim Terrorists*. New York: Oxford University Press, 2011.

Kutty, Faisal. "The Myth and Reality of Shari'a Courts in Canada: A Delayed Opportunity for the Indigenization of Islamic Legal Rulings. *University of St. Thomas Law Journal* 7, no. 3 (2010): 599–602.

Leaman, Oliver. "Apostasy." In *The Oxford Encyclopedia of the Islamic World*, edited by John L. Esposito. New York: Oxford University Press, 2009.

Leichtman, Mara A. "Shi'i Islam in West Africa." In *Oxford Islamic Studies Online*.

Llewellyn, Othman Abd-ar Rahman. "The Basis for a Discipline of Islamic Environmental Law." In *Islam and Ecology: A Bestowed Trust*, edited by Richard C. Foltz, Frederick M. Denny, and Azizan Baharuddin, 185–248. Cambridge, MA: Harvard University Press, 2003.

Lowry, Joseph. "Theft," In *Encyclopaedia of the Qur'ān*, Vol. V, edited by Jane Dammen McAuliffe. Leiden: Brill, 2006.

Luban, Daniel. "Forget 'Ground Zero Mosque,' It's the Great Sharia Conspiracy," Inter Press Service, September 16, 2010.

Macfarlane, Julie. *Islamic Divorce in North America: A Shari'a Path in a Secular Society*. New York: Oxford University Press, 2012.

Macfarlane, Julie. "'Shari'a Law' Coming to a Courthouse Near You?: What Shari'a Really Means to American Muslims." Report to the Institute for Social Policy and Understanding, Washington, DC, January 30, 2012.

Mach, Daniel, and Jamil Dakwar. "Anti-Sharia Law: A Solution in Search of a Problem." *HuffPost Religion*, May 20, 2011.

Maguire, Daniel C., ed. *Sacred Rights: The Case for Contraception and Abortion in World Religions*. New York: Oxford University Press, 2003.

Maguire, Daniel C., and Sa'diyya Shaikh. *Violence against Women in Contemporary World Religions: Roots and Cures*. Cleveland, OH: Pilgrim Press, 2007.

Marzouki, Nadia. "Conversion as Statelessness: A Study of Contemporary Algerian Conversions to Evangelical Christianity." *Middle East Law and Governance* 4 (2012): 69–105.

Masud, Muhammad Khalid, and Brinkley Messick. *Islamic Legal Interpretation: Muftis and Their Fatwas*. Cambridge, MA: Harvard University Press, 1996.

Masud, Muhammad Khalid, Rudolph Peters, and David S. Powers. *Dispensing Justice in Islam: Qadis and Their Judgments*. Leiden: Brill, 2012.

Mayer, Ann Elizabeth. "Inheritance." In *The Oxford Encyclopedia of the Islamic World*, edited by John L. Esposito. New York: Oxford University Press, 2009.

McAuliffe, Jane Dammen, ed. *Encyclopaedia of the Qur'ān*, Vol. 1. Leiden: Brill, 2001.

Mir-Hosseini, Ziba, Mulki Al-Sharmani, and Jana Rumminger, eds. *Men in Charge? Rethinking Authority in Muslim Legal Tradition.* Oxford: OneWorld, 2015.

Mir-Hosseini, Ziba, Kari Vogt, Lena Larsen, and Christian Moe, eds. *Gender and Equality in Muslim Family Law: Justice and Ethics in the Islamic Legal Tradition.* London: I.B. Tauris, 2013.

"Misr: Sahwa Azhariyya lil-Hadd min Fuda al-Fatawa (Egypt: Azhar Awakening on the Limit of Fatwa Chaos)," al-Sharq al-Awsat, September 2012.

Moors, Annelies. *Women, Property, and Islam: Palestinian Experiences, 1920–1990.* New York: Cambridge University Press, 1995.

Moussali, Ahmad S. *The Islamic Quest for Democracy, Pluralism, and Human Rights.* Gainesville, FL: University Press of Florida, 2001.

Musallam, B.F. *Sex and Society in Islam.* New York: Cambridge University Press, 1983.

"Muslim Americans: Middle Class and Mostly Mainstream." Pew Research Center, May 22, 2007.

"Muslims and Islam: Key Findings from the U.S. and around the World." Pew Research Center, February 17, 2017, http://www.pewresearch.org/fact-tank/2017/02/27/muslims-and-islam-key-findings-in-the-u-s-and-around-the-world.

Mydans, Seth. "Blame Men, Not Allah, Islamic Feminists Say." *The New York Times*, October 10, 1996.

Nasr, Seyyed Hossein. "Islam, the Contemporary Islamic World, and the Environmental Crisis." In *Islam and Ecology: A Bestowed Trust*, edited by Richard C. Foltz, Frederick M. Denny, and Azizan Baharuddin, 85–106. Cambridge, MA: Harvard University Press, 2003.

Nasr, Seyyed Hossein. *Man and Nature: The Spiritual Crisis of Modern Man.* Chicago: ABC International Group, Inc., 1997.

Nasr, Seyyed Hossein, Editor-in-Chief. *The Study Quran: A New Translation and Commentary,* General Editors Caner K. Dagli, Maria Massi Dakake, Joseph E.B. Lumbard, and Mohammed Rustom, Assistant Editor. New York: HarperOne, 2015.

Omer, Atalia, R. Scott Appleby, and David Little, eds. *The Oxford Handbook of Religion, Conflict, and Peacebuilding*. New York: Oxford University Press, 2015.

O'Sullivan, Declan. "Egyptian Cases of Blasphemy and Apostasy against Islam: Rakfir al-Muslim." *The International Journal of Human Rights* 7, no. 2 (2003): 97–137.

Ozdemir, Ibrahim. "Toward an Understanding of Environmental Ethics from a Qur'anic Perspective." In *Islam and Ecology: A Bestowed Trust*, edited by Richard C. Foltz, Frederick M. Denny, and Azizan Baharuddin, 3–38. Cambridge, MA: Harvard University Press, 2003.

"Paper 6: Islamic Inheritance Laws and Systems." UN-HABITAT, 2005.

Patel, Fazia, Matthew Duss, and Amos Toh. "Foreign Law Bans: Legal Uncertainties and Practical Problems." Center for American Progress and Brennan Center for Justice, May 2013.

Pearl, David Stephen. "Hudud." In *The Oxford Encyclopedia of the Modern Islamic World*, edited by John L. Esposito. New York: Oxford University Press, 1995.

Peters, Rudolph. *Crime and Punishment in Islamic Law: Theory and Practice from the Sixteenth to the Twenty-First Century*. New York: Cambridge University Press, 2005.

Peters, Rudolph. "Hudud." In *The Oxford Encyclopedia of Islam and Women*, edited by Natana J. DeLong-Bas. New York: Oxford University Press, 2013.

Peters, Rudolph. "Hudud." In *The Oxford Encyclopedia of the Islamic World*, edited by John L. Esposito. New York: Oxford University Press, 2009.

Peters, Rudolph. "The Islamization of Criminal Law: A Comparative Analysis." *Die Welt des Islams* 34, no. 2 (November 1994): 246–74.

Peters, Rudolph. *Jihad in Classical and Modern Islam*, updated ed. with a Section on Jihad in the 21st Century. Princeton: Markus Wiener Publishers, 2005.

Polgreen, Lydia. "Timbuktu Endured Terror under Harsh Shariah Law." *The New York Times*, February 1, 2013.

Poll by Institute for Social Policy and Understanding, "American Muslim Poll: Participation, Priorities, and Facing Prejudice in the 2016 Elections." March 2016

Powers, David S. "Appeal." In *The Encyclopedia of Islam*, 3rd ed., edited by Kate Fleet, Gudrun Krämer, Denis Matringe, John Nawas and Everett Rowson. Leiden: Brill, 2007.

Powers, David S. "On Judicial Review in Islamic Law." *Law & Society Review* 26, no. 2 (1992): 315–42.

Al-Qaradawi, Yusuf. *The Lawful and the Prohibited in Islam*, trans. Kamal El-Helbawy, M. Moinuddin Siddiqui, and Syed Shukry, trans. reviewed by Ahmad Zaki Hammad. New Delhi: Kitab Bhavan, 2006.

Al-Qaradawi, Yusuf. *Al-Tatarruf al-Almani fi Muwajat al-Islam (The Extremes of Secularism in Confrontation with Islam)*. Cairo: Dar al-Shuruq, 2001.

Quraishi, Asifa, and Frank Vogel, eds. *The Islamic Marriage Contract: Case Studies in Islamic Family Law*. Cambridge, MA: Islamic Legal Studies Program, Harvard Law School, 2009.

Quraishi-Landes, Asifa. "Five Myths about Sharia." *The Washington Post*, June 24, 2016.

Quraishi-Landes, Asifa. "Her Honor: An Islamic Critique of the Rape Laws of Pakistan from a Woman-Sensitive Perspective." *Michigan Journal of International Law* 18, no. 287 (1997).

Quraishi-Landes, Asifa. "How to Create an Islamic Government – Not an Islamic State." *Middle East Eye*, February 17, 2017.

Quraishi-Landes, Asifa. "Islamic Constitutionalism: Not Secular. Not Theocratic. Not Impossible." *Rutgers Journal of Law & Religion* 16 (2015): 553–79.

Quraishi-Landes, Asifa. "Rumors of the Sharia Threat Are Greatly Exaggerated: What American Judges Really Do with Islamic Family Law in Their Courtrooms." *New York Law School Review* 57, no. 245 (2013).

Quraishi-Landes, Asifa. "The Sharia Problem with Sharia Legislation." *Ohio North University Law Review*, Vol. 41, (2015).

Quraishi-Landes, Asifa. "Who Says Shari'a Demands Stoning of Women? A Description of Islamic Law and Constitutionalism." *Berkeley Journal of Middle Eastern & Islamic Law* 1 (2008): 163–77.

Qutb, Sayyid. *Social Justice in Islam*, trans. John B. Hardie, trans. rev. and introduction by Hamid Algar. Oneonta, NY: Islamic Publications International, 2000.

Rabb, Intisar. "Courts," subentry in "Law." In *The Oxford Encyclopedia of the Modern Islamic World*, edited by John L. Esposito. New York: Oxford University Press, 1995.

Rabb, Intisar. *Doubt in Islamic Law: Maxims, Interpretation, and Islamic Criminal Law*. New York: Cambridge University Press, 2014.

Raines, John C., and Daniel C. Maguire. *What Men Owe to Women: Men's Voices from World Religions*. Albany, NY: State University of New York Press, 2001.

Ramadan, Hisham. "On Islamic Punishment." In *Understanding Islamic Law: From Classical to Contemporary*, edited by Hisham Ramadan. New York: Alta Mira Press, 2006.

Ramadan, Hisham, ed. *Understanding Islamic Law: From Classical to Contemporary*. New York: Alta Mira Press, 2006.

Ramadan, Tariq. *Radical Reform: Islamic Ethics and Liberation*. New York: Oxford University Press, 2009.

Ramadan, Tariq. *Western Muslims and the Future of Islam*. New York: Oxford University Press, 2004.

"Rape Laws: Crime and Clarity." *The Economist*, September 1, 2012.

Religious Freedom Education Project of the First Amendment Center and the Interfaith Alliance Islamic Understanding. "What Is the Truth About American Muslims? Questions and Answers." Publication date unclear, but cites material published as recently as 2011.

Rodenback, Max. "No God but God: The War within Islam." *The New York Times*, May 29, 2005.

Rosenberg, Tina. "Editorial Observer: Mutilating Africa's Daughters: Laws Unenforced, Practices Unchanged." *The New York Times*, July 5, 2004.

Rosenthal, Franz. *Gambling in Islam*. Leiden: Brill, 1975.

Sachedina, Abdulaziz. *Islamic Biomedical Ethics: Principles and Application*. New York: Oxford University Press, 2009.

Sachedina, Abdulaziz. *The Islamic Roots of Democratic Pluralism*. New York: Oxford University Press, 2001.

Saeed, Abdullah. "Reflections on the Establishment of Sharia Courts in Australia." In *Sharia in the West*, edited by Rex Ahdar and Nicholas Aroney. New York: Oxford University Press, 2010.

Said, Abdul Aziz, Nathan C. Funk, and Ayse S. Kadayifci, eds. *Peace and Conflict Resolution in Islam: Precept and Practice*. Lanham, MD: University Press of America, 2001.

Salmi, Ralph H., Cesar Adib Majul, and George K. Tanham. *Islam and Conflict Resolution: Theories and Practices*. Lanham, MD: University Press of America, 1998.

Sanders, Paula. "Clitoridectomy." In *The Oxford Encyclopedia of the Islamic World*, edited by John L. Esposito. New York: Oxford University Press, 2009.

Schacht, Joseph. *An Introduction to Islamic Law*. Oxford: Clarendon Press, 1964.

Scharffs, Brett G. "International Law and the Defamation of Religion Conundrum." *The Review of Faith & International Affairs* 11, no. 1 (2013): 66–75.

Semerdjian, Elyse. "Zinah." In *The Oxford Encyclopedia of the Islamic World*, edited by John L. Esposito. New York: Oxford University Press, 2009.

Shahar, Ido. "Legal Pluralism and the Study of Shari'a Courts." *Islamic Law and Society* 15 (2008): 112–41.

Sharkey, Heather J. "Christians among Muslims: The Church Missionary Society in the Northern Sudan." *The Journal of African History* 43 (2002): 51–75.

Sharkey, Heather J. "Empire and Muslim Conversion: Historical Reflections on Christian Missions in Egypt." *Islam and Christian-Muslim Relations* 16, no. 1 (2005): 43–60.

Sonbol, Amira El-Azhary. *Women of Jordan: Islam, Labor, and the Law*. Syracuse: Syracuse University Press, 2003.

Sonbol, Amira El-Azhary, ed. *Beyond the Exotic: Women's Histories in Islamic Societies*. Syracuse: Syracuse University Press, 2005.

Sonbol, Amira El-Azhary, ed. *Gulf Women*. Syracuse: Syracuse University Press, 2012.

Sonbol, Amira El Azhary, ed. *Women, the Family, and Divorce Laws in Islamic History*. Syracuse: Syracuse University Press, 1996.

Sonneveld, Nadia. *Khul' Divorce in Egypt: Public Debates, Judicial Practices, and Everyday Lives*. Cairo: The American University in Cairo Press, 2012.

Sonneveld, Nadia, and Monika Lindbekk, eds. *Women Judges in the Muslim World: A Comparative Study of Discourse and Practice*. Leiden: Brill, 2017.

Soroush, Abdolkarim. *Reason, Freedom and Democracy in Islam*, trans. and ed. Mahmoud Sadri and Ahmad Sadri. New York: Oxford University Press, 2000.

Spectorsky, Susan A., trans. *Chapters on Marriage and Divorce: Responses of Ibn Hanbal and Ibn Rahwayh*. Austin: University of Texas Press, 1993.

Stephan, Maria J., ed. *Civilian Jihad: Nonviolent Struggle, Democratization, and Governance in the Middle East*. New York: Palgrave Macmillan, 2009.

Sterett, Brittany. "Tunisia Praised for Efforts to Protect Women's Rights." U.S. Department of State Bureau on International Infonation Programs, June 10, 2005.

"Stoning Victim 'Begged for Mercy,'" *BBC News*, November 4, 2008.

Tamimi, Azzam S. *Rachid Ghannouchi. A Democrat within Islam*. New York: Oxford University Press, 2001.

Tucker, Judith E. *In the House of Law: Gender and Islamic Law in Ottoman Syria and Palestine*. Berkeley: University of California Press, 1998.

Tucker, Judith E. *Women, Family, and Gender in Islamic Law*. New York: Cambridge University Press, 2008.

Turner, Howard R. *Science in Medieval Islam: An Illustrated Introduction*. Austin: University of Texas Press, 1995.

Twining, William, ed. *Human Rights, Southern Voices: Francis Deng, Abdullahi An-Na'im, Yash Ghai, and Upendra Baxi*. New York: Cambridge University Press, 2009.

Uddin, Asma T. "Blasphemy Laws in Muslim-Majority Countries." *The Review of Faith & International Affairs* 9, no. 2 (2011): 47–55.

Usmani, Muhammad Taqi. "The Islamization of Laws in Pakistan: The Cases of Hudud Ordinances." *The Muslim World* 96 (April 2006).

Van Bijsterveld, Sophie. "Negotiating the Unfamiliar." In *Shari'a in the West*, edited by Rex Ahdar and Nicholas Aroney. New York: Oxford University Press, 2010.

Vischer, Robert K. "The Dangers of Anti-Sharia Laws." *First Things* (March 2012).

Vogel, Frank. *Islamic Law and Legal System: Studies on Saudi Arabia*. Leiden: Brill, 2000.

Vogel, Frank E. "Saudi Arabia: Public, Civil, and Individual Shari'a in Law and Politics." In *Shari'a Politics: Islamic Law and Society in the Modern World*, edited by Robert W. Hefner. Bloomington, IN: Indiana University Press, 2011.

Vogel, Frank E., and Samuel L. Hayes III. *Islamic Law and Finance: Religion, Risk, and Return*. Leiden: Brill, 1998.

Wadud, Amina. *Inside the Gender Jihad: Women's Reform in Islam*. Oxford: OneWorld, 2006.

Wadud, Amina. *Qur'an and Woman: Rereading the Sacred Text from a Woman's Perspective*. New York: Oxford University Press, 1999.

Walker, Paul E. "Taqiyah." In *The Oxford Encyclopedia of the Modern Islamic World*, edited by John L. Esposito. New York: Oxford University Press, 1995.

Weimann, Gunnar J. "Judicial Practice in Islamic Criminal Law in Nigeria – A Tentative Overview." *Islamic Law and Society* 14, no. 2 (2007).

Welchman, Lynn. *Women and Muslim Family Laws in Arab States: A Comparative Overview of Textual Development and Advocacy*. Amsterdam: Amsterdam University Press, 2007.

Welchman, Lynn, ed. *Women's Rights and Islamic Family Law*. London: Zed Books, 2004.

Wensinck, A.J. "Khamr." In *The Encyclopedia of Islam*, 2nd ed, edited by P. J. Bearman, Th. Bianquis, C. E. Bosworth, E. van Donzel, W. P. Heinrichs et al. Leiden: E. J. Brill, 1960–2005.

Wiederhold, Lutz. "Blasphemy against the Prophet Muhammad and His Companions (Sabb al-Rasul, Sabb al-Sahabah): The Introduction of the Topic into Shafi'i Legal Literature and Its Relevance for Legal Practice under Mamluk Rule." *Journal of Semitic Studies* 42, no. 1 (1997): 39–70.

Williams, Julie. *Islam: Understanding the History, Beliefs, and Culture.* Berkeley Heights, NJ: Enslow Publishers, 2008.

Williams, Rt. Rev. Dr. Rowan. "Civil and Religious Law in England: A Religious Perspective." In *Shari'a in the West*, edited by Rex Ahdar and Nicholas Aroney. New York: Oxford University Press, 2010.

Wilson, Rodney. *Economic Development in the Middle East*, 2nd ed. New York: Routledge, 2010.

Wilson, Rodney. *Islam and Economic Policy: An Introduction.* Edinburgh: Edinburgh University Press, 2015.

Wilson, Rodney. *Legal, Regulatory, and Governance Issues in Islamic Finance.* Edinburgh: Edinburgh University Press, 2012.

"The World's Muslims: Religion, Politics and Society." Pew Research Center, April 30, 2013, http://www.pewforum.org/2013/04/30/the-worlds-muslims-religion-politics-society-overview.

Wurth, Anita. "The Normativity of the Factual: On the Everyday Construction of Shari'a in a Yemeni Family Court." In *Shari'a: Islamic Law in the Contemporary Context*, edited by Abbas Amanat and Frank Griffel. Stanford, CA: Stanford University Press, 2007.

www.ammanmessage.com.

www.lettertobaghdadi.com.

Yamani, Maha A.Z. *Polygamy and Law in Contemporary Saudi Arabia.* Reading: Ithaca Press, 2008.

Al-Yaqeen Institute for Islamic Research. https://yaqeeninstitute.org/en/homepage.

Yount, Kathryn M. "Resources, Family Organization, and Domestic Violence against Married Women in Minya, Egypt." *Journal of Marriage and Family* 67, no. 3 (August 2005): 579–96.

Zaman, Sarah. "The Stigma of Reporting a Rape in Pakistan." *PBS: Frontline*, May 28, 2013.

Ziadeh, Farhat J. "Criminal Law." In *The Oxford Encyclopedia of the Modern Islamic World*, edited by John L. Esposito. New York: Oxford University Press, 1995.

INDEX

mahr (dower), 25, 106, 108–9

makruh (discouraged)
    actions, 56–57

Malik, Anas ibn, 42, 48

Maliki school, 48
    divorce and, 53
    on evidence of illicit sex, 75

Mamluk regime, 48, 151

Mamun (caliph), 77

maqasid al-Shariah (principles/
        objectives of Shariah),
        31–32, 41–42
    as applied to fiqh, 34
    defined, 2
    ijtihad and, 38
    reform and, 42–46
    tajdid and, 42–46
    Western influence on, 45

market inspector (muhtasib), 64

marriage (nikah, zawaj), 16,
        24–25, 106–17
    arranged, 114–16
    child, 116–17
    consent to, 106–7
    of desire (mutah), 109–10
    forced, 115–16
    mahr and, 25, 106, 108–9
    misfar (travel
        marriage), 109–10
    misyar (pleasure
        marriage), 109–10
    to non-Muslims, 113–14
    polygyny and, 111–13
    reform and, 45
    responsibilities of, 106–7

Shariah courts and, 66

marriage gift, 25, 106, 108–9

martyrdom, 181–84

maslahah (common good)
    abortion and, 289
    approach to Shariah and, 19
    banking practices and, 239
    capitalism and, 250–52
    charity and, 243–44
    contracts of sale and, 247
    crime and, 186, 195
    defined, 2
    democracy and, 143
    environmental issues and, 266
    as focus of fiqh, 35
    freedom of religion and, 156
    freedom of speech and, 153
    global financial market
        and, 256–58
    government and, 132–33, 143
    human rights and, 147, 149
    interest/usury and, 231, 235
    istislah and, 38
    jihad and, 179
    legal outcomes and, 38, 86
    medical research and, 269
    medicine and, 270–71
    non-Muslims and, 165, 167
    obedience to civil authority
        and, 142
    poverty and, 252
    property rights and, 245
    reform and, 43–44, 46
    Shariah courts and, 87
    slavery and, 153